T0291375

The Global Management of Creativity

In the past, 'Global Management' meant optimizing production and commercialization activities around the world in an international business context. With the emergence and rise of the creative economy, the global game has changed.

This book is about the global management of creativity and related innovation processes, and examines how companies, organizations and institutions can foster the transformation of an original idea to its successful execution and international diffusion. *The Global Management of Creativity* gives a clear framework for analyzing creativeness in organizations in an international context, and pinpointing important key elements that should be tracked. Comprising expert contributions and written by a wide array of leading scholars in economics, management of innovation and creativity, this book is an insightful resource.

This volume provides empirical and theoretical material for managers, students and academics in the field of international management of creativity and innovation. It is also suitable for those who are interested in industrial economics, management of technology, and innovation and industrial studies.

Marcus Wagner is a Full Professor at the University of Augsburg, Germany, where he holds the Chair in Management, Innovation and International Business and is an associate member of the Bureau d'Economie Théorique et Appliquée, where he held an Intra-European Marie Curie Fellowship from 2006 to 2008.

Jaume Valls-Pasola is Professor of Management and Business Administration. After a period of 12 years at the University of Girona, in October 2006 he joined the University of Barcelona, Spain, where he is currently responsible for the UB Entrepreneurship Chair and coordinates the UB Business and Management Research Group.

Thierry Burger-Helmchen is a researcher at BETA (Bureau d'Economie Théorique et Appliquée, UMR 7522 – CNRS) and Dean of the Department of Economics and Management at the University of Strasbourg, France.

Routledge Studies in Global Competition
Edited by John Cantwell, Rutgers, the State University
of New Jersey, USA, and David Mowery,
University of California, Berkeley, USA

For a full list of titles in this series, please visit www.routledge.com/Routledge-
Studies-in-Global-Competition/book-series/RSGC

The Global Management of Creativity

Edited by Marcus Wagner,
Jaume Valls-Pasola and
Thierry Burger-Helmchen

Routledge
Taylor & Francis Group

LONDON AND NEW YORK

First published 2017
by Routledge
2 Park Square, Milton Park, Abingdon, Oxon OX14 4RN

and by Routledge
711 Third Avenue, New York, NY 10017

Routledge is an imprint of the Taylor & Francis Group, an informa business

British Library Cataloguing in Publication Data
A catalogue record for this book is available from the British Library

Library of Congress Cataloging in Publication Data
Names: Wagner, Marcus, 1973- editor. | Valls Pasola, Jaume, editor. |
    Burger-Helmchen, Thierry, editor.
Title: The global management of creativity / [edited by] Marcus Wagner,
    Jaume Valls Pasola and Thierry Burger-Helmchen.
Description: Abingdon, Oxon ; New York, NY : Routledge, 2017. |
    Includes index.
Identifiers: LCCN 2016029546| ISBN 9781138910164 (hardback) |
    ISBN 9781315693552 (ebook)
Subjects: LCSH: Creative ability in business. | Diffusion of innovations. |
    Technological innovations—Management.
Classification: LCC HD53 .G5473 2017 | DDC 658.3/14—dc23
LC record available at https://lccn.loc.gov/2016029546

ISBN: 978-1-138-91016-4 (hbk)
ISBN: 978-1-315-69355-2 (ebk)

Typeset in Times New Roman
by Swales & Willis Ltd, Exeter, Devon, UK

FSC
www.fsc.org
MIX
Paper from
responsible sources
FSC® C013604

Printed and bound by CPI Group (UK) Ltd, Croydon, CR0 4YY

Contents

Figures

Tables

Contributors

Arman Avadikyan has a PhD in Economics. He is a research engineer at BETA (Bureau d'Economie Théorique et Appliquée, UMR 7522 – CNRS), a research unit of the University of Strasbourg, the University of Lorraine and the CNRS (France). His current research work focuses on innovation management, sustainable technologies and S&T policy.

Thierry Burger-Helmchen (PhD in Management Science, University of Strasbourg) is a researcher at BETA (Bureau d'Economie Théorique et Appliquée, UMR 7522 – CNRS) and Dean of the Department of Economics and Management at the University of Strasbourg, France. His research topics are entrepreneurship and innovation management. He analyses the economic impact of creativity notably in the video game industry. He teaches Strategy of SMEs and Managerial Economics at the University of Strasbourg.

Patrick Cohendet is Professor of Economics at HEC Montréal, Canada, and was previously a professor at the University of Strasbourg, France. His research interests include economics of innovation, technology management, knowledge management, theory of the firm and economics of creativity. He is the author or co-author of 15 books and over 60 articles in refereed journals. He has conducted a series of economic studies on innovation and economics of knowledge (measurement of spin-offs, evaluation of the economic benefits of R&D projects, evaluation of technology transfer, etc.). These studies were carried out by his research laboratory BETA (Bureau d'Economie Théorique et Appliquée, UMR 7522 – CNRS) and Mosaic at HEC Montréal for different European and North American organizations such as the European Commission, the EU, OECD, Council of Europe and the Canadian Space Agency.

Evelyn García is Managing Partner of Kayros Institute and Vice-president of the Association of International Mobility Experts, member of the Chair in Business Internationalization, Diversity and Professional Development of the Comillas Pontifical University (ICADE University, Spain). She has developed her career at several prestigious consulting firms (PwC and E&Y) and she was Head of Corporate Mobility Area and International Talent on Acciona Group. Evelyn is an expert in the design of policies and models of International

Mobility, International Careers and development of Cultural Intelligence with over 15 years experience in International Mobility in more than 60 countries. She is a frequent lecturer and teaches courses at ICADE about Global Talent Management and International Mobility.

David Grandadam has a PhD in Economics from the University of Strasbourg, France. He is currently a researcher at the Mosaic research lab at HEC Montreal, Canada. His research concentrates on the economics and management of ideas, with a particular focus on the fields of arts and science.

Claude Guittard has a PhD in Business Studies from the University of Strasbourg, France. He works as a researcher at BETA (Bureau d'Economie Théorique et Appliquée, UMR 7522 – CNRS) and is Associate Professor at the Department of Economics and Management at the University of Strasbourg. His work tries to answer the general question of 'how to use IT to manage knowledge'. From this perspective he has written several articles about knowledge creation and transfer on the Internet and the role of community of practice in IT entrepreneurship or, more recently, about crowdsourcing, or the definition of IT experts.

Jean-Alain Héraud is Professor of Economics at the University of Strasbourg, France. He was head of BETA (Bureau d'Economie Théorique et Appliquée, UMR 7522 – CNRS) from 1991 to 2000, and of the Department of Economics and Management of Université de Strasbourg from 2008 to 2012. As member of BETA, he specializes in economics of innovation and science and technology policy and has worked also in specific fields like regional development, training and employment, energy systems and technology foresight. In recent years he has organized or participated in several collective studies on multi-level and multi-actor governance of science and technology, in particular within European research programs. In France, he has been involved in national studies and experiences on the design of regional innovation policies, as well as on cross-border cooperation schemes (in the Upper-Rhine area). His present activities are particularly focusing on the field of creative and knowledge-based development of territories.

Erik E. Lehmann is a full professor of Management and Organization at the University of Augsburg, Germany. From 2004 to 2005 he joined the Max Planck Institute as an assistant director. Together with Silvio Vismara (University of Bergamo, Italy) he directs the CISAlpino Institute for Comparative Studies in Europe (CCSE). Lehmann's research is focused on the links between corporate governance in family and entrepreneurial firms, innovation, public policy, education and innovation systems, financial constraints and regional and global competition. His research has been published in leading academic journals including *Review of Finance, Research Policy, Entrepreneurship Theory and Practice, Journal of Economic Behavior and Organization, Small Business Economics: An Entrepreneurship Journal, Journal of Small Business Management, Review of Accounting and Finance* and *Journal of Technology Transfer*, among others.

Chahira Mehouachi is preparing a PhD in Strategy at Université Paris-Dauphine, France. She is an assistant professor at ISG Paris Business School. She is also associate researcher at MOSAIC (Pôle Créativité & Innovation) at HEC Montréal, Canada. Her current research is centred on the issues of creativity and innovation management and inter-organizational cooperation within creative industries.

Emmanuel Muller has been active for 20 years in France and Germany in the fields of innovation and knowledge economics. He is coordinating the evoREG chair devoted to innovation policy and research in the Upper Rhine and is associated with BETA (Bureau d'Economie Théorique et Appliquée, UMR 7522 – CNRS, University of Strasbourg, France) and the Fraunhofer Institute for Systems and Innovation Research ISI (Karlsruhe, Germany). Apart from teaching and publishing in the fields of innovation economics, management and policy he performs contract research mainly on the issues of regional innovation systems, knowledge-intensive business services (KIBS) and creative economics.

Moritz Müller is Assistant Professor at the Faculty of Economics and Management of the University of Strasbourg and researcher at BETA (Bureau d'Economie Théorique et Appliquée, UMR 7522 – CNRS), which is a research laboratory of the University of Strasbourg, the University of Lorraine and the French National Centre for Scientific Research (CNRS) in France. He gratefully acknowledges financial support from the Chair in Economic Policy, ECON, KIT, in Germany. The research of Moritz Müller centres on the implications of human interaction in industrial as well as science systems.

Montserrat Pareja-Eastaway (PhD in Applied Economics, Universitat Autònoma de Barcelona, Spain) is Associate Professor of the Department of Economics at the University of Barcelona (UB), Spain. She is the coordinator of the research group 'Creativity, Innovation and Urban Transformation' (CRIT) at the Faculty of Economics and Business (UB). Dr Pareja-Eastaway devotes her research to the analysis of urban problems and, in particular, their impact on social and economic issues. She has extensive experience coordinating international and national research programmes. She is currently involved in CREASPACE, a research project funded by the Spanish Government (2016–2020) about spaces of creation and new modes of production of creative sectors. Since 2010 she has been Vice-Chair of the European Network for Housing Research and coordinates the working group 'Housing and Urban Sustainability'.

Julien Pénin is a researcher at BETA (Bureau d'Economie Théorique et Appliquée, UMR 7522 – CNRS). He has authored and co-authored many publications related to the economics and management of patents, open innovation and open source. Julien Pénin teaches Economics and Management of Innovation at the Department of Economics and Management at the University of Strasbourg, France.

Thierry Rayna is a professor of Economics and Innovation at Novancia Business School Paris, France. Earlier, he spent ten years in the United Kingdom, where he held academic positions at Imperial College London, the London School of Economics, University College London, and the University of Cambridge. His research investigates the consequences of technological change and digitization for intellectual property strategies, business models, and innovation ecosystems. He has served as an advisor for national and international organizations, as well as for major companies in the media, telecommunications, and cultural industries. He also mentors start-ups.

Marc Rocas is Associate Professor at University of Barcelona, Spain, where he teaches Strategic Management. Marc works as a consultant in the fields of Intercultural Management and Diversity Management. His research interests are cultural intelligence, organizational behaviour, international mobility of talent, entrepreneurship, and innovation management.

Eric Schenk is Associate Professor in Management at INSA Graduate School of Science and Technology of Strasbourg and an associate researcher at BETA (Bureau d'Economie Théorique et Appliquée, UMR 7522 – CNRS). His research focuses on innovation management and the questions related to competences. His recent work deals with the management of experts and of creativity.

Nikolaus Seitz is a research and teaching assistant at the Chair of Management and Organization at the University of Augsburg, Germany. His research aims at developing a better understanding of entrepreneurship-driven development strategies, innovation milieus and the role of (sub-)culture in creativity and knowledge-spillovers and start-up growth. Besides several book and conference contributions, his work has been published in the *Journal of Technology Transfer* and the *Journal of International Business and Economics*.

Laurent Simon, PhD, is Associate Professor in Management at HEC Montréal, Canada. His research activities aim at developing a better understanding of the design and management of collaborative, creative and innovative processes in organizations, with a specific focus on techno-creative industries (video games and media), artistic organizations, cultural industries and professional services. He co-chairs Mosaic, a research group dedicated to the study of the management of creation in an innovation society, a partnership with business organizations (Bell, Ubisoft Montreal, National Bank, Hydro-Québec, Cirque du Soleil and more).

Ludmila Striukova is a senior lecturer in the School of Management at University College London, UK. Her previous experience includes working as a market analyst for a statistical agency and as a researcher at King's College, University of London. She has published extensively in the area of innovation and technology management, and her research work has been used in numerous EU and national government reports. She has also used her telecommunications engineering background to mentor and advise technology-based start-ups and multinational corporations.

Jaume Valls-Pasola is Professor of Management and Business Administration at the University of Barcelona (UB), Spain, where he is responsible for the UB Entrepreneurship Chair and coordinates the UB Business and Management Research Group. His research interests are in the fields of innovation management, creativity, and entrepreneurship. His main teaching activities are related to innovation management and business creation processes.

Juan Vidaechea is a PhD candidate in the Management of Culture and Heritage programme at the Universitat de Barcelona, Spain. His PhD project explores the conditions for the emergence, generation and exchange of knowledge with symbolic component in temporal or permanent creative communities. He has conducted the research study 'Factories of creativity in Barcelona: What kind of middleground devices?', and has been involved in UB's research project INNRED. He has been a lecturer at the Universitat de Barcelona, was awarded the Universitat de Barcelona's Extraordinary Completion of Master's Degree Prize in the Cultural Management degree (2013) and has obtained a Culturex scholarship granted by the Spanish Secretary of the State for Culture in 2015.

Marcus Wagner is a full professor at the University of Augsburg, Germany, where he holds the Chair in Management, Innovation and International Business and is an associate member of the Bureau d'Economie Théorique et Appliquée, where he held an Intra-European Marie Curie Fellowship from 2006 to 2008. Prior to his position in Augsburg, he was professor at the University of Würzburg (Chair in Entrepreneurship and Management, 2009 to 2014), assistant professor in technology and innovation management at Munich University of Technology (2005 to 2009) and a senior manager in the semiconductor industry. His research interests are entrepreneurship and innovation, international management, sustainability and strategic management, with several works on this having been published in *Journal of Business Venturing*, *Journal of International Business Studies*, *Long Range Planning* and *Research Policy*, amongst others.

Wilfried Zidorn is associated with the Universidad de las Americas in Ecuador as a visiting scholar and part-time professor for Entrepreneurship. Prior to these roles, he was a senior business project manager for Credit Suisse in Switzerland and a research assistant at the University of Würzburg, Germany. His research interests are entrepreneurship and innovation management, strategic and sustainable management in developing countries and business development within the renewable energy industry.

Foreword

Innovation in a world of rapid change

The only thing constant is change – attributed to Heraclitus of Ephesus, 535–475 BC

We live in a period of rapid change. While this has always been true, as evidenced by the above rather clichéd quote, the increased pace of innovation and consequent reduced cycle times have altered the global economy in fundamental ways. If one were forced to put a finger on one single seismic shift that underlies this change it would have to be the widespread diffusion of the Internet at the turn of the century. It is perhaps the leading cause of the transition from the twentieth-century managerial economy to the twenty-first-century entrepreneurial economy. Like the steam engine, electric power and the internal combustion engine, the Internet is the latest general-purpose technology that is transforming every aspect of society.

From this perspective, the most important effect of the new digital economy is that it has led to a drastic reduction in spatial transaction costs. This has drastically changed the organization of business. Most value is now created in global value chains (GVCs): worldwide networks that weave together low-value, standardized (repetitive) activities undertaken in emerging economies with high value, specialized (non-repetitive) activities performed in advanced economies. Orchestrators typically control the knowledge-intensive intangibles that accrue the lion's share of value created, accounting for the rising share of intangibles in global valued added. GVCs are made up of two generic types of firms – specializers that focus on narrower and narrower niches and orchestrators that design the final customer value proposition and coordinate the multifarious activities and eco-system of constituent organizations. Knowledge is the mainspring of GVCs and therefore the relevant actors implement a diverse array of innovation tools. However, the nature and organization of these tools is still little understood.

Consequently, this volume that addresses current themes in global innovation and creativity is a welcome effort. The editors and authors highlight and analyse key elements of the new, complex, spatially dispersed global economy, including open innovation and the encouragement and harnessing of creativity. These efforts have led to a wide variety of new phenomena that need to be understood and placed within the theoretical framework of innovation: incubators, accelerators, idea contests, idea boxes, portals, communities of beta-testers, open data, intrapreneurship programmes, corporate venture capital, crowd-sourcing and crowd-funding just to name a few. Explaining the rise of new and emerging phenomena often requires modifying extant theory in order to develop new theoretical insights. I see this volume as part of this process. Therefore, I laud both the editors and the authors for providing the innovation research community with this valuable new resource.

Ram Mudambi, *Temple University*
Philadelphia, 2016

Foreword

Open innovation and the global creativity challenge

As an international business scholar with a distinctive interest in the globalization of innovation and R&D, I have had the chance to talk with a number of corporate managers. During these conversations, all of them, irrespective of sector and location of their corporate operations, pointed out the need to create and look for opportunities to share ideas and liaise with stakeholders, start-ups and universities in order for their companies to innovate and stay competitive. In addition to managers, academics and consultants are by now aware of the corporate imperative 'innovate or die' and increasingly conscious of the dramatic relevance of ideas generated outside a firm's boundaries for, in Henry Chesbrough's words, creating and profiting from technology. Interactions with the external business ecosystem are also strongly encouraged by policy makers willing to nurture the blooming of 'born global' entrepreneurial ventures and start-ups, which are an active part of the open innovation and co-creation process.

Attention on creativity and open innovation has widely informed studies by academics, professionals and media, which have discussed drivers, effects and contingencies of the creation process, and adoption of an open innovation model. This book is different, however, and well overdue. It is about the global dimension of open innovation and co-creation processes. During the conversations on the cross-border dimension of the innovation process I engaged at international conferences and outlets, I have realized over the years that the discussion on managing creativity globally has remained disconnected from the debate on the open innovation model.

For this reason, I happily welcome this volume that contributes to enhance our understanding of the main concerns of creativity management at a global scale by explicitly connecting global management and the open innovation model in an increasingly cross-cultural digitalized world. In particular, I applaud the editors and the authors in neatly identifying culture and the developments of information and communication technologies as key tools that facilitate the process and management of creativity globally. I strongly recommend *The Global Management of Creativity* to managers, academic, consultants as well as policy makers, who will benefit from an integrated understanding of global management of creativity, learn about a set of challenging issues for twenty-first-century management, and appreciate global opportunities arising from megatrends such as digitalization.

Global corporate players as well as world-class universities look for open innovation collaboration, and a thorough grasp of the 'global management of creativity' is critical to ride the wave, and creating and profiting from technology.

Grazia D. Santangelo, Jean Monnet Chair International Business
for European Union, University of Catania
Catania, 2016

Acknowledgements

This book was put into motion in autumn 2014 when the publisher accepted the proposal submitted by the Augsburg-Barcelona-Strasbourg academic network. But, the edition has become a reality, obviously, because of the contribution of the 21 authors that have prepared the nine chapters of its contents. They answered with enthusiasm the call we sent out and they participated in the research workshop that was organized in order to develop the final steps of this collective project. Coming from different countries and different institutions, the contributors collaborated and evaluated each other's works with great professionalism. Hosting a workshop in Augsburg was also a very pleasant moment and insightful for all participants whose works were improved during these two days of discussion.

A final push in order to adjust to the common guidelines after the workshop was critical for the coherence and quality of the whole text. There is no doubt that this publication would not have been possible without the huge effort of all the authors. As editors of the book we are thankful to all of them.

We are also indebted to the staff of the Augsburg University's Chair of Management, Innovation and International Business who contributed substantially to the success of the publication process through organizing a research workshop on 'Global Management of Creativity in the Digital Age' that took place on 18 and 19 February 2016. Specifically, we would like to thank Armin Anzenbacher, Regina Dietmair, Hüseyin Doluca, Anna-Lena Hoffmann and Stephanie Lange. We are grateful for financial support to the workshop by the Institute for Digitization Research (specifically Daniel Veit), the Lechwerke AG, the Faculty of Business Administration and Economics Competence Center for Global Business and Law and the Chair of Organization and Management, and for the latter two specifically Erik Lehmann.

We would also like to express our gratitude to our universities for their support in the project, namely, Strasbourg University, Augsburg University and the University of Barcelona. From the Strasbourg University side we would like to acknowledge the support of Ms Anne Leitzgen (Groupe Schmidt), M. Ivan Steyert (Socomec) and M. Frédéric Creplet (Voirin-Conseil en management) for our activities under the chair in Management of Creativity headed by Patrick Llerena. In Barcelona, we are grateful to Banco de Santander for supporting our activities through the Entrepreneurship Chair. In Augsburg, special thanks go to

Regina Dietmair for her continued support for the project activities and especially for preparing the index of the book.

Finally, we thank the staff at Routledge, who gave us the opportunity to publish this book. A special thank you is extended to Emily Kindleysides and Laura Johnson at Routledge for their confidence and support of the production of this book.

Introduction

Thierry Burger-Helmchen, Jaume Valls-Pasola and Marcus Wagner

During the last decades of the twentieth century the academic recognition of the innovation-competitiveness link took place. The new product economy and the management of innovation displaced production management from the top rankings of main managerial concerns and creative value chain management became more and more a core management topic. Over the last decade or so, two new themes entered the mainstream: creativity and open innovation. These two subjects have gained great currency among managers but also academics, consultants and policy makers.

They are at the core of the innovation/competitiveness research field and they reflect deep changes in the way we face innovation going further than a process orientation for value creation chains and that of the product-service innovation process. They show the increasing importance, within the innovative processes, of structuring the generation and collection of ideas and of opening the company to the exchange of knowledge in a radical way in order to shorten time-to-market, optimize resources and nurture the ideation processes. In other words, the interaction with the external business ecosystem is decisive for being competitive.

Nowadays, it is widely accepted that without open innovation strategies organizations cannot compete at the global scale and that this approach is no longer a simple opening to bidirectional knowledge exchanges. It is much more. It comprises a wide scope of possible actions, inside and outside the organization, that are crucial for the collection and development of ideas. Amongst these activities we can mention: idea contests, idea boxes, portals, communities of beta-testers, open data, intrapreneurship programmes, licensing or corporate venturing. Start-up partnership programmes are also a relevant strategy. More and more innovative start-ups are forming part of these open innovation and co-creation processes.

This is especially the case for the recent phenomenon of the so-called 'born global' entrepreneurial ventures and start-ups. They are truly innovative and have a speeded process of internationalization in which the scalability of the activity developed forms part of its business DNA. They can carry out partnership strategies with big companies, can be the object of acquisition strategies, can attract important investments or simply can nurture the innovative processes of different ecosystems and orienting their specialization. In addition, a growing number of start-ups can be found in the social field, as well as in the cultural, artistic and entertainment sectors. In a global creativity scenario where we are interdisciplinary approaches and creative industries are obviously at the centre of the blooming of the creative economy.

This blooming takes place in a context of extraordinary developments in the field of Information and Communication technologies (ICT) that push for a non-reversible digitalization scenario of the management procedures. Or, in other words, the way to address the processes of innovation changes and take into consideration the role of creativity and of the ideation processes in a more intensive and structured way. Ideas and new concepts are no longer the result of brainstorming strategies but they have to be managed in a more systematic way. Information systems, ICT platforms and applications programming interfaces are key tools in such systematization. Creativity is at the core of the 'co' approaches that lead these major changes in innovation management: collaboration, cooperation . . . But, probably, the most significant example of these changes is 'co-creation'. A process where co-ideation and co-design are often pushed by computing tools and computer platforms that allow global scale interaction with the users and their strong and active involvement in co-creation through these platforms.

This book tries to contribute to a better understanding of the main concerns of creativity management at a global scale. We hope that the 'trip' that we propose to the reader through nine chapters will help him to immerse in a set of challenging issues that are, from our point of view, key issues for twenty-first century management researchers. This 'trip', has been promoted and organized by an academic team from three European universities where management research groups specializing in innovation, creativity and entrepreneurship are located. Prior to outlining the contents of the book briefly in order to conclude this introduction we would like to provide the reader with a short overview of these three research units.

BETA (Bureau d'Economie Théorique et Appliquée) is a research laboratory of the University of Strasbourg, University of Lorraine and the French National Centre for Scientific Research CNRS. It was created in 1972 and it became an 'associate' member of CNRS in 1985. BETA's activities cover a wide range of topics dealing with basic as well as applied scientific research in the fields of economics and management science. Historically, the laboratory developed its research program along several research directions based on micro- and macro-economic theories, and is heir to a local tradition of history of economic thought. It has also developed a number of focus areas, often resulting from the fruitful interaction of 'theoretical' approaches and 'applied' approaches – as expressed in its name – such as the economics of innovation, management of technology and organizations, environmental economics, socio-economic approaches of education, training and employment and, more recently, historical economics and cliometrics.

The result has been the creation of collective competences from years of practice with different methodologies: modelling techniques, econometrics, methods of technology evaluation and foresight, experimental economics, to mention only a few. In July 2016 BETA numbered some 120 staff members with permanent positions (mainly professors and assistant professors of the university, researchers, administrative and technical personnel) and over 80 non-permanent staff (associate members, PhD students and post-docs). Since 2010 several developments have taken place in the domain of economics and management of creativity. In particular, BETA is now successfully supported by three local companies: Groupe Schmit, Socomec and Voirin-Conseil en management, through a Chair in Management of Creativity. It has allowed BETA and the Faculty of Economics and Management to organize a Fall School in Management of Creativity and structure an Academy of Management of Creativity and Innovation.

Since its creation, 10 years ago, the Entrepreneurship Chair of the University of Barcelona has worked acutely in subjects related with entrepreneurship, creativity and Innovation. These activities have been carried out in the framework of the Business and Management Department jointly with the research group of the same name that is associated to it. The group, as a permanent research unit, has been recognized as a consolidated research group, a label awarded to high-quality research groups by the regional government (Generalitat of Catalonia). It has 28 researchers and over 20 non-permanent staff (mainly PhD students). In addition to the subjects already mentioned, there are four additional research lines: international business, marketing, quality management and operations management.

Concerning creativity and entrepreneurship more recent projects cover fields like creativity and gastronomy, entrepreneurship success and failure and open innovation and innovation performance. Since 2009 the Chair organizes, every year, jointly with HEC Montreal the International Summer School on Creativity Management in an Innovation society, which gathers during two weeks 60 international participants on an intensive creativity management program. The group is a member of the Entrepreneurship Observatory of the Spanish University System and takes part in different international networks like RedEmprendia and the Yunus Social Business Centre Initiative.

At Augsburg University the Chair of Management, Innovation and International Business conducts research in the areas of corporate sustainability, innovation and international/strategic management, with much work being at the intersections of these. This is important since through the emergence of a digital age characterized by complex product-service systems and 'lot size 1'-matched product and labor markets firms have to manage creative activities in geographically and culturally globalized value chains and production networks. Beyond this, global management also has a broader meaning since with more efficient markets for technology and increasingly digital products, firms face novel questions on how to organize.

This concerns the possibility of open innovation, implying an increase of alliances and acquisitions. It also relates to ambidexterity, and global management in the sense of balancing exploration and exploitation activities to embrace new possibilities arising from megatrends such as digitalization. Therefore, global management of creativity is understood at the chair as a multi-level concept, and thus as a simultaneous requirement for international management, innovation management and strategic management to coordinate activities and orchestrate assets towards global optima in a creative (i.e. entrepreneurial and sustainable) manner. The chair carries out work on this in close cooperation and interaction with Augsburg University's Center for Entrepreneurship, the Münchener Kreis, and SCANCOR at Stanford University.

Overall, this introduction has hopefully clarified the need for an integrated understanding of global management of creativity in the face of new trends in value chain management and open innovation. This also includes the notion of a wide and encompassing definition of creativity that links to exploration and breakthrough as well operational (i.e. non-breakthrough) forms of creativity linked more to exploitation.

At a general level, the papers of this volume fall in two broad areas, namely five chapters with an innovation and creativity focus and four chapters with a focus on culture and creativity. We used this bisection for our chapter structure, starting out initially with three chapters focusing on innovation and creativity. To make the reading more varied, this is followed by the four chapters focusing on culture and creativity. The book concludes with two more chapters that return to the innovation and creativity focus. However, within this binary division, other more fine-grained divisions become visible as is exemplified by the following matrix:

Table 0.1 Topic-related structure of contributions

Ambidexterity	**Cultural Creativity**
Heraud and Muller	*Lehmann and Seitz*
Wagner and Zidorn	*Rocas and García*
Knowledge Spaces	**Open Innovation**
Mehouachi, Grandadam, Cohendet and Simon	*Avadikyan and Muller*
Vidaechea and Pareja-Eastaway	*Rayna and Striukova*
	Schenk, Guittard and Pénin

These concluding remarks of the introduction hopefully help the readers to navigate the different chapters of this edited volume and to easily identify those areas of highest interest to them. It is also our wish that the book will trigger further research in this important and topical area of management research that today is so vital for the success of firms, as well as the sustainable development of countries and regions.

1 How and when does open innovation affect creativity?

Eric Schenk, Claude Guittard and Julien Pénin

Introduction

Over the last decade, open innovation (hereinafter referred to as 'OI') has received increasing attention from both researchers and practitioners. The focus has been mainly placed on business model aspects of OI, which include IP issues, access to external resources and markets, absorptive capacity, etc. This chapter more specifically addresses the impact of OI on individual and organizational creativity.

In our view, creativity encompasses individuals' ability to generate new relevant ideas and concepts, as well as out-of-the-box problem solving capabilities. There is a usually a general (often implicit) consensus that OI has a positive effect on creativity. By opening up their boundaries and interacting with other actors, firms may avoid falling into an incremental trap and/or avoid the innovator dilemma (Christensen, 1997). Moreover, the literature shows that openness and information sharing may have a positive effect on problem solving (Boudreau and Lakhani, 2013; Brabham, 2008).

However, OI involves many different modalities. It can be highly or weakly interactive, market or non-market based, formal or informal, exploration or exploitation oriented, etc. Depending on the modality that is chosen, the implications for creativity may be different. OI may sometimes enhance creativity but also, in other cases and contexts, have no impact at all, or even a negative impact on it. For instance, when a pharmaceutical multinational buys a licence for a life science start-up company, it usually has no impact on creativity. On the contrary, OI can be seen here as a consequence of the lack of creativity of the pharmaceutical firm, which therefore obliges it to compensate and buy a licence.

The objective of this chapter is therefore to use the existing literature and case studies in order to discuss how and when OI affects creativity. An important point in our reasoning is that, since creativity is described as an ability, OI must affect firms' innovative process, routines and knowledge in order to increase it. If it only aims to develop new technology that can be exploited without changing routines and the innovation process, then OI, although it may increase the innovative performance of the process, will have no impact on its actors' creativity. This leads us to distinguish two radically different types of OI modalities: the ones that only aim at reorganizing the innovation process (and follow a pure logic of resource allocation) and the ones that aim at co-creating new resources. In our view, only the second ones can have a significant effect on OI actors' creativity (although the first ones can significantly improve the efficiency of the innovation process).

In the following section, we introduce the concepts of creativity and OI that are used in this chapter. We then present OI modalities targeted at resource allocation and question their impact on firms' creativity, with the example of markets for technology and crowdsourcing. In the next step, we consider cases where OI sustains resource co-creation and show that in these cases, the effect on creativity can be significant. The example of knowledge communities is used to back the argument. The last section concludes.

What do we mean by creativity and open innovation?

Providing a comprehensive review of creativity and OI goes beyond the scope of this chapter. However, given the multiplicity of approaches in the literature, it is important to clarify in which way we use these concepts.

Creativity and the innovation process

Although innovation is known to have various potential targets, we mainly focus on product innovation and the new product development process (e.g., Pahl *et al.*, 2007; Ulrich and Eppinger, 2012). However, as shown, for instance, by Lenfle (2005), some insights into product development can also be applied for an analysis of new service development. New product development is often viewed as a 'stage-gate' process (e.g., Cooper and Edgett, 2012). First, the ideation phase is a period in which new concepts emerge. This phase, sometimes referred to as the Fuzzy Front End (Khurana and Rosenthal, 1998; Gassmann and Schweitzer, 2013; Cohendet *et al.*, 2013), usually gives room to creativity, for instance, by the use of brainstorming methods or crowdsourcing. After this first step, some concepts are selected and a phase of business analysis is entered in which market as well as financial opportunities are assessed. After the business case analysis, another selection takes place leading to the development phase for a few projects. The aim of the development phase is to find cost effective and reliable ways to implement the concepts that have been selected previously. Therefore, this phase is very much problem solving oriented. The last steps imply the testing and validation of previously developed concepts and solutions, and finally the market launch.

Our general assumption is that creativity is required throughout the innovation process. In the early stages, creativity is targeted towards the emergence of new ideas. This process can be rather open and unstructured (hence the term 'fuzzy front end') and it is related to a rather classical view of creativity (emergence of novel useful ideas). Later in the innovation funnel, creativity is employed in the problem solving process. Indeed, solving new problems often implies the ability to think out of the box and to depart from methods and techniques that are usually employed).

Creativity can be viewed as the outcome of an individual process. According to the componential theory of creativity (Amabile, 1996, 1998; Amabile *et al.*, 1996), individual creativity is related to domain specific skill, creative thinking skills, intrinsic task motivation and, finally, the social environment. Domain specific skills refer to competence and expertise which are largely tacit and acquired though personal experience (Ericsson *et al.*, 2007; Bootz *et al.*, 2015). Creative thinking skills include traits of personality, cognitive characteristics such as reasoning and attitude towards risk, and the ability to think 'out of the box'. Intrinsic motivators include task enjoyment (Deci, 1975) and autonomy, mastery and purpose (Pink, 2015). Finally, environmental factors refer to the work environment, which includes relationships with colleagues and the hierarchy, but also the job design and incentive schemes of the organization. Creativity is therefore influenced by individual, idiosyncratic factors, as well as by external factors. It can be noticed that the environmental factors can have a positive or a negative impact on creativity (Amabile and Kramer, 2011). For instance, according to the overjustification effect (Deci *et al.*, 1999), extrinsic motivators can impede creativity by crowding out intrinsic motivation.

A complementary approach to creativity is proposed by Woodman *et al.* (1993) who define organizational creativity as the ability of an organization to stimulate interactions between individuals in a complex social setting. Organizational creativity depends on individual characteristics, group characteristics and organizational characteristics. Recent studies (Hargadon and Bechky 2006; Parjanen, 2012) have further analysed the notion of group creativity. For instance, according to Parjanen (2012), collective or group creativity can be stimulated by the strategy of the organization, the type of leadership, the organizational culture, and the tools and methods supporting creativity. According to these authors, group creativity is relevant for complex tasks that require multiple skills, and which cannot be dealt with individually. In this context, social interactions and knowledge sharing are especially useful in overcoming individual perceptions (Nonaka and Takeuchi, 1995).

A primer on open innovation

OI is an umbrella term that means that the innovation process is interactive since innovators today can no longer remain isolated or entirely self-reliant (Chesbrough, 2003; Pénin *et al.*, 2013). OI is thus opposed to the romantic vision of the lone entrepreneur who heroically breaks down all barriers in order to bring the innovation to the market. On the contrary, in OI logic, the entrepreneur interacts with his or her environment at different stages of the innovation process, forging links with other innovation stakeholders, public research centres, suppliers, customers or even actual or potential competitors. OI is thus more or less synonymous with collaborative, modular or collective innovation, many terms that are sometimes found in the literature and which mean that innovation is a matter of collaboration and more or less formal interactions.

The modalities of OI can be very different (see Table 1.1): formation of a research joint venture between different organizations, exchange of intellectual property licences, formation of patent pools, agreements on industrial standards, formation of innovative clusters, outsourcing of problems on Internet platforms (crowdsourcing), interactions with open source communities, etc. Jullien and

Table 1.1 Types of open innovation (Jullien and Pénin, 2014)

	Open innovation 1.0	Open innovation 2.0
"Outside-in"	Licensing-in, Spin-ins	Crowdsourcing
Mixed or coupled	Co-conception, Co-development Research consortium Research joint venture	Innovation with communities / open source
"Inside-out"	Licensing-out, Spin-outs	Online market places / eBay for ideas

Pénin (2014) provide a classification of OI modalities according to the importance they give to ICTs (OI 1.0 versus 2.0) and the inside-out versus outside-in nature of knowledge flows.

Indeed, the literature generally distinguishes two sides of OI: the 'inside-out' and the 'outside-in'. Both sides are based on the direction of knowledge and information flows between the company and its environment. Inside-out means that the knowledge flows from the inside to the outside of the company, i.e., it outsources knowledge and technology internally developed by granting licences, creating spin-offs or revealing trade secrets to a collaboration partner. Outside-in means that the knowledge flows from outside to inside, i.e., that the company absorbs knowledge developed by others, for example, by buying intellectual property licences, absorbing other companies or by setting up 'crowdsourcing' contests. Often, the OI process is also called coupled, that is to say, it mixes both types of knowledge flows, as is the case, for example, during bilateral collaboration in R&D where both partners generally exchange individual information.

Chesbrough does not hesitate to speak of a new paradigm in order to describe the rupture induced by OI. But for other authors it is possible to find examples of OI during most periods of the past, thus suggesting that the OI concept is nothing more than a recycling of previous concepts, a very successful marketing operation, i.e., 'old wine in new bottles' (Trott and Hartmann, 2009). However, OI still carries original elements. In particular, the emphasis put by Chesbrough on the inside-out aspect and the importance of open business models are absolutely new. Moreover, the use of ICTs, and especially the Internet, has changed the situation by allowing OI to be far more open and interactive today than in the past. ICTs multiply the possibilities of remote interactions and facilitate the links between several partners and the development of innovative communities. The modalities of OI today are therefore sometimes very different from those that could be observed even in the last few decades. To illustrate this change, Jullien and Pénin (2014) speak of OI 2.0 versus 1.0 (see also Rayna and Striukova, 2015).

Open innovation as a pure resource allocation process

Seeking to understand if OI improves organizational creativity in the innovation process, we distinguish between two very different cases of OI: OI as a pure resource allocation process and OI as a knowledge co-creation process. We argue in this section that in the first case, the impact on organizational creativity is likely to be marginal.

Resource allocation versus knowledge co-creation

Many cases of OI only aim at better allocating the resources used in the innovation process. It therefore follows a pure logic of optimization of existing resources which does not affect, or only marginally, the cognitive capacity of the actors in the innovation process. For instance, many examples of crowdsourcing of inventive or creative activities or of in-licensing only aim, for the company that crowdsources a problem or buys a patent licence, to substitute internal R&D with external R&D. Similarly, many bilateral collaborative agreements only aim at improving the exploitation of an already existing invention by, for instance, optimizing the supply chain, etc.

In this case, OI is a way to make the innovation process more efficient. In the end, thanks to OI, the global innovative performance of the system is improved and more innovations reach the market, but companies that open up their boundaries as a way to better allocate resources do not become more creative. It may be a way for them to outsource creative work and access more creative things.

On the other hand, some cases of OI, such as, for instance, research joint ventures or open source communities, primarily aim at creating new knowledge by merging different competences and making heterogeneous people work together, thus impacting their cognitive capacity. Those modalities of OI are much more exploratory and within these contexts it is likely that OI not only improves the global innovative performance of the system, but also enhances the creativity of participants because it obliges them to interact actively with other participants. This will be developed later in the chapter.

In the case of a pure resource allocation process, OI does not significantly improve creativity. Rather, OI is a consequence of the lack of creativity of the actors in the innovation process. It can offer them a short-term solution to their lack of creativity, but does not affect their cognitive capacity and does not improve their ability to think out of the box, introduce new concepts, radically test new solutions, etc.

It is possible that the specialization effect induced by a better allocation of resources enhances, to some extent, the skills of actors involved in the innovation process. Yet, we believe that this positive effect is usually overcome by the negative effect of specialization which traps innovators into separate boxes. Indeed, the division of labour and specialization induced by OI contributes to reducing a global problem, which requires interaction between very different participants (thus eventually obliging them to 'think different') in a series of independent local boxes, thus reducing interactions between heterogeneous actors and narrowing their research scope. Specialization, even in the case of inventive and complex activities, is likely to reduce the creative impulse of those who perform them.

Markets for technology: does a division of labour and technology specialization increase creativity?

The example of markets for technology is, we believe, quite emblematic in understanding the weak impact of OI on creativity when it is performed in a pure logic of resource allocation. Over the last two decades, developed countries have observed the growth of markets in which organizations trade technology (Arora *et al.*, 2001; Arora and Gambardella, 2010). In markets for technology, technology sellers (often a technological firm, start-up, or research organization (public or private) develop new technologies which they sell to technology buyers, usually manufacturing firms which then embody these technologies within the manufacturing products that they sell. Markets for technology are greatly facilitated by the existence of intellectual property rights that ensure the flow of technology from sellers to buyers (Arora and Merges, 2004; Pénin, 2012).

Markets for technology are thus clearly a case of OI in which some companies perform inside-out by selling technologies to other companies who perform outside-in. Furthermore, it is also clearly a case of a pure resource allocation process since companies do not work together in order to co-create something. Markets are a way to efficiently allocate resources.

A major consequence of markets for technology is facilitating the division of innovative labour across firms involved in the innovation process and fostering specialization. The fact that markets promote division of labour and vertical specialization has been acknowledged at least since the pioneering work of Adam Smith. Thus, the development of markets for technology, as imperfect as they are, leads to a major reorganization of research activities. It promotes the appearance of upstream firms, highly efficient in research, specializing in the development of new technologies that they then sell to downstream manufacturing firms. In other words, markets for technology improve the organization of innovative labour. Consequently, they are considered beneficial for the global performance of the system, i.e., they lead to more innovations. This is perfectly illustrated by the case of pharmaceuticals illustrated in Box 1.1.

Box 1.1   The case of biotech start-ups and big pharmaceutical companies

The example of the pharmaceutical sector illustrates the link, or absence of a link, between markets for technology and creativity. The biotechnology revolution that began in the 1970s in the US has profoundly changed the landscape of the pharmaceutical industry. Big pharmaceutical companies, which earlier were doing most of their applied research internally, are now engaged in a logic of division of labour with small biotech companies (Hamdouch and Depret, 2001). Many of their research activities, including the identification of new molecules, are now largely outsourced and carried out by biotechnology start-up companies, which then license them to large pharmaceutical groups who develop and market the drug.

Big pharmaceutical companies and start-up firms, often presented as competing actors, are therefore rather perfectly complementary, as evidenced by the high number of collaborative agreements between the two (Hagedoorn, 2002). This division of labour leads to the increased specialization of each player in its core competencies. A very flexible and dynamic start-up company can focus on scientific excellence. In contrast, large pharmacy groups focus on financing clinical testing and marketing the drug, tasks that are difficult for small start-ups to perform.

Similar transformation has been observed in electronics and more specifically, semiconductors. The organization of this industry has been affected in the 1980s by the arrival of new types of actors, 'fabless' companies. The purpose of these 'fabless' companies is to limit the amount of mobilized physical capital by focusing on innovation and creativity. They therefore specialize in the design of new chips and R&D as well as marketing and distribution. In sum, 'fabless' companies are only creators of electronic components (designers) whose production is then outsourced to foundries (or 'fabs'), essentially located in South East Asia.

Both in pharmaceuticals and electronics, this new division of labour, based on the principles of OI, may improve the innovation performance of firms. However, it is not clear whether it has improved the creativity of the actors. Do big pharmaceuticals companies become more creative when they outsource part of their research to start-up firms? This is unlikely if they do not also massively invest in order to mix their own competences with those of the start-ups. Do start-up companies become more creative when they specialize in a limited number of research domains in order to provide manufacturing firms with efficient research solutions? Once again, we believe that this specialization, on the contrary, locks them in a given technological trajectory, thus reducing their ability to broaden their minds and do things differently.

But can we say that markets for technology lead to more creativity? Markets for technology optimize, in a sense, the allocation of creative resources. They lead to a better use of existing resources (including knowledge and workers' skills) and make organizations more efficient, more productive but not more creative (specialization increases productivity, not creativity). Thanks to markets for technology, individuals and firms can become more specialized and efficient. However, these gains in specialization may even negatively affect their creativity since specialization, i.e., the reproduction of similar tasks not even linked to routine activities but to inventive activities, can hardly train people to think differently, quite the opposite. It is possible that people are more creative during start-ups that are more flexible, less bureaucratic and give more space to personal involvement. However, this effect must be balanced by the specialization effect, the fact that those companies have, by definition, a narrow view of their research domains which will damage their creativity.

Crowdsourcing and innovation contests

An interesting way to seek creativity outside the boundaries of the firm is to use crowdsourcing. Generally speaking, crowdsourcing reflects the fact of outsourcing, via an Internet platform, a task to 'the crowd' (i.e., a large number of individuals that are *a priori* unknown). The literature shows that crowdsourcing can be applied in different ways in order to perform various tasks (see e.g., Estellés-Arolas and Gonzáles-Ladrón de Guevara, 2012; Pénin and Burger-Helmchen, 2011; Schenk and Guittard, 2011).

In creativity-oriented tasks such as designing a logo, crowdsourcing can access the creativity of Internet users distributed around the globe. While these creative tasks sometimes need special professional skills, they are also accessible for non-professionals or event users of the firm's products (Poetz and Schreier, 2012). Therefore, crowdsourcing is a way to reach professionals at a lower cost, but also to build a closer customer relationship. For instance, crowdsourcing is successfully implemented by the Lego Company (Box 1.2).

Box 1.2   Crowdsourcing by the Lego company

We focus on the Lego Group's implementation of crowdsourcing through the Lego Ideas project (a more comprehensive presentation of Lego's innovation approach is provided in Chapter 2 of this book). The Lego Group is a Danish company whose main product is the famous Lego toy. This toy can create all kinds of 3D objects from plastic bricks, either sold as generic 'brix boxes' or as more complex sets representing specific universes (e.g., Star Wars). Today, The Lego Group is a world leader in the toy market (No. 1 worldwide in 2015). Experts from 'Brand Finance' consider the Lego company the most powerful one in the world ahead of Apple or Google. Lego appears as a highly identified and recognized global brand.

Following the severe crisis that the company faced in early 2000 and with the emergence of spontaneous coordination by fans, especially through web forums, Lego has chosen to open its product development process. The Cuusoo project was first tested in the Japanese market from 2008 to 2011. Following the success of this first experiment, the project was launched worldwide in 2011.

The operating principle is quite simple. Any registered user can propose a new 'Lego set' and users in the community have the opportunity to give support to projects through their vote. When a project has reached 10,000 votes (originally 1000, but given the unexpected success of the platform, the threshold was raised), the project enters the final stage of the process. A dedicated Lego team then decides if the model can be

---

developed and market launched. The model creator receives 1 per cent of the revenue generated by the model.

The Lego Ideas platform is a real success. At the beginning of 2016, more than 16,000 projects have been displayed on the platform, 13 models coming from the crowdsourcing competition have been launched on the market and 9 projects are under internal review.

However, a question that is still open is whether this crowdsourcing initiative contributes to improving the creativity of the Lego company or whether it is merely a very efficient manner to harness the creativity of outside contributors. For Lego, the next step might therefore be to try to turn this crowdsourcing platform into a real communitarian mode of knowledge production in which Lego creators and researchers actively work with people from the crowd (i.e., to transform crowdsourcing into a real case of co-creation as discussed by Rayna and Striukova in Chapter 2).

Crowdsourcing also fosters innovation because it is a particularly effective way to solve complex problems that cannot be resolved internally (Brabham, 2008; Jeppesen and Lakhani, 2010; Pénin and Burger-Helmchen, 2012). Crowdsourcing can be used to access expert problem solving skills that are sometimes absent from the firm's nexus of partners and competitors (Boudreau and Lakhani, 2013). Therefore, under certain conditions, crowdsourcing is a way to implement distant search (Afuah and Tucci, 2012). These conditions are, among others, the ability to access a large population of potential contributors, the ability to formulate problems in a precise way, and the ability to absorb and implement external knowledge in the innovation process.

In other words, if crowdsourcing can be an effective way to capture creativity outside the firm, in our view, in its simplest form, it does not improve the creative processes inside the company itself. Creativity is outsourced rather than integrated into the culture of the organization. In order to enhance creativity, crowdsourcing should be viewed by companies not as a simple resource allocation process, but rather as a resource co-creation process in which the company works hand-in-hand with the crowd.

Open innovation as a knowledge co-creation process

Facilitating conditions

When implemented in a pure logic of resource allocation, OI can scarcely impact the creativity of organizations involved in the innovation process. Yet, this may not be the case when OI is implemented in a logic of knowledge co-creation. In this case, organizations have to work together, agree on common objectives, pool resources and understand the other party to some extent. OI here can be a powerful instrument for boosting the creativity of companies that implement it. However, this still requires a series of facilitating conditions to be met. Here we explore the role of 1) the objective of collaboration; 2) its modalities, and 3) the type of partners. Our conclusions (still very preliminary) are shown in Table 1.2.

As to the objective of collaboration, as stated earlier in the paper, it is obviously important to distinguish cases where actors only aim to better exploit an existing resource (collaboration in an exploitative logic such as optimization of the distribution chain, etc.) from cases where they explicitly aim to explore new problems, i.e., produce new knowledge. In the first case, it is likely that external resources brought by partners mostly substitute internal ones, thus leaving the cognitive ability of OI participants largely unaffected. In the second case, on the other hand, companies must develop exploratory joint research projects that will largely affect their cognitive capacities and eventually their creativity.

As to the modalities of collaboration, OI can be more or less formalized, open and interactive. In the case of open source communities, there is no formal hierarchy (the structure is entirely informal), the process is completely open, in the sense that everybody can contribute, and interactivity is potentially high (people can exchange almost simultaneously online). Conversely, in the case of bilateral collaboration between two companies, formalization is usually high (collaboration is contractualized), collaboration is controlled, in the sense that information and knowledge are protected by patents and secrecy and do not spill over to other companies, and interactivity is quite limited (meetings are spaced in time). As regards creativity, it is likely that a context that is more informal, more open and more interactive is more favourable as illustrated by the case of open source communities (see Box 1.3).

Finally, in order to understand the link between OI and creativity, it is also important to take into account the distance (cultural, cognitive, etc.) between OI participants. Interactions between very close actors may not significantly improve their creativity since it may not introduce new visions, problems or instruments. Creativity may therefore require interactions between very different participants whose confrontation may provoke the emergence of new thinking. However, distance may also impede communication and the ability to develop common projects.

An inverse U-shape relationship between creativity and distance has been put forward in the case of inter-firms alliances (see 'Inter-firms innovation alliances' below) where cognitive distance has been seen as an important parameter, both for the emergence of trust and the knowledge creation process. Cognitive distance is a way to represent resource and knowledge heterogeneity between partners (Nooteboom 1999; Nooteboom *et al.*, 2007). On the one hand, in a partnership the 'value of novelty' increases with cognitive distance, since cooperation between distant partners is likely to yield an outcome that was not achievable without cooperation. On the other had the 'ability to cooperate' will decrease when the cognitive distance increases, due to differences between partners with regard to technological knowledge and systems of meanings and interpretation (Nooteboom, 1999; Nooteboom *et al.*, 2007). As underlined by the literature, cognitive distance does not only decrease the knowledge absorption capacity, thereby complicating collaboration. Cognitive distance also increases the value of collaboration in terms of

Table 1.2 Facilitating conditions: when does OI affect creativity?

	Weak impact on actors' creativity	*Possible strong impact on actors' creativity*
Objective of collaboration	Exploitation	Exploration
Degree of interactivity	Low interactivity	High interactivity
Degree of openness	Closed	Open
Degree of formalization	High level of initial formalization	Low level of initial formalization
Distance (cultural, cognitive, sectoral, etc.)	Too small or too important	Important

novelty and creativity: 'in cooperating with others in alliances there is a trade-off to be made between the opportunity of novelty value and the risk of misunderstanding' (Nooteboom *et al.*, 2007, p. 1030).

A related question is linked to the type of collaborators who may enhance a firm's creativity. Obviously, standard collaboration with customers, suppliers or competitors may prove efficient in solving current optimization problems. Yet, their effect on firms' creativity is questionable. In order to improve the ability of the company to introduce new modes of thinking, collaboration with additional partners, such as public research organizations, firms in sectors with nothing in common, etc., may be necessary.

Inter-firms innovation alliances

Innovation partnerships and inter-organizational alliances are a very common way to implement OI. Drawing from the work of Penrose (Penrose, 1959), the resource-based approach (Wernerfelt, 1984; Barney, 1991) has emphasized the fact that resource heterogeneity is a powerful explanation of performance differences across firms. In this context, firms seeking to combine these heterogeneous resources are likely to form alliances and partnerships (Hagedoorn, 1993; Prahalad and Hamel, 1990; Nooteboom, 1999), especially in the domain of innovation. Powell *et al.* (1996) argue that in a context of increasing technology complexity and knowledge creation, alliances go beyond the usual make-or-buy decision. Innovation partnerships can take several forms of varying complexity. Contractual R&D agreements or technology exchange agreements can be seen as being rather simple since they imply one-direction knowledge flows. On the other hand, R&D joint ventures or interfirm networks are more complex since they imply resource sharing and bilateral knowledge flows (Burt, 1992; Hargadon and Sutton, 1997).

Hagedoorn (1993) explores the rationales underlying firms' participation in these various innovation partnerships. While some partnerships are focused on cost reduction with a short-term perspective, others have a 'long-term' strategic aim (Hagedoorn, 1993). Besides knowledge complementarities that help cope with technology complexity and reduce the risks and costs of R&D, partnerships are also motivated by the willingness of participants to capture a partner's tacit knowledge and benefit from technology transfer, and by market access perspectives (e.g., entry in foreign markets).

Partnerships can be seen as a strategic way to pool resources (Teece, 1986), but they can also be viewed as a mode of social learning. According to Brown and Duguid (1991), social learning is bound to the learning context, and knowledge creation takes place in evolving social settings. Rather than being opposed to each other, strategic and social learning views are intertwined (Powell *et al.*, 1996). Indeed, the ability of firms to draw benefit from innovation alliances and partnerships appears as the self-enforcing result of a learning process that implies internal capacities and organizational routines.

Considering alliances and partnerships in a social learning perspective, internal and external knowledge should not be considered as substitutes but rather as complements: although external knowledge obviously benefits from external R&D, internal knowledge is required to assess external R&D capabilities. Therefore, partnerships should not be viewed solely as a way of compensating for the lack of internal competences (Powell *et al.*, 1996). Moreover, building successful alliances is a competence per se. Collaboration does actually strengthen this internal competence as well as the perspective of subsequent successful collaboration. Hence, self-enforcing cycles of partnership building exist (Powell *et al.*, 1996).

Alliances and partnerships can have a significant impact on firms' creativity since they imply joint R&D activities and inter-organizational creativity, i.e., the creation of novelty though repeated interactions with R&D partners. In a partnership, each participant is likely to benefit from external knowledge flows and assesses external knowledge according to its own knowledge base. Moreover, partnerships and collaborations expand the horizons of individuals within the firm and increase the awareness of new perspectives. Partnerships can be classified as 'coupled processes' of OI and we can argue that their impact goes beyond simple 'outside-in' knowledge transfers. First, partnerships entail the production of joint work and imply collective creativity processes that take place across organizations. These inter-organizational creativity processes are likely to nourish each firm's knowledge base and creative potential. Second, partnerships foster a mechanism of 'learning-by-collaborating' whereby collaboration routines and abilities are built and increase the probability of future successful collaboration (Powell *et al.*, 1996). Indeed, rather than one-shot collaborations, R&D partnerships usually take place in networks that reinforce and evolve over time. While IP is an important aspect in such alliances, they also strongly rely on mutual knowledge and trust (Nooteboom, 2000; Krishnan *et al.*, 2006).

Knowledge communities as creativity enhancers

In addition to formalized partnership modes, companies can also build creative processes with communities outside the company. Since the seminal book of Lave and Wenger (1991), communities have been a topic of interest in innovation management and organization science (see e.g., Amin and Cohendet, 2004; Cohendet *et al.*, 2010; Harvey *et al.*, 2013). Communities rely on shared standards and norms and they aim to produce knowledge. They distinguish themselves from project teams in several respects (McDermott and Archibald, 2010): they have no fixed duration, their boundaries are not clearly defined, and they are not ruled by contracts or other formal incentives, but rather by trust, reputation, and mutual engagement. There is consensus over the fact that the management of communities entails a subtle balance between autonomy and control (Borzillo *et al.*, 2008).

As shown by recent studies, communities have been the drivers of creativity and innovation in various sectors (Burger-Helmchen and Cohendet, 2011; Cohendet *et al.*, 2010; Harvey *et al.*, 2015). These authors develop the idea that communities create a link between the relatively disorganized world of ideation and creativity, and the structured world of the organization. The authors also use the terms 'underground', 'middleground' and 'upperground' to characterize these sets:

- The underground is composed of individuals and groups conducting creative activities in various domains (scientific, technological, artistic).
- The upperground consists of project-driven companies and organizations that obey economic rules and constraints.
- The middleground consists of communities which make the creativity produced at underground level available to the upperground.

Creativity emerges as the outcome of interactions between the underground, communities and formal organizations such as companies. The latter do not simply outsource the process of creativity, but they set an original open process for creativity. This phenomenon has been studied extensively in the development of open source software (Box 1.3) or video game development (Grandadam *et al.*, 2013; Burger-Helmchen and Cohendet, 2011). But it can be extended to many other sectors. For instance, the scientific world is full of examples of start-ups or multinationals building creative processes based on academic research communities. For instance, in Chapter 8 of this book, Avadikyan and Müller show how the involvement of multiple communities contributes to the development of a large scale research facility.

To sum up, we believe that innovation with communities can be a formidable way for companies to enhance their creativity. However, as shown by Bach *et al.* (2010) in the music and video game sectors, this may require companies to adapt some of their strategies to the needs of communities, especially in terms of intellectual property rights.

Box 1.3 Open source software

Open source software (OSS, e.g., von Krogh and von Hippel, 2006) is a category of computer software whose source code can be modified and freely distributed. The concept of OSS is an evolution of the free software movement started by Richard Stallman in the early 1980s with the GNU

(continued)

(continued)

project. According to Stallman, free software must guarantee freedom to access, modify and distribute source codes. The free software foundation developed a specific licensing scheme to ensure this freedom: the GNU general public licence (also called GPL licence), which still remains a benchmark for open source software licensing. This type of licence ensures that software is 'copyleft'. In 1992, Linus Torvalds released software that became emblematic for the community: Linux.

The free software paradigm shifted in 1997, when Eric Raymond published his book *The Cathedral and the Bazaar*. In this manifesto, Raymond supports the idea that the accessibility and openness of source codes helps improve software through collective efforts within the developer community. This view led to the emergence of the Open Source Initiative in 1998. Raymond's approach is above all pragmatic. He considers that the opening of source code induces an improvement in the quality of software, including the elimination of bugs ('given enough eyeballs, all bugs are shallow'). The most famous OSS are Linux, Firefox, Apache/Open Office, Android. Most open source projects are accessible on the Sourceforge platform (http://sourceforge.net).

OSS stands as an archetype of the collective production model based on communities. Von Hippel and von Krogh (2003) show that OSS developers are mainly motivated by belonging to a community and the quality of their shared collective production. In this 'private-collective' model, knowledge sharing is based on reciprocity within the community of contributors. With regard to the motivations of OSS contributors, Lerner and Tirole (2002) and von Krogh *et al.* (2012) have shown that besides classical motivations, community membership is a powerful driver of implication in OSS development.

OSS development is primarily conducted by independent programmers grouped into virtual communities. These communities have developed famous independent programs such as Linux or Firefox. However, very large companies such as Google cooperate with these communities to innovate. Android developed by Google is developed from the Linux kernel. Some Google developers are actively involved in OSS communities that allow Google to develop cross creativity with the OSS communities.

Open source software therefore provides a nice illustration of a context in which the motivations of participants, their freedom, the open dimension of projects and low level of formalization seem very efficient in harnessing the creativity of people all around the world and continuously developing new, original and reliable software.

Concluding remarks

The idea put forward in this chapter is deliberately provocative: it questions the link between OI and creativity and shows that participating in OI processes does not necessarily increase firms' creativity. It is important to bear this in mind because too often today, especially in the business community, OI is seen as a miracle solution to almost every problem. The stream of innovative products of your firm dries up? Engage in OI! Your products are getting old fashioned? Engage in OI! Your competitors seem more creative? Engage in OI! etc.

What we wanted to show here is that very often OI works more like a short-term patch than a long-term solution. In particular, the outcome obviously depends on the kind of OI in which the company is involved. It is important to bear in mind that the concept of OI includes very different practices with necessarily heterogeneous outcomes on creativity. In most OI modalities, and for understandable reasons, companies maintain a high level of control and formalization. Intellectual property rights and secrecy remain major challenges (since to open up its boundaries can be dangerous and can lead to knowledge spillovers, for instance, companies that adopt open innovation may paradoxically be tempted to strengthen their intellectual property policy and increase their level of control over employees). This does not necessarily offer a context that is conducive to creativity.

Very often, OI is practised in an unambitious way, in a logic of short-term exploitation, which obviously has little effect on the creative potential of the firm in the longer term. To open up its boundaries does not guarantee creativity, and a relatively closed organization is not necessarily a guarantee of lack of creativity. To illustrate this point, we can quote the case of Apple, often presented as a symbol of the closed innovation model, the do-it-yourself mentality, and yet still considered by many as one of the most creative companies in the world. Xerox PARC, a rather closed yet extremely creative place and the source of most inventions at the basis of the PC environment, is another case in point. If Xerox PARC has been criticized, it is not for its lack of creativity, but rather for its lack of economic vision and inability to convert inventions into commercial success. OI is invoked here in a purely exploitation sense!

To open up its boundaries may even, in some cases, have a negative impact on creativity by impacting, for example, employees' motivation. In particular, the practice based on 'outside-in', aiming to exploit internally developed solutions (by doing crowdsourcing, licensing-in, spin-ins) can be potentially devastating for internal researchers who find themselves in competition with the rest of the world. Procter & Gamble, for example, claims that if an internal search team is not able to complete a project on time, the project will be made available online and users will be able to propose solutions. It is easy to understand that depending on the context and the management practices that accompany them, practices like this may encourage or, conversely, discourage creators!

In conclusion, OI in itself, when this concept is considered globally, has no automatic link with creativity. Everything is based on how companies practise OI.

References

Afuah, A. and Tucci, C. L. (2012). 'Crowdsourcing as a solution to distant search', *Academy of Management Review*, 37(3), 355–375.

Amabile, T. M. (1996). *Creativity in Context*, Boulder, CO: Westview Press.

Amabile, T. M. (1998). 'How to kill creativity', *Harvard Business Review*, 76, 76–87.

Amabile, T. M., Conti, R., Coon, H., Lazenby, J. and Herron, M. (1996). 'Assessing the work environment for creativity', *Academy of Management Journal*, 39(5), 1154–1184.

Amabile, T. M. and Kramer, S. J. (2011). *The Progress Principle, Using Small Wins to Ignite Joy, Engagement, and Creativity at Work*, Boston, MA: Harvard Business Review Press.

Amin, A. and Cohendet, P. (2004). *Architectures of Knowledge: Firms, Capabilities and Communities*, New York: Oxford University Press.

Arora, A. and Gambardella, A. (2010). 'Ideas for rent: An overview of markets for technology', *Industrial and Corporate Change*, 19, 775–803.

Arora, A., Fosfuri, A. and Gambardella, A. (2001). *Markets for Technology: The Economics of Innovation and Corporate Strategy*, Cambridge, MA: MIT Press.

Arora, A. and Merges, R. (2004). 'Specialized supply firms, property rights and firm boundaries', *Industrial and Corporate Change*, 13, 451–475.

Avadikyan, A. and Müeller, M. (2016). 'Management of creativity in a large-scale research facility', in M. Wagner, J. Valls-Pasola and T. Burger-Helmchen, *Global Management of Creativity*, London: Routledge.

Bach, L., Cohendet, P., Pénin, J. and Simon, L. (2010). 'Creative industries and the IPR dilemma between appropriation and creation: Some insights from the videogame and music industries', *Management International*, 14(3), 59–72.

Barney, J. B. (1991). 'Firm resources and sustained competitive advantage', *Journal of Management*, 17(1), 99–120.

Bootz, J.-P., Lièvre, P. and Schenk, E. (2015). 'Solicitation of experts in an undetermined environment: The case of a polar exploration', *Journal of Knowledge Management*, 19(5), 900–911.

Borzillo, S., Probst, G. and Raisch, S. (2008). *The Governance Paradox: Balancing Autonomy and Control in Managing Communities of Practice*. Academy of Management Best Papers Proceedings.

Boudreau, K. J. and Lakhani, K. R. (2013). 'Using the crowd as an innovation partner', *Harvard Business Review*, 91(4), 60–69.

Brabham, D. (2008). 'Crowdsourcing as a model for problem solving: An introduction and cases', *Convergence: The International Journal of Research into New Media Technologies*, 14(1), 75–90.

Brown, J. S. and Duguid, P. (1991). 'Organizational learning and communities-of-practice: Toward a unified view of working, learning, and innovation', *Organization Science*, 2(1), 40–57.

Burger-Helmchen, T. and Cohendet, P. (2011). 'User communities and social software in the video game industry', *Long Range Planning*, 44(5–6), 317–343.

Burt, R. S. (1992). *Structural Holes: The Social Structure of Competition*, Cambridge, MA: Harvard University Press.

Chesbrough, H. W. (2003). 'The era of open innovation', *MIT Sloan Management Review*, 44(3), 34–41.

Christensen, C.M., 1997, *The Innovator's Dilemma: When New Technologies Cause Great Firms to Fail*, Boston, MA: Harvard Business Press.

Cohendet, P., Llerena, P. and Simon, L. (2010). 'The innovative firm: Nexus of communities and creativity', *Revue d'Economie Industrielle*, 129–130, 139–170.

Cohendet, P., Harvey, J.-F. and Simon, L. (2013). 'Managing creativity in the firm: The fuzzy front end of innovation and dynamic capabilities', in T. Burger-Helmchen (Ed.), *The Economics of Creativity: Ideas, Firms and Markets*, New York: Routledge, pp. 131–150.

Cooper, R. G. and Edgett, S. J. (2012). 'Best practices in the idea-to-launch process and its governance', *Research-Technology Management*, 55(2), 43–54.

Deci, E. L. (1975). *Intrinsic Motivation*, New York: Plenum.

Deci, E. L., Koestner, R. and Ryan, R. M. (1999). 'A meta-analytic review of experiments examining the effects of extrinsic rewards on intrinsic motivation', *Psychological Bulletin*, 125, 627–668.

Ericsson, K. A, Prietula, M. J. and Cokely, E. T. (2007). 'The making of an expert', *Harvard Business Review*, July–August, 114–121.

Estellés-Arolas, E. and González-Ladrón-de-Guevara, F. (2012). 'Towards an integrated crowdsourcing definition', *Journal of Information Science*, 38, 189–200.

Gassmann, O. and Schweitzer, F. (2013). *Management of the Fuzzy Front End of Innovation*, New York: Springer.

Grandadam, D., Cohendet and P., Simon, L. (2013). 'Places, spaces and the dynamics of Creativity: The video game industry in Montreal', *Regional Studies*, 47(10), 1701–1714.

Hagedoorn, J. (2002). 'Inter-firm R&D partnerships: An overview of major trends and patterns since 1960', *Research Policy*, 31(4), 477–492.

Hagedoorn, J. (1993). 'Understanding the rationale of strategic technology partnering: Inter-organizational modes of cooperation and sectoral differences', *Strategic Management Journal*, 14(5), 371–385.

Hamdouch, A. and Depret, M.-H. (2001). *La nouvelle économie industrielle de la pharmacie: structures industrielles, dynamique d'innovation et stratégies commerciales*, Paris: Elsevier.

Hargadon, A. B. and Bechky, B. A. (2006). 'When collections of creatives become creative collectives: A field study of problem solving at work', *Organization Science*, 17(4), 484–500.

Hargadon, A. and Sutton, R. I. (1997). 'Technology brokering and innovation in a product development firm', *Administrative Science Quarterly*, 42, 716–749.

Harvey, J.-F., Cohendet, P., Simon, L. and Borzillo, S. (2015). 'Knowing communities in the front end of innovation', *Research-Technology Management*, January–February, 46–54.

Harvey, J.-F., Cohendet, P., Simon, L. and Dubois, L.-E. (2013). 'Another cog in the machine: Designing communities of practice in professional bureaucracies', *European Management Journal*, 31(1), 27–40.

Jeppesen, L. B. and Lakhani, K. R. (2010). 'Marginality and problem-solving effectiveness in broadcast search', *Organization Science*, 21(5), 1016–1033.

Jullien, N. and Pénin, J. (2014). 'Innovation ouverte', in F. Tannery, J. P. Denis, T. Hafsi, A-C. Martinet (Eds.), *Encyclopédie de la Stratégie*, Paris: Vuibert, pp. 701–714.

Khurana, A. and Rosenthal, S. R. (1998). 'Towards holistic "front ends" in new product development', *The Journal of Product Innovation Management*, 15(1), 57–74.

Krishnan, R., Martin, X. and Noorderhaven, N. G. (2006). 'When does trust matter to alliance performance', *Academy of Management Journal*, 49(5), 894–917.

Lave, J. and Wenger, E. (1991). *Situated Learning: Legitimate Peripheral Participation*, Cambridge: Cambridge University Press.

Lenfle, S. (2005). 'L'innovation dans les services: Les apports de la théorie de la conception', *Économies et Sociétés*, 39, 11–12.

Lerner, J. and Tirole, J. (2002). 'Some simple economics of open source', *Journal of Industrial Economics*, 52(2), 197–234.

McDermott, R. and Archibald, D. (2010). 'Harnessing your staff's informal network', *Harvard Business Review*, March, 1–7.

Nonaka, I. and Takeushi, H. (1995). *The Knowledge-Creating Company: How the Japanese Companies Create the Dynamic of Innovation*, New York: Oxford University Press.

Nooteboom, B. (1999). *Inter-firm Alliances: Analysis and Design*, London: Routledge.

Nooteboom, B., Vanhaverbeke W. P., Duysters G. M., Gilsing V. A., van den Oord A. J. (2007). 'Optimal cognitive distance and absorptive capacity', *Research Policy*, 36(7), 1016–1034.

Pahl, G., Beitz, W., Feldhusen, J. and Grote, K.-H. (2007). *Engineering Design: A Systematic Approach*, 3rd edition, London: Springer.

Parjanen, S. (2012). 'Experiencing creativity in the organization: From individual creativity to collective creativity', *Interdisciplinary Journal of Information, Knowledge, and Management*, 7, 109–128.

Pénin, J. (2012). 'Strategic uses of patents in markets for technology: A story of fabless firms, brokers and trolls', *Journal of Economic Behavior and Organization*, 85, 633–641.

Pénin, J. and Burger-Helmchen, T. (2011). 'Crowdsourcing of inventive activities: Definition and limits', *International Journal of Innovation and Sustainable Development*, 5(2/3), 246–263.

Pénin, J. and Burger-Helmchen, T. (2012). 'Crowdsourcing d'activités inventives et frontières des organisations', *Management International,* 16, 101–112.

Pénin, J., Burger-Helmchen, T., Dintrich, A., Guittard, C. and Schenk, E. (2013), *L'innovation ouverte: Définition, pratiques et perspectives*, Paris: CCI Paris, Collection Prospective et Entreprise.

Penrose, E. T. (1959). *The Theory of the Growth of the Firm*, 3rd edition, New York: Oxford University Press.

Pink, D. (2015). *Drive: The Surprising Truth about What Motivates Us*, New York: Riverhead Books.

Poetz, M. K. and Schreier, M. (2012). 'The value of crowdsourcing: Can users really compete with professionals in generating new product ideas?', *Journal of Product Innovation Management*, 29(2), 245–256.

Powell, W. W., Koput, K. W. and Smith-Doerr, L. (1996). 'Interorganizational collaboration and the locus of innovation: Networks of learning in biotechnology', *Administrative Science Quarterly*, 41, 116–145.

Prahalad, C. K. and Hamel, G. (1990). 'The core competence of the corporation', *Harvard Business Review*, 68(3), May–June, 79–93.

Raymond, E. (1997). *The Cathedral and the Bazaar*, Cambridge: O'Reilly.

Rayna, T. and Striukova, L. (2015). 'Open innovation 2.0: Is co-creation the ultimate challenge?', *International Journal of Technology Management*, 69(1), 38–53.

Schenk, E. and Guittard, C. (2011). 'Towards a characterization of crowdsourcing practices', *Journal of Innovation Economics and Management*, 7(1), 93–107.

Teece, D. (1986). 'Profiting from technological innovation: Implications for integration, collaboration, licensing and public policy', *Research Policy*, 15, 285–305.

Trott, P. and Hartmann, D. (2009). 'Why "Open Innovation" is old wine in new bottles', *International Journal of Innovation Management*, 13(4), 715–736.

Ulrich, K. T. and Eppinger, S. D. (2012). *Product Design and Development*, 5th edition, New York: McGraw-Hill.

von Hippel, E. and von Krogh, G. (2003). 'Open-source software and the "private-collective" innovation model: Issues for organization science', *Organization Science*, 14(2), 209–223.

von Krogh, G., Haeflinger, S., Spaeth, S. and Wallin, M. W. (2012), 'Carrots and rainbows: Motivation and social practice in open source development', *MIS Quarterly*, 36(10), 1–28.

von Krogh, G. and von Hippel, E. (2006). 'The promise of research on open source software', *Management Science*, 52, 975–983.

Wernerfelt, B. (1984). 'A resource-based view of the firm', *Strategic Management Journal*, 5(2), 171–180.

Woodman, R. W., Sawyer, J. E. and Griffin, R. W. (1993). 'Toward a theory of organizational creativity', *Academy of Management Review*, 18, 293–321.

2 Managing co-creation within global creative processes

A framework

Thierry Rayna and Ludmila Striukova

Introduction

While there is a widespread belief, both amongst academics and practitioners, that open innovation provides great benefits for firms who adopt it, it often comes at the cost of making creative processes more complex and harder to manage. This is particularly the case when users, and just not industrial partners, are taking a significant part in the creative process.

Co-creation is an active, creative and social collaborative process between firms and users aimed at creating value (Piller *et al.*, 2010). Co-creation can take many forms and relates to potentially any part of the creative process, whether ideation, product design, production and even in some cases distribution. While co-creation was seldom used in the past, the rapid progresses in ICTs have enabled increasingly advanced forms of collaboration between firms and users and, as a result, co-creation is now often considered as a key source of competitive advantage. The ever-growing use of crowdsourcing, mass-customisation, co-design and 'open-source'-like collaboration certainly shows how important co-creation has become.

While co-creation has indeed great advantages, managing co-creative processes is a complex matter. Not only can co-creation take many forms (sponsored, autonomous), it also involves different types of collaborations (depending on whether activities are integrated to differentiated) and may have different goals (is the outcome of co-creation mass-marketed? Is it a custom order?). Consequently, managing co-creation efficiently requires a global view of the creative process. This is critical to create adequate incentives and overcome the challenges at hand.

By providing a comprehensive framework of co-creation, this chapter aims to provide a better understanding of co-creative processes. This framework is then used to identify challenges and opportunities related to co-creation management within global creative process.

This chapter is organised as follows. The first section provides an overview of co-creation. The second section introduces the co-creation framework. The third section presents four case studies of co-creation (Hasbro, Lego, Digits2Widgets and Digital Forming). The co-creation framework is used in each of these four cases to identify challenges related to IP, motivation and management costs. This section is followed by concluding remarks.

Co-creation: an overview

Co-creation was originally defined by Kambil *et al.* (1996) as co-creation of value by a firm's customers. In this early work, co-creation is not seen as the production of a joint product or service with customers, but instead a situation where the actions of customers enable the firm to create more value. For instance, Kambil *et al.* (1996) mention the case of Amazon, which even in its infancy (1994) offered discussion groups and user generated reviews, both of which enable Amazon to co-create value with customers by enabling them to help other customers finding new books they might like.

As later on noted in Prahalad and Ramaswamy (2004b), co-creation undermines the traditional vision of the value chain. For instance, in the traditionally vision only the firms create value, not the customers. As a matter of fact, Prahalad and Ramaswamy (2004a) emphasised that for a long time the interactions between customers and companies were not seen as a source of value creation.

Building up on the definition provided by Kambil *et al.* (1996), Prahalad and Ramaswamy (2004a) define co-creation as a joint creation of value between a firm and its customers. Co-creation is about customers co-constructing the service experience and joint problem definition and problem solving. Prahalad and Ramaswamy (2004a) focus mainly on the medical sectors, where customers (patients) play a key role, by communicating information, feedback and wishes, in co-creating a unique service experience. Unlike Kambil *et al.* (1996), Prahalad and Ramaswamy (2004a) emphasise that co-creation is not about pleasing the customers or delivering a 'lavishly good' customer service. Customers need to play an active role in fine-tuning the service experience.

Piller and Ihl (2009) and Piller *et al.* (2010) move away from co-creation as just a means to enhance user experience. Instead, they define co-creation as an active, creative and social collaborative process between producers and users aimed at creating value for customers. Piller *et al.* (2010) emphasise that customer co-creation does take place during the development process of products and that it implies that customers actively take part in the design of a new offering.

Hence, co-creation with customers can take place at two different stages in the production process:

1   Product design: consumers suggest a design, create their own design or improve/amend an existing design.
2   Product manufacturing/ distribution: consumers manufacture products themselves (for example, using a 3D printer) and might even distribute it.

The actual contribution of consumers depends on the type of co-creation practice set up by the firms. Furthermore, even when both options are available, some consumers participate only in one of the co-creation stages, whereas some both co-design and co-manufacture.

The fact that co-creation relates to customers taking part in either product design or manufacturing and distribution enables a first distinction to be drawn between co-creation and user innovation. Indeed, user innovation typically relates to the design stage of a product (von Hippel, 1978; von Hippel and Katz, 2002). A further distinction between user innovation and co-creation is that the former necessarily implies that people engaging in user innovation are, by definition, users of the product. In contrast, people engaging in co-creation are not necessarily users of the product themselves (for instance, designers of Threadless t-shirts do not necessarily intend to wear them). Thus, while there are cases when co-creation and user innovation overlap, the two are not identical.

Since co-creation implies an active role for both consumers and firms, Zwass (2010) distinguishes between autonomous and sponsored co-creation. Autonomous co-creation means that individuals or consumer communities produce value through voluntary activities, which they conduct independently from established organisations (even though they might be doing so using tools or platforms provided by these organisations). For instance, the apps and hacks developed by the iOS 'jailbreak' community relate to autonomous co-creation. These apps and hacks clearly create value (some have been so popular that Apple has subsequently built in similar developments in the iOS operating system), but are not sanctioned by Apple (which has actively tried to prevent 'jailbreaking'), though they use tools (the developer kit and compilers) provided by Apple.

In contrast, sponsored co-creation relates to co-creation activities conducted by individuals or consumer communities at the initiative of an organisation. One of the most famous examples of sponsored co-creation is crowdsourcing. Coined by Howe (2006), crowdsourcing is defined as a new web-based business model that uses a distributed network of individuals to find creative solutions for existing problems. Crowdsourcing practices may vary depending on processes of examining contributions (Geiger *et al.*, 2011) or marketing applications (Whitla, 2009). Crowdfunding has also been, over the past years, an increasingly popular way to involve consumers in the production process. This form of co-creation also relates to consumer involvement in the production process (though the resource provided by consumers is cash, which is then used to pay for manufacturing, instead of actual manufacturing).

While co-creation can take place between companies and individual consumers, co-creation communities are also formed between consumers. Such communities, generally referred to as 'communities of creation' (Sawhney and Prandelli, 2000) or 'communities of co-design' (Piller *et al.*, 2004), create common knowledge and value not only for the members of the community, but also for 'outsiders'. Co-creation communities can be extremely valuable as they can provide a company with a range of new ideas and help to save on R&D, which is especially critical when the development of products and technologies are beyond company's resources.

Co-creation is often mentioned alongside other concepts, such as open innovation and mass customisation. Whereas co-creation is generally considered as the customer-related part of open innovation (Piller *et al.*, 2010; Rayna and Striukova, 2015), mass customisation only leads to co-creation if customers have an actual input in the creative process. As noted in Prahalad and Ramaswamy (2004a), when a company offers a set of predetermined options the customers can choose from, and then manufactures the resulting product on demand, this form of mass customisation is not co-creation because customers do not have any input, besides indicating a choice of options.

Managing co-creation: a framework

Co-creation represents a great opportunity for firms and society alike, to the point that it is considered by some as the 'next stage' of capitalism (Ritzer and Jurgenson, 2010; Prahalad and Ramaswamy, 2004a; Tapscott and Williams, 2006). However, just like any form of open innovation, co-creation comes with associated management challenges (mainly related to incentives, costs and IPR issues).

As emphasised in the previous section, co-creation can take many forms. Each form creates different management challenges (for instance, the challenges of mass-customisation and crowdsourcing are quite different) and, therefore, understanding the actual nature of a particular co-creation activity is of critical importance.

Rayna and Striukova (2015) introduced a typology of co-creation that can be used as a basis for a framework enabling one to identify and overcome management challenges. A key issue related to co-creation is whether the roles and actions of customers in the production process can be identified and measured.

In regard to co-creative processes, the respective roles of the firm and the customers can either be considered as *integrated* or *differentiated*. Roles are *differentiated* (in which case firms' and customers' activities can be seen as vertically integrated) when firms and customers have distinct roles in the co-creation process, for instance, when customers design a product that is then manufactured by the firm. Many cases of crowdsourcing also fall in this category.

In contrast, in some co-creative processes, the respective roles of firms and customers relate to the same part of the production process. For instance, both firms and customers can engage in the design process, in which case, roles are effectively *integrated*. There may still be some degree of specialisation, though. For instance, the firm might have provided a base template that customers are asked to modify and complete, or customers might have provided a two-dimensional drawing that the firm then turns into a three-dimensional object. Open source software is also a clear case of *integrated* co-creation, since both firms and customers engage in joint software development.

In the latter case, it is still possible to track and assess the output of each contributor (Concurrent Versions Systems, or CVS, typically enable the tracking of changes made by all the participants in a software development project, even when thousands of them engage in co-creative software development). However, in some cases it is simply impossible to untangle the contributions of firms and customers, or when it is, it is impossible to assess the actual weight of each respective contribution in the final output. This is, for instance, the case when firms and customers simultaneously engage in co-design (in which case the situation is akin to an instrumental jam), or in a case of mass customisation such as the one offered by Digital Forming (one of the cases discussed in detail in the following section), where customers are offered unlimited (albeit bounded) free-form transformation of the original design created by the firm. In such a case, when respective contributions cannot be untangled or their respective weight in the final output cannot be assessed, roles are totally *integrated* and co-creation can be categorised as *pure co-creation*.

Thus, co-creation, with regard to inputs (i.e. contributions), can take many forms ranging from purely *integrated* to purely *differentiated*. As will be demonstrated in the following section, challenges related to incentives, management costs (including transaction costs) and IP are usually quite different depending on the type and level of integration. Generally speaking, as noted by Rayna and Striukova (2015), all things remaining equal, *integrated* co-creation creates more challenges in all dimensions, simply due to the fact that highly horizontally integrated co-creation has similar features to the contribution to a public good. It can be added that the scale of participation also plays a critical role, and management issues (whether motivation, IP or costs) rise with the number of customers engaging in the co-creation process. Just like in the case of a public good, free riding is more likely to arise when the number of contributors gets high. Likewise, in this latter case, monitoring and enforcement costs, as well as IP attribution and management issues, are expected to be more prevalent.

Thus, for a firm engaging in co-creation it is critical to assess whether co-creation corresponds to a clear and separate contribution of customers or whether it is a joint collaborative effort with customers. However, the occurrence of the role integration issues (related to *input*) discussed above also depends on the nature of the *output* of the co-creative process. Indeed, depending on whether the *output* is meant for the mass market or whether, instead, it is meant for a particular individual, management issues are likely to strongly differ. In the former case, the input is valuable to one, whereas in the latter case, the output is valuable to many.

As noted by Rayna and Striukova (2015) and as will be demonstrated in the following section, IP issues are more likely to be prevalent when the output is destined for mass production/distribution rather than when it is customised and tailored for a particular individual. Even when contributions are fully horizontally integrated, the matter of IP ownership seldom matters in the case of a customised output (for instance, people rarely argue over the IP ownership of a co-designed wedding cake). Likewise, motivational issues (and the resulting increase in monitoring and enforcement costs) are less likely to occur when the output is customised than when it is meant for the masses (free riding is a much less rational behaviour when the resulting product is meant exclusively for you).

Figure 2.1 presents the framework that will be used to analyse the case studies introduced in the next section. This framework is based on the two dimensions (input–output) discussed above and enables us to categorise co-creation depending on its degree of role integration and target market. It is important to note that this framework does not simply define four cases (corresponding each to one quadrant), but, instead, a continuum of cases, each related to a different level of integration and customisation.

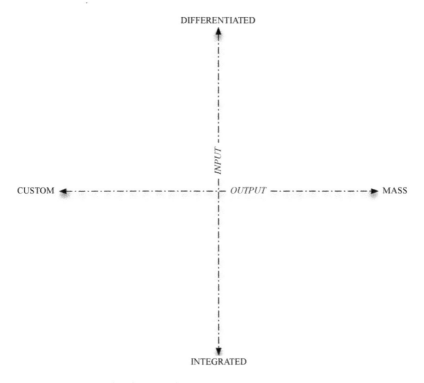

Figure 2.1 Co-creation framework.

Case studies

Hasbro

Hasbro is a US toy and games multinational and one of the largest toymakers worldwide. As with other toy manufacturers, Hasbro also produces films and TV series/cartoons that are used to support the sales of its toys.

While Hasbro is a fairly traditional company, it has recently started to make use of co-creation. In summer 2014, Hasbro teamed up with Shapeways, one of the world's leading online 3D printing platforms, to create Super Fan Art, an online platform that enables fans to sell their creations inspired from the different characters of Hasbro's cartoons (Figure 2.2).

Hasbro had, indeed, noticed autonomous co-creation attempts by fans of some of its franchises, as 3D models of Hasbro's toys started to appear on online 3D model sharing platforms, such as Thingiverse. However, these 3D models were often not just mere copies of existing Hasbro's toys, but instead original creations made by fans.

Unlike other companies that have tried to prevent co-creation (for instance, HBO forced the removal of a Game of Thrones inspired smartphone dock, despite

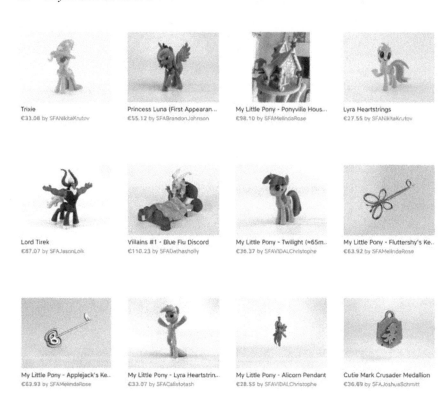

Trixie
€33.08 by SFANikitaKrutov

Princess Luna (First Appearan...
€55.12 by SFABrandonJohnson

My Little Pony - Ponyville Hous...
€98.10 by SFAMelindaRose

Lyra Heartstrings
€27.55 by SFANikitaKrutov

Lord Tirek
€87.07 by SFAJasonLoik

Villains #1 - Blue Flu Discord
€110.23 by SFADathasholly

My Little Pony - Twilight (≈65m...
€38.37 by SFAVIDALChristophe

My Little Pony - Fluttershy's Ke...
€63.92 by SFAMelindaRose

My Little Pony - Applejack's Ke...
€63.93 by SFAMelindaRose

My Little Pony - Lyra Heartstrin...
€33.07 by SFACallistotash

My Little Pony - Alicorn Pendant
€28.55 by SFAVIDALChristophe

Cutie Mark Crusader Medallion
€36.69 by SFAJoshuaSchmitt

Figure 2.2 Co-created objects by fans of Hasbro's My Little Pony franchise on Shapeways.

the creator offering to pay for a licence), Hasbro realised its large potential in terms of value creation.

By opening the Super Fan Art platform, Hasbro enabled a switch from autonomous to sponsored co-creation. One of the key advantages of doing so is that Hasbro then became in control of the co-created products (for instance, terms and conditions of Super Fan Art explicitly forbid violent or obscene content), which was not the case for autonomous co-creation (unless Hasbro kept sending the lawyers to attempt removing *a posteriori* potentially harmful content).

Yet, simply opening a platform was not enough to ensure that co-creation would take place through that platform, rather than continuing autonomously. Managing motivation is critical when engaging in co-creation. While Hasbro fans were obviously intrinsically motivated, since they were already carrying out autonomous co-creation, Hasbro had to find a way to motivate them to join the sponsored platform, as opposed to doing it autonomously. Hasbro did that by allowing co-creators to sell the resulting product on Shapeways.

So far, Hasbro has provided co-creators with a large degree of freedom. Aside from a couple of sensible rules (e.g. interdiction of violent and obscene content), co-creators are free to create any kind of object inspired by the Hasbro franchises.

As a result, a wide range of objects has been created: figurines, jewellery, accessories, etc. Furthermore, fans are free to choose the selling price of their creation (Shapeways provides them with the manufacturing cost, which corresponds to the cost of 3D printing, packaging and shipping the object, to which co-creating fans add a margin of their choice – Hasbro takes a small percentage of the total price). This strategy has provided strong incentives for fans to join the sponsored co-creation platform and ensured that autonomous co-creation remains minimal, thereby granting Hasbro a near total monitoring and control over the resulting co-created products.

Using our framework introduced gives a clearer view of the type of co-creation Hasbro is engaged in. In regard to the respective contributions (*input*), the roles of Hasbro and its fans are quite *integrated*, since both engage in design (manufacturing is carried out by a third party). Yet, this is not a case of *pure co-creation*, as the roles of Hasbro and the fans are still, despite being both related to design, fairly differentiated. Hasbro has provided the original two-dimensional drawings of the characters (through the cartoons) as well as a limited number of three-dimensional objects (the toys manufactured by Hasbro). The fans produce three-dimensional objects inspired by the cartoons and (occasionally) the toys.

In regard to *output*, co-creating fans are not the (only) target of the co-created objects. Furthermore, the Super Fan Art platform, run by Shapeways, does not enable final customers to customise the co-created objects. Because of that, the co-creation Hasbro is engaged in leans more towards *mass* than *customisation*. Yet, it should be noted that while several customers are likely to see value in the co-created objects, it nonetheless corresponds to rather small niches consisting of fans who see an appeal in objects that are different from the otherwise mass produced and mass distributed Hasbro toys and merchandising (for instance, some fans might want a figurine of a character that has a fairly minor role in the cartoon, or want a different figurine, with a different posture, of one of the heroes in the cartoon).

So, overall, this particular case of sponsored co-creation carried out by Hasbro is mildly *integrated* and mildly *mass*. In regard to the management challenges that such a type of co-creation entails, it can be noted that, as mentioned above, the right provided to fans to sell and set their own prices provides strong incentives for them to engage in co-creation. On the firm's side, however, there could potentially be an issue if the co-created objects were to become so popular that they would cannibalise the sales of regular toys and merchandising, on which Hasbro has a far greater margin. In this case, however, since the co-created products have mainly a niche appeal (and co-creation is only mildly *mass*), this is unlikely to be the case. Furthermore, if a particular co-created product were to become very popular, Hasbro could strike a deal with the co-creator and have the product mass manufactured instead of being 3D printed. Since the cost of mass manufacturing is significantly lower than the cost of 3D printing, this would lead to a 'win-win' situation, as both parties could have a greater margin.

In regard to IP management, the sponsored co-creation platform has enabled Hasbro to keep things fairly simple, as the Super Fan Art platform is a single selling point. Consequently, this has enabled Hasbro to grant licences to the co-creator, but only for sales on the dedicated platform. Co-creators retain the IP related to their contribution in the co-created object (unlike many cases of crowdsourcing or co-creation where customers are required to transfer all IP to the firm). Again, this simple IP management is due to the fact that co-created products are sold exclusively on the Super Fan Art platform and any additional form of sales (e.g. Hasbro mass manufacturing the objects and selling them in stores or the co-creator selling the object through other platforms) would require negotiating additional IP licences from the other side. In such a case, however, reaching an agreement on the licence fee can be potentially challenging, as actual IP attribution can be an issue, because roles are horizontally integrated and both firms and fans have engaged in design. Assessing the weight of the respective contributions in the value created by the co-created object is likely to pose a significant challenge.

Concerning the risks and costs involved with this particular form of co-creation, the sponsored platform and the control it provides Hasbro with (in particular, in relation to curation) makes them fairly minimal. However, this is only the case because co-creators have strong incentives to co-create through this platform, rather than doing it autonomously via other platforms. Such strong incentives are related to the large degree of freedom granted by Hasbro to co-creators and to the fact that Hasbro only retains a very small part of the proceeds. In turn, that implies that co-creation has to remain a fairly minor part of Hasbro's business, as otherwise the company would have to increase either control or markup (actually, potentially both), which would decrease co-creators' incentives to go down the sponsored route. So, again, the fact that this particular co-creation is only of mildly *mass* appeal has been highly instrumental in its success.

Lego

The Lego Group's history dates back to 1949. In addition to having produced more than 600 billion Lego parts over these years, Lego has also created its culture with movies, games and six Legoland amusement parks. It also has millions of faithful followers, both children and adults.

Lego is one of pioneers in customer co-creation, its original co-creation project, Lego MindStorms, was launched in 1998. Since then it has become the best-selling product in Lego's history.

MindStorms, a building and programming robotics tool set, grew out of the Lego's collaboration with MIT. A tiny portable computer is embedded inside a traditional Lego brick, which enables it to interact with the physical world through sensors and motors. In addition to being used by children, the technology is also used by some businesses as a rapid prototyping tool.

After MindStorms was introduced to the market, more than 1000 users 'hacked' the kit and customised it to improve its performance and to add new functions. Originally, Lego tried to fight the autonomous co-creation efforts of its customers, and even sent cease and desist letters. Eventually, Lego decided not to sue anyone for writing a new code for the product and distributing it for free, and even created a discussion forum where users could share their ideas.

This decision led to the creation of the full MindStorms ecosystem: in addition to the official forum, sites with the pictures of My Own Creations (MOCs) and detailed instructions to replicate these creations were created, books were written on how to build and programme Lego bots and even new start-ups selling MindStorms compatible sensors and hardware were launched. Considering that the project attracted many adult customers, who were not the original Lego's target market, the sales went up and there was even nothing on stock for Christmas.

Considering the successful use of co-creation for the first version of MindStorms, Lego decided to use it again when it decided to develop a second version in 2004. Since the second version was supposed to be very different, there was a risk that if the whole crowd of users was integrated as developers, the project might be taken to a completely different direction than Lego had envisaged and, moreover, that this direction might be wrong. In order to mitigate this risk, Lego's chose the sponsored co-creation route. The decision was taken to use five lead users, who were chosen by browsing MindStorms forums looking for the users who were praised by the community. The four programmers (the fifth one never replied to the original email) collaborated with Lego for one year. They were not paid for their work, but were offered a free kit and the company's gratitude. Their silence was crucial for the success of the project and, indeed, during the whole year no information leaked to the crowd. The main motivation at the time was having the privilege to be one of the creators of the new product. The second stage was to engage 100 users to test the beta version and despite the fact that users had to pay for the own kits (though at a reduced price) Lego received around 10,000 applications. Once 100 users were chosen, the next question was the time and effort Lego would have to spend in order to monitor and control the testers. The solution was to put respected forum members in charge of this task.

Around the same time (in 2005) Lego launched a Design byME service under the name Lego Factory. The service allowed users to design their own models (including the boxes), to upload them to Lego's site and have them manufactured and delivered to them; they could also view the designs of others, add and remove bricks to them and also have them manufactured. Millions of models were built over the years, however, due to its very high price tag (despite a limited number of bricks that were available for design), only a small fraction of the models were ordered to be manufactured and the service was closed in 2012.

The next co-creation project, which started in 2006, was very different in nature, as it involved one partner only. Together with an architect, Adam Reed Tucker, who was designing and building models of famous landmarks as a hobby, Lego launched the Lego Architecture brand. As of today, more than 30 sets have been released. As with the MindStorms project Lego turned autonomous co-creation into sponsored creation.

In 2008 Lego, together with a Japanese website Cuusoo, launched Lego Cuusoo. The website allowed users to submit ideas that would have a potential to be turned into commercial products. Originally, the site was only available in Japan, but became international in 2011. It was transferred to Lego Ideas in 2014. The site already has more than 100,000 registered users.

Users submit a written description of the idea and a sample Lego model. Currently, there are around 9,000 projects listed on the site. Once the project reaches 10,000 supports (originally 1000 for Cuusoo) it becomes eligible for production. The first 1,000 supports should be reached within one year; in this case, an additional six months will be granted to reach 5,000. If 5,000 is reached within the remaining time, users are granted an additional six months to reach 10,000. If the project does not reach the required number of supports within the time limit, it is archived, but can be resubmitted again (but voting will start from scratch).

If the project is accepted for production, the original designer receives 1 per cent of the royalties (including from a third-party intellectual property such as a game, a TV show or a film), as well as five copies of the final set and his or her name on the box. The projects are then reviewed in batches three times per year and, if cleared for production, are developed and manufactured. The projects are evaluated by a team of Lego designers, product managers and other key employees. The evaluation is based on the concept presented in the description, photos of the model, as well as potential market estimation.

Since the launch of Lego Ideas in 2014, 67 projects have reached the 10,000 threshold. Eight sets have been approved (six have already been released), 23 projects are under review, and the remaining 36 were rejected (Figure 2.3).

One of the projects that was rejected is based on My Little Pony. As the IP is owned by Lego's competitor (Hasbro), it was impossible to obtain a licence. Also, if two projects with overlapping concepts reach 10,000 supports in the same review period, only one project will be chosen. This was the case when two Dr Who projects created by two different users reached 10,000 (one of them posted on 26 February 2014 and the other one on 28 February 2014).

The chances of a submitted project being accepted are, therefore, rather slim. The quality of the project matters, but so does its marketing. Participants discuss on Lego forums that sometimes marketing their project on the Internet is much more labour intensive than actually designing the model itself. Despite the chances of success being rather small, around 10 new projects are submitted every day. The site can be used by Lego's fans to test their ideas, as often comments left by other users include suggestions on how the project could be improved.

If the project is accepted, Lego designers refine the product and it takes around six months from the time it is accepted to the time it is available for sale. Both production and sales of the sets co-developed via Lego Ideas are in volumes comparable to the sets developed internally. If the project is selected and produced, it is possible Lego will start a new theme based on it, however, this production will be independent from the Lego Ideas and additional compensation is not offered.

All IPRs generated by users are assigned to Lego (including copyright, design right and patent right). Users keep the right to promote their work, but cannot sell neither digital nor physical versions of submitted projects. If the project is removed before Lego's approval, Lego still keeps the rights for three years. If the project is refused and/or archived the rights are returned back to the user. However, Lego keeps a non-exclusive right to display these ideas on its website.

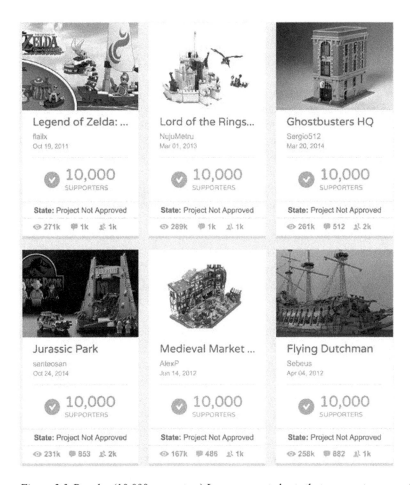

Figure 2.3 Popular (10,000 supporters) Lego co-created sets that were not approved.

Using our framework, we can understand better which type of co-creation Lego is engaged in. In terms of *input*, apart from the first version of MindStorms, when Lego was caught off guard, it is usually *integrated*. As to *output*, Lego was involved in custom co-creation only once, though the official statement says that the company might reconsider its decision to provide customised products in the future, its current focus is on the *mass* side.

Digits2Widgets

Digits2Widgets (D2W), a 3D printing bureau, was established in 2008. It was a creative spin-off of the leading dental practice Dawood & Tanner, which started to use 3D printing in its dental treatment in 2005 to recreate the architecture of the face, jaw and skeleton.

The D2W team of experts come from multidisciplinary backgrounds, comprising an architect, model makers, product, jewellery and industrial designers, a games developer and an artist. The medical roots of the start-up also mean that the bureau has access to a dental/maxillofacial surgeon, medical physicist and a medical software developer.

One of the main services provided by D2W is 3D printing. The company operates multiple 3D printers, including the capability to 3D print full-colour objects and objects in nylon. However, D2W emphasises that its service is not 3D printing, but 'working with people' helping them at any stage of their creative path. As D2W clients request different services when they approach the company, all their co-creation activities are sponsored.

Digits2Widgets' clients include architects, product designers, engineers, fashion designers, jewellers, artists and makers who come from Europe and North America. Clients' needs as well as their expertise in 3D printing vary a lot. Therefore, the projects D2W work on can range from very simple to very sophisticated. Their customers can bring a sketch, a 2D CAD file, or a 3D CAD file that needs refining; D2W will then take it from any stage to a 3D printable CAD file.

When customers already have a CAD file they would like to be 3D printed, D2W can help with fixing these files. Actually, all files that are sent to the bureau are checked to ensure the data can be 3D printed to the highest quality. The service is free if it is a basic file analysis and/or repair; more complicated repairs are charged at £30 per hour. D2W helps its customers avoid these costs by providing them with fixing guides for each of the materials they use: nylon, multi colour and wax.

D2W also provides a range of scanning services, such as structured white light scanning (which produces high quality scans of medium to large size objects, photogrammetry (where a large number of photographs of an object is combined to produce a CAD file), CT scanning (often including internal details). The cost of scanning is £90 plus VAT for the first hour and £50 plus VAT per hour thereafter.

The pricing structure of D2W is quite different from other printing bureaus, as it encourages customers to prepare optimally packed files. CAD is used to pack objects in 'virtual suitcases'. When nylon printing is used, a box is printed with objects inside it, which saves D2W employees time, as the box can be given directly to the customers and no time is wasted sorting the objects after the printing process.

The fact that the cost of 3D printing depends on volume means that there are a lot of projects when D2W works together with its customers to make the design more efficient and consequently more elegant to make separately printed parts fit together. An example of a co-creation project aimed at decreasing the volume is a 3D printed bird-nesting box, which was developed in collaboration with a design firm. In order to reduce the cost of production the volume of a standard bird-nesting box had to be decreased, which was done by breaking the form down into the minimum number of flat pack elements. The new design, which exploited the flexible properties of the nylon material, had the same finished form but could be printed at a fraction of the cost.

In addition to printing services, D2W offers consultancy to help companies and individuals unleash the potential of 3D printing. D2W emphasises that it is trying to make not only well designed but also purposeful things. They do not want their customers to 3D print just for the sake of it, and if 3D printing cannot meet the demand of their customers they tell them so directly. On the other hand, since their strategy is focused on understanding the purpose of the project, when 3D printing cannot be applied in the way customers envisage, it can still be applied to other parts of customers' projects.

Before signing a contract, D2W usually demonstrates to its customers the current capabilities of 3D printing and shows them the print rooms to show customers the day-to-day logistics of running industrial 3D printers. Likewise, when D2W employees lack expertise they do refer to their clients. Clients can visit the bureau and get inspired by good examples of 3D printing. A spare space in the rear of the workshop is located as co-space occupied by those who are working on 3D-related work, generating a nexus of advanced 3D design.

The risks of co-creation are very low for D2W, as it has a very transparent intellectual property policy. It does not discuss details of projects and uploaded files cannot be downloaded by third parties. For those customers looking for confidentiality, the company offers to sign a standard or customers' own individual non-disclosure agreements. On the other hand, customers are asked to make sure that all materials they present to D2W are free from any third party intellectual property claims and they are warned that D2W is not liable against all liabilities, costs, expenses, damages or losses.

D2W keeps all materials in which original works are created by D2W. These works are available for future reproduction (by the same customer); a license agreement can be signed when there is a transfer of ownership of these materials. Customers retain IP on any material they supply.

By applying the framework introduced earlier, one can see that in terms of *input*, the roles of D2W and its clients are *integrated*, since D2W's core business is providing services. As to *output*, D2W's services, being tailored according to the need of individual clients, are about *customisation*.

Digital Forming

Digital Forming is a company that was founded in 2008 and that specialises in mass customisation. Currently, its main product is an online mass customisation platform that operates as SaaS (Software as a Service) and that is used by large companies and independent designers alike. While in the former case, the customisation interface is integrated into the companies' websites, Digital Forming also operates an online shop enabling the independent designers to sell their objects.

The key idea of Digital Forming is that customers should be given as much freedom as possible, while retaining the functionality of the customised object. Consequently, customers are provided with a wide array of free-form customisation options (which means that the shape of the object can be radically altered – even completely transformed), while setting boundaries so that the object remains functional and manufacturable (as the customised object is then 3D printed). For instance, the overall shape of a lemon squeezer can be heavily transformed for as long as the lemon squeezing part retains a certain shape. Same thing goes with a lamp shade: it can be heavily customised, as long as there is still enough space for the light bulb in the middle.

The Digital Forming platform relies on two different pieces of software. The first one, ODO, enables designers to set up customisation options for their three-dimensional objects, as well as the limits that should not be exceeded when modifying the shape of the object. The second piece of software is called UCODO and provides an online interface enabling customers to customise the object. Options offered through this interface are quite extensive. Multiple sliders enable one to radically alter the shape and colour of the object. Different shape options can also be provided (e.g. different shapes for the foot of a lamp), which can also be customised. Once the object has been customised, an order is placed and the object is 3D printed and shipped to the customer.

Digital Forming acts as an intermediary between the firms that provide the 3D objects and the customers. A cost algorithm is used to calculate in real time, as the customers modify the object, the cost of manufacturing. The firms that supply the 3D objects are free to choose the mark-up (as well as minimum price) for their objects. In the case of smaller firms or independent designers that use Digital Forming's online store, Digital Forming takes a commission on the sales.

Based on the co-creation framework introduced earlier, it is clear that the co-creation enabled by Digital Forming belongs to the *customised/integrated* case (lower left quadrant in Figure 2.1). The fact that co-creation results in a customised object helps alleviate a significant number of management issues, which would be otherwise prevalent. In particular, because customers can radically alter the shape of the object, IP attribution is significantly challenging. But because the co-created object is only sold to the customer who co-created it and not to the mass market, this is essentially a non-issue, as customers are very unlikely to worry about IP in this case (and, as a matter of fact, no IP is attributed to customers when they engage in co-design). However, IP issues would arise if the firms using Digital Forming technology were tempted to mass market a particular co-created object (for instance, because the resulting co-created object is particularly well designed).

Because the output of co-creation is a customised object, there are also very few challenges related to motivation (customers co-design for themselves, so are intrinsically motivated) or to management costs (since customers do not need to be incentivised and this is bilateral co-creation).

Concluding remarks

The four cases presented in the previous section were chosen because they all relate to situations where co-creation takes place during the creative process (as opposed to manufacturing or distribution processes). Yet, they clearly show that even in this particular case, co-creation can take many forms and, hence, to give rise to different management challenges. Using the co-creation framework has enabled us to clarify some of these issues.

In all these four cases, co-creation was, in regard to input, *integrated*. Yet, the actual degree of integration varies. In two cases (Lego, Digits2Widgets), while firms and customers do engage in co-design, their roles are actually quite distinct and complementary. Consequently, the contribution of each party towards the final output can easily be assessed. In contrast, in the two other cases (Hasbro, Digital Forming), the roles are far more integrated, although contributions are sequential (i.e. the firm provides an initial design that customers then modify). In the Hasbro case, the objects created by the customers entail different levels of creativity on their part. Some objects, especially figurines, appear to be merely a three-dimensional rendering of a particular scene in a cartoon, while other objects display a significant creative input of the co-creating customer (for instance, in the case of jewellery). In the case of Digital Forming, while also sequential, the co-creative process is strongly integrated and it is generally not possible to assess the weight of respective contributions in the value of the final output. Digital Forming is thus the most integrated of all four cases, followed (in decreasing order) by Hasbro, Lego and Digits2Widgets.

With regard to outputs, two of the cases (Digital Forming, Digits2Widgets) are essentially on the *customised* side. The other two (Lego, Hasbro) are on the *mass* side, with Lego clearly aiming at the mass market, since the winning co-created Lego sets are then mass manufactured and distributed worldwide on a large scale. By contrast, Hasbro's fan art objects are in most cases niche products.

Concerning the management challenges, the four case studies have illustrated potential motivational pitfalls, as well as ways to overcome them. Of course, such motivational issues are unlikely to arise when co-creation leads to a customised object (at least as long as the co-creation is carried out by the customer herself) and, as a matter of fact, motivational issues appear to be non-existent in the Digital Forming and Digits2Widgets cases. In the two other cases (Hasbro and Lego), motivational challenges could arise (in particular, customers could decide to engage in autonomous co-creation instead of using the sanctioned platform). To alleviate such issues and to foster customer engagement, both Hasbro and Lego have devised incentive schemes. Hasbro enables co-creating customers to sell the resulting product at a price of their choosing. Lego offers both financial (1 per cent of the royalties) and non-financial (name printed on the box, five boxes of the set) incentives to the co-creating customers. While such incentives help overcoming motivational issues in the *mass* cases of co-creation, finding the right balance between incentives and profitability may be an issue and can actually depend on the extent of the mass appeal of the co-created product. As was shown in the Hasbro case, the incentives provided by Hasbro would be too costly for Hasbro if the co-created products had a large mass appeal. Because they are niche products, however, and unlikely to cannibalise Hasbro's regular toy range, the current high incentive scheme strikes the right balance.

In regard to Intellectual Property, IP assignment issues are present to some extent in all four cases. Digital Forming and Hasbro are the two most radical cases, because they correspond to the most integrated forms of co-creation. In the case of Digital Forming, however, because the co-creation output is a customised product, this becomes less of an issue, since the object is only manufactured once for the particular customer who engaged in co-creation. In the three other cases (Hasbro, Digits2Widgets and Lego), while it may be possible to attribute IP based on the contributions of customers, such IP is nonetheless dependent on other IP. For instance, while the IP over a three-dimensional object inspired by one of Hasbro's cartoon character may be attributed to the co-creating customers, the IP in question can only be used with a licence granted by Hasbro. Lego and Digits2Widgets also display similar overlapping IP issues (although for the latter, this is most likely a non-issue, due to the customised nature of the product). In two of the four cases (Hasbro, Digits2Widgets) co-creating customers actually retain their IP, while in the two other cases (Lego, Digital Forming), IP is transferred entirely to the company.

These four cases also have enabled the identification of a further issue related to IP. Indeed, looking at the Lego projects that have reached the 10,000 supporter threshold but have not been accepted, one finds that the vast majority of them (32 out of 36) correspond to projects that involve third party IP that Lego would have to licence in (and which could potentially be refused). Such third party IP issues are also present in all other three cases.

Regarding management costs, as identified in Rayna and Striukova (2015), they relate mainly to search costs (e.g. curation costs) in the two *mass* cases, though Lego also crowdsources part of the search process (since only projects supported by 10,000 customers are examined by Lego teams). In the two *custom* cases, one would expect instead negotiation costs to arise. While this certainly is the case for Digits2Widgets, Digital Forming's platform automation and interface enable this issue to be alleviated. In all four cases, the sequentiality of co-creation enables to minimise coordination costs.

Based on four case studies, this chapter has shown that understanding the nature of co-creation is of critical importance. The co-creation framework provided enables the understanding of not only existing challenges, but also envisaging challenges that could arise if the nature of a particular co-creation activity were to change. Managing co-creation within global creative processes requires a precise understanding of the nature of each particular co-creation process and the framework provided can be used for this purpose, which enables adequate management practices to be designed.

However, while understanding the nature of co-creation is undoubtedly of critical importance, it is important to note that this may not be sufficient to leverage co-creation, i.e. capture the value resulting from the co-creation activities. As noted by Rayna and Striukova (2015), transaction costs are a significant hurdle when engaging in co-creation and both intellectual and social capital play a critical role. For instance, tacit knowledge impacts significantly coordination costs and, thereby, engagement in co-creation (in this respect, co-creation in the Lego case appears to be hindered by the fact that consumers do not really understand what the 'rules of the game' are). In regard to social capital, norms and routines also play an important role and the fact that people engaging in co-creation are located outside of the firm can make it hard for them to adopt the routines and norms of the firm (and conversely, it may be difficult for the firms to adapt their routines and norms to those prevailing in the community). As discussed by Rayna and Striukova (2015), these issues are particularly prevalent in the cases when roles are more integrated, regardless of whether the output is customised or meant for the mass market.

A further issue concerning the management of co-creation, and which is likely to become increasingly prevalent in the coming years, is related to the growing access of consumers to manufacturing and distribution technologies (Rayna *et al.*, 2015). Looking at the four cases presented in this chapter, it is clear that co-creation can remain 'under control' because consumers (aside from a few hobbyists) do not yet have the means to manufacture Lego sets or Little Ponies. The fact that they still need go through a platform (such as Shapeways or DigitalForming), through a mass manufacturer (Lego) or throughout a service bureau (Digits2Widgets) to have customised products manufactured enables firms to retain some control. However, what will happen when, eventually, manufacturing capabilities will be (potentially) in the hands of everyone? As noted by Rayna and Striukova (2016), value capture is likely to become extremely challenging when it will be possible to manufacture at home (or at least locally) products of a similar quality as those currently manufactured 'professionally'.

If consumers can design (as a group), manufacture and distribute on their own, what role is there left for firms? Toffler (1981) noted that we are progressively moving away from the 'industrial age' that has prevailed since the 19th century towards an 'information age'. While in the former corporations are the key organisation in the economy (because of the necessary concentration of means of production that traditional manufacturing technologies entail), this is no longer the case when the key resource in the economy becomes information. In this case, Toffler conjectures that communities become the key organisation. And this is indeed what has happened online, with communities taking over the production of content (Facebook, YouTube, Instagram, etc.) and, more recently, of services (Airbnb, Uber pop, Blablacar). While production has remained in the hands of companies, the advent of technologies such as 3D printing, which are characterised by a constant cost per unit (and, hence, do not require concentration to achieve economies of scale) is getting us ever closer to a tipping point where the transition towards the 'information age' will spread to the whole economy.

When this happens, our entire economic, legal and social systems will have to be rethought. Indeed, if one of the key aspects of capitalism is the concentration of ownership of means of production, one can only wonder what happens when means of production are widespread and available to everyone. Likewise, what happens with IP laws when creation is no longer the act of one or a couple of individuals, but instead is carried out by an entire community that constantly remixes and improves existing creations? Finally, what happens to value capture when value is created mainly by communities and no longer by firms?

The past couple of years have shown that becoming a platform (e.g. Apple, Facebook, Airbnb, Uber, Blablacar) is a way (and perhaps, eventually, the only way) for firms to capture a significant amount of value in a community-driven environment. But considering that this leaves room for only a couple of firms, what happen to the rest of them?

Thus, considering the question of management of co-creation is certainly a way, in the short and middle term, to accommodate technological trends and consumer behavioural changes, and, thereby, to generate competitive advantage. It goes beyond that, however, and in the long term, understanding co-creation management issues enables one to reflect upon the radical transformations that each and every firm will necessarily have to undergo.

References

Geiger, D., Seedorf, S., Schulze, T., Nickerson, R. and Schader, M. (2011). Managing the crowd: Towards a taxonomy of crowdsourcing processes. In *Proceedings of: Americas Conference on Information Systems (AMCIS)*, pp. 1–11. Detroit, Michigan.

Howe, J. (2006). The rise of crowdsourcing. *Wired Magazine*, 14(6): 1–4.

Kambil, A., Ginsberg, A. and Bloch, M. (1996). Re-inventing value propositions. Stern Working Paper IS-96–21, New York University.

Piller, F. T. and Ihl, C. (2009). *Open Innovation with Customers. Foundations, Competences and International Trends*. Trend Study within the BMBF Project 'International Monitoring'. RWTH Aachen University: Aachen.

Piller, F., Ihl, C., Fuller, J. and Stotko, C. (2004). Toolkits for open innovation: The case of mobile phone games. In *System Sciences, 2004. Proceedings of the 37th Annual Hawaii International Conference on*, pp. 1–10. IEEE.

Piller, F., Ihl, C. and Vossen, A. (2010). A typology of customer co-creation in the innovation process. *Available at SSRN 1732127*.

Prahalad, C. and Ramaswamy, V. (2004a). Co-creation experiences: The next practice in value creation. *Journal of Interactive Marketing*, 18(3): 5–14.

Prahalad, C. K. and Ramaswamy, V. (2004b). *The Future of Competition: Co-creating Unique Value with Customers*. Boston, MA: Harvard Business School Press.

Rayna, T. and Striukova, L. (2015). Open innovation 2.0: Is co-creation the ultimate challenge? *International Journal of Technology Management*, 69(1): 38–53.

Rayna, T. and Striukova, L. (2016). From rapid prototyping to home fabrication: How 3D printing is changing business model innovation. *Technological Forecasting and Social Change*, 102: 214–224.

Rayna, T., Striukova, L. and Darlington, J. (2015). Co-creation and user innovation: The role of online 3D printing platforms. *Journal of Engineering and Technology Management*, 37: 90–102.

Ritzer, G. and Jurgenson, N. (2010). Production, consumption, prosumption: The nature of capitalism in the age of the digital 'prosumer'. *Journal of Consumer Culture*, 10(1): 13–36.

Sawhney, M. and Prandelli, E. (2000). Communities of creation: Managing distributed innovation in turbulent markets. *California Management Review*, 42(4): 24–54.

Tapscott, D. and Williams, A. D. (2006). *Wikinomics: How Mass Collaboration Changes Everything*. New York: Portfolio.

Toffler, A. (1981). *The Third Wave*. New York: Bantam Books.

von Hippel, E. (1978). A customer-active paradigm for industrial product idea generation. *Research Policy*, 7(3): 240–266.

von Hippel, E. and Katz, R. (2002). Shifting innovation to users via toolkits. *Management Science*, 48(7): 821–833.

Whitla, P. (2009). Crowdsourcing and its application in marketing activities. *Contemporary Management Research*, 5(1): 15–28.

Zwass, V. (2010). Co-creation: Toward a taxonomy and an integrated research perspective. *International Journal of Electronic Commerce*, 15(1): 11–48.

3 Cultural intelligence and the management of creativity

A proposed framework

Marc Rocas and Evelyn García

The management of creativity is a strategic field nowadays as more and more companies face a rapidly changing environment fuelled by digitization; globalization; new business models based providers and consumers being connected through social networks; the coexistence of several very different consecutive generations (i.e. baby boomers, generation X, the millennial generation and the Gen2020 generation); and new consumer habits.

Since the last two decades of the twentieth century, the world has become more and more interconnected due to globalization. Globalization has led to an increasing number of interactions with other cultures. This means that a larger number of individuals interact daily with others from different cultural backgrounds. At the same time, this increasing global competition results in more and more industries adding innovation capabilities in order to use their resources more efficiently. Organizations need to manage the ability to adapt their employees to this new competitive environment in order to gain competitive advantage. This means that both companies and employees have to develop the capacity to work in different cultural environments. This ability has been identified as 'cultural competence'.

Whaley and Davis (2007) define **cultural competence** as a set of problem-solving skills including abilities to recognize intercultural dynamics and acquire knowledge and internalize it in order to routinely use it with diverse groups. Within intercultural competences, cultural intelligence (CQ) has been recently regarded as the most important competence for succeeding in the international environment (Alon and Higgins, 2005; Triandis, 2006).

This chapter provides a framework for managing creativity. It suggests using the construct of cultural intelligence as a tool, both for designing a strategic plan in order to boost creativity in organizations and for writing a research proposal on this matter. The framework reviews the relationship between cultural intelligence and creativity through common elements included in several theories related to **individual, team and organization levels**.

Creativity in a global context

The growing international expansion experienced by companies means that the skills that employees have to work in a global market become one of the main keys to the success of a company. Intercultural interactions within organizations are everywhere in today's marketplace: dealing with suppliers, dealing with customers, managing subsidiaries abroad, but also inside the company, obtaining the best performance from multicultural teams.

In this context, it is important to be able to manage change effectively and globally implement new market strategies. In order to generate new ideas, companies need to manage creativity in a broad sense.

According to Amabile (1982: 997), creativity is defined as '*the generation of novel ideas that are useful and appropriate*'. Innovation can therefore be seen as a stage of the creative process and defined as the '*implementation of a new and possibly problem-solving idea, practice or material artifact (e.g. a product) which is regarded as new*' (Martins and Martins, 2002: 67). The creativity stage of this process refers to idea generation, and both idea generation and implementation and creativity and innovation are strongly related and introduce new ways of doing things at work (Anderson *et al.*, 2014).

Although creativity is a universal human attribute, it is also multifaceted. As seen from Amabile's definition, there are at least three different elements to consider: novelty, usefulness and suitability. These three elements are culturally dependent. Culture has a profound influence on the expression and conceptualization of creativity, involving historical, societal and individual factors (Rudowicz, 2003). We refer to culture as a shared system of cognitions, behaviours, customs, values, rules and symbols concerning the manner in which a set of people interact with their social and physical environment (Triandis, 1996).

According to the investment theory of creativity, proposed by Sternberg and Lubart (1991, 1996), creative people '*buy low and sell high*'. Buying low means fighting resistance for those new or undervalued ideas that have growth potential; selling high means releasing novel ideas after they have gained value. These new ideas are possible solutions chosen as candidates to solve a problem.

The way the problems are defined or the perceived resistance for novelty varies across cultures (Lubart and Sternberg, 1998). Lubart and Sternberg (1998) maintain that creativity is not in the person or in the culture, but in the interaction between the two. As Rudowicz (2003) exposes, Csikszentmihalyi (1988, 1999) has further proposed that creativity is a process resulting from an interaction between three main forces: the culture that stores and transmits the selected ideas, values and beliefs to the next generations; the social system that selects which behaviours, values and information are worth preserving; and the individual who brings about some transformation to the social and cultural domain.

Rudowicz (2003) identifies some differences between Western and Eastern cultures regarding especially implicit theories of creativity, i.e., those derived from individuals' belief systems. She also sets down the motivational qualities, cognitive traits and personality characteristics, common in both cultures, that shape a creative person. Motivational characteristics for creative people give us an energetic, active, motivated, inquisitive, curious, adventurous, ambitious, and self-confident person. Cognitive traits give us the ability to make connections, the ability to develop awareness and interpret the environment and grasp abstract ideas. Personality characteristics include skills such as free spirit or assertiveness.

We focus our attention on the way of thinking and behaviour that encourages creativity, both from a manager's and an employee's point of view, and the importance that cultural intelligence has in managing creativity.

Employees working in a global context, and especially managers working in multinational companies, need to learn how to develop a specialized way of thinking. This specialized way of thinking has been referred to by some scholars as *'global mindset'*. Srinivas (1995) defines *'global mindset'* as a way of approaching the world from a broad perspective, composed of eight dimensions: a curiosity and concern with context; acceptance of complexity and its contradictions; diversity consciousness and sensitivity; seeking opportunity in surprises and uncertainties; faith in organizational processes; focus on continuous improvement; extended time perspective; and systems thinking.

Creativity implementation

Most companies are nowadays immersed in a continuous challenging procedure. Some of these challenges appear because of the existing intercultural environment in today's organizations. The term 'intercultural' refers here not only to interactions between people from different ethnical cultures, but also to different organizational cultures that appear in a company or up and down its value chain. Some of those challenges are related to communication misunderstandings, the integration of virtual teams, differences in work styles, or simply to different ideas about how the management of creativity should be developed.

Both creativity and intercultural executions, defined as those behaviours and outcomes related to exposure to intercultural situations, can be seen from two different points of view: as a concern of organizational behaviour and/or from an individual approach.

Organizational behaviour

Although there is general agreement on the important role that creativity and innovation play in today's organizations, there is no consensus about how to implement a culture of creativity in a company's culture.

When we refer to culture, we also take into account organizational culture. Organizations have their own values, codes of conduct and beliefs. Schein (2004) distinguishes three levels of culture in organizations, going from the very visible to the very tacit and invisible: observable artefacts, espoused values and basic underlying assumptions. Observable artefacts include everything from a physical layer – what you see, hear, feel when entering an organization. Although they are easy to observe, they are hard to decipher accurately. Espoused values are norms, ideologies, codes of conduct, mission and vision statements, and goals explicitly exposed by the organization. Basic underlying assumptions are mostly unconscious and determine perceptions, feelings and behaviour. They are explained throughout the history of the company and/or the culture of its founders. Schein (2004: 17) defines culture in organizations as:

> *a pattern of shared tacit assumptions that was learned by a group as it solved its problems of external adaptation and internal integration, that has worked well enough to be considered valid and, therefore, to be taught to new members as the correct way to perceive, think, and feel in relation to those problems.*

Martins and Terblanche (2003) identify five determinants of organizational culture that influence creativity and innovation: a strategy that promotes the development and implementation of new products and services; a structure that promotes creativity, sustained by values like flexibility, freedom, cooperative teamwork and effective team's composition; support mechanisms that boost creativity, such as rewards and recognitions; a behaviour that encourages innovation, where a culture of failure or knowledge management are important drivers for creativity; and an organizational culture that supports a clear and transparent communication based on trust. We will read below how cultural intelligence involves these types of behaviour in organizations, especially in multicultural teams.

Individual cultural competence and creativity

The definition of cultural capabilities has attracted increasing attention from researchers (Caligiuri and Tarique, 2012; Lovvorn and Chen, 2011; Thomas and Inkson, 2005). Firms focus on recruiting the best professionals. Our knowledge-based economy means that human resources now become critical in a company for gaining competitive advantage. So, in this context, cultural intelligence is motivated by the effect of globalization in the workplace; the need to understand why some professionals are more successful than others on their international assignments; and the need to manage the employees' capability to work effectively across cultures. In fact, cultural intelligence is defined as *'an individual's capability to function and manage effectively in culturally diverse settings'* (Earley and Ang, 2003).

Cultural intelligence

Ang and Inkpen (2008) suggest that cultural intelligence complements other forms of intelligence (i.e. social, emotional and cognitive intelligences) and provides the explanation when coping with diversity and functioning in new cultural settings. Earley and Ang (2003) developed the construct of cultural intelligence from Sternberg and Detterman's (1986) multi-loci theory of intelligence, and identified four relevant dimensions for explaining how to function and manage effectively in intercultural environments: a metacognitive, a cognitive, a motivational and a behavioural dimension.

Van Dyne *et al.* (2012) refined four dimensions of CQ and presented eleven sub-dimensions as an expanded conceptualization. We will summarize all four dimensions and eleven subdomains below.

- Metacognitive dimension reflects the thinking processes that an individual uses to acquire cultural knowledge and understanding. It reflects the awareness that a person has about how culture influences his or her own behaviour, regarding the interpretation of the facts made when in intercultural situations. Three sub-dimensions are identified: planning, awareness and checking. Planning is defined as the formulation of strategies before intercultural interaction occurs. It involves developing action plans including specific actions and behaviours in order to achieve predetermined goals. Awareness is defined as knowing about cultural thinking and knowledge of oneself and others in real time. Home culture acts as a cultural anchor and influences our mental processes and behaviour. Awareness implies knowing how cultural aspects of the situation could be influencing our own personal behaviour and the behaviour of others, and applying chosen aspects from our cultural values, experience, perception of the situation and past experience to our planning. It implies being able to consciously suspend judgment according to one's own cultural values, until enough information is available to take decisions. Checking is defined as the process of reviewing previous assumptions and mental models, comparing them with inputs from intercultural encounters and adapting decisions, if needed, according to this new information.
- The cognitive dimension refers to knowledge of the economic, legal and social aspects of different cultures. Since the existence of universal values that meet the basic needs of human beings (Triandis, 1994), it should be noted that different cultures have evolved over time, giving different answers to these fundamental needs and originated ways of organizing society that match each particular vision of them. The culture of each country determines the mode of thinking and behaviour of its members (Hofstede *et al.*, 1991). Individuals with a high cognitive CQ have a deep knowledge of the rules, practices and conventions that characterize different cultures (Earley and Ang, 2003); understand the political and economic systems, institutions and cultural values; and show advanced systems cognitive categorization, through which they can conceptualize systems of universal values and recognize similarities and differences between cultures. They are able to understand the culture of others and predict the behaviour of its members based on external cultural values, facilitating cultural interactions. Van Dyne *et al.* (2012) distinguish two sub-dimensions for cognitive CQ: cultural-general knowledge and context-specific knowledge. Cultural-general knowledge is defined as the knowledge of the universal elements that form a culture. It implies knowledge of the various economic, legal, political and religious systems, the role of male-female roles, different languages, but also a knowledge of values, beliefs, norms and assumptions shared in a group and even rules to express non-verbal (gestures, facial expressions) behaviours or forms of communication (direct vs indirect communication). In the scope of

organizations, both cultural-general knowledge and context-specific knowledge can be matched with Schein's basic underlying assumptions (Schein, 2004). Context-specific knowledge is defined as general knowledge of cultural values in a specific environment. These general rules have been widely used for teaching purposes, based mainly on cultural value categorization from several scholars (Hofstede *et al.*, 1991; Meyer, 2014; Livermore, 2013).

- Motivational CQ is defined as the ability of a person to direct attention and energy toward understanding other cultures and how to behave in different cultural environments. It refers to the motivation and willingness of an individual to adapt to different cultural situations. Three sub-dimensions are distinguished for motivational CQ: intrinsic motivation, extrinsic motivation and self-efficacy to adjust. Intrinsic motivation involves an individual's enjoyment and satisfaction facing new situations and working with people from several cultures. Extrinsic motivation is caused by the appreciation of the benefits offered by having intercultural experiences such as employability, possible promotions and professional exposure. Self-efficacy to adjust is the belief that one can be effective in a particular task in intercultural contexts and it implies self-confidence and perseverance (Bandura, 1977).

- Behavioural CQ reflects the ability to adapt one's own behaviour when interacting with people from different cultures. Behavioural CQ can be divided into three sub-dimensions: verbal behaviour, non-verbal behaviour and speech acts. Verbal behaviour implies the ability to be flexible when it comes to expression by varying the tone of voice we use, or the use of pauses and silences, speaking faster or slower or still more or less formally. Non-verbal behaviour implies the ability to vary gestures, facial expressions and body language, standing at a distance or closer when talking to other people or body or eye contact. Speech acts are defined as the used communication style and imply the ability to change the way we communicate certain types of messages such as requests, invitations, apologies, how to give thanks or show disagreement. It includes the type of words used, the degree of openness, and the direct or indirect way of putting it.

Cultural intelligence and creativity: common elements

As previously stated, this chapter helps to understand the relationship between cultural intelligence and the management of creativity by developing a conceptual framework based on a list of identified common elements. These common elements are developed below.

Individual cultural intelligence and creativity

Personality traits

Simonton (2000) describes creative people as individuals inclined to be independent, non-conformist, unconventional, likely to have wide interests, open to new experiences and risk seeking. Csikszentmihalyi (1996) points out some character-istics that creative people show: a great deal of physical energy; the combining of playfulness, discipline and responsability; they tend to be both extroverted and introverted; they are humble and proud at the same time; they are both rebellious and conservative; and very passionate about their work. Sung and Choi (2009) find a relationship between the Big Five personality traits and creativity, moderated by extrinsic motivation. Extraversion and openness to experience have significant effects on individual creativity. Extraversion refers to an individual's tendency to be energetic, enthusiastic and ambitious. Openness to experience refers to the extent to which individuals are imaginative, broad-minded, curious, and non-traditional. It enables individuals to move from traditional beliefs to new ways of thinking, since they tend to be flexible and accept different points of view. But Sung and Choi (2009) identify extraversion as the most powerful Big Five trait for predicting creativity, since extraverts are full of energy and enthusiasm, boosting proactive behaviour for facing problems and enhancing communication.

In the same way, although the cultural intelligence construct and Big Five traits are different concepts, there is a relationship between them. The personal-ity traits of an individual describe how a person typically behaves in different situations over time (Costa and McCrae, 1992). We can determine which person-ality traits remain stable over time and do not vary in different cultural contexts. Cultural intelligence, on the other hand, determines changes in a person's behav-iour according to the situation and cultural context which he/she is involved in. Then, given that personality influences the choice of behaviour, some per-sonality traits may be related to the different aspects of cultural intelligence. In fact, Ang, Van Dyne and Koh (2006) find significant links between conscien-tiousness and metacognitive CQ; between agreeableness and emotional stability with behavioural CQ; between extraversion with cognitive, motivational and behavioural CQ; and between openness to experience with all four factors of CQ. Agreeableness refers to an individual's trusting nature, tolerance and good nature. Conscientiousness refers to the extent to which individuals are purpose-ful, hardworking and persistent. Emotional stability refers to the individual's degree of calmness, self-confidence and security.

Motivation

As already seen, Amabile (1998) identifies expertise, skills and motivation as components of creativity, but supports intrinsic motivation as being the one that explains a better propensity to creativity. Amabile defines the '*Intrinsic Motivation Principle of Creativity*' as a factor that explains that people will be more creative when they feel motivated primarily by the interest, challenge and satisfaction of the work itself.

Creativity is not a behaviour observed now and then, but a habit (Sternberg, 2012: 3), defined as '*an acquired behaviour pattern*'. Sternberg summarizes this behaviour as four ways of acting: looking for ways to see problems that oth-ers do not see; taking risks; standing up for one's own beliefs; and seeking to overcome obstacles and challenges to one's views. Stenberg and Lubart proposed the '*Investment Theory of Creativity*' for explaining the resources needed for being creative (Sternberg and Lubart, 1996; Sternberg, 2006, 2012; Sternberg and Lubart, 1991). According to the investment theory, creative individuals select ideas that are not known or out of favour but have growth potential, and they persist and manage to overcome the initial resistance. Stenberg and Lubart identify six resources for creativity: intellectual abilities for generating new ideas, analysing them and selling the ideas to others; knowledge to move forward, but also for deciding when to apply past experiences to new challenges; styles of thinking globally to recognize the important questions; specific personality traits, such as self-efficacy and willingness to overcome obstacles, tolerate ambiguity and take risks; intrinsic motivation; and a supporting and rewarding environment for boosting creative ideas. However, in the same way as explained before, most creative individuals are those who develop divergent thinking (ability to generate multiple solutions in a given situation). Some of these six resources for creativity are directly linked to some of the CQ dimensions. Deciding when to apply past experiences to new challenges is also applicable to new intercultural encounters. This resource is linked to awareness. Being aware implies distinguishing and extracting remarkable information from all the perceived inputs. Taking decisions about applying available resources or not has to do with perception and the ability to suspend judgment. Individuals with high metacognitive CQ show this resource. Self-efficacy, intrinsic motivation and resilience are competencies that have to do with motivational CQ.

Prabhu, Sutton and Sauser (2008) emphasize the importance of intrinsic and extrinsic motivation as mediators of the relationship between creativity and three personality traits: openness of experience, self-efficacy and perseverance. Creativity is closely related to openness to experience and self-efficacy; extrinsic motivation completely moderates the relationship between creativity and perseverance; and intrinsic motivation completely mediates the relationship between creativity and self-efficacy. Motivation is extremely important in creativity because it drives an individual to persist in problem solving. '*Creative potential is not fulfilled unless the individual (and his or her social support) is motivated to do so, and creative solutions are not found unless the individual is motivated to apply his or her skills*' (Runco, 2005: 609).

Language

Shannon and Begley (2008) propose that language skills are related to cognitive and behavioural CQ. Given that a language reflects norms, conventions and norms from a culture, it transmits cultural knowledge. Regarding cognitive CQ, Shannon and Begley state that those individuals with high-level ability in multiple languages have a key for accessing core values from different cultures, and, therefore, acquiring more knowledge of other cultures. As far as behavioural CQ is concerned, since it has to do with verbal and non-verbal communication, it is clear that speaking a language enables an individual to establish a direct verbal communication with people from other cultures. Hommel *et al.* (2011) suggest that bilingualism is related with the specific processes and mechanisms that underlie creativity. They suggest that bilinguals perform better in creative activities associated with convergent thinking, i.e. illumination, where ideas come together to form a possible solution, and verification, where those possible chosen solutions are evaluated. These scholars suggest that this is consistent with previous results which show how monolinguals outperform bilinguals in verbal fluency tasks.

Cultural agility

Caligiuri (2013: 6) explains that successful global professionals show what she calls cultural agile competences, defined as '*the ability to quickly, comfortably and successfully work in cross-cultural and international environments*'. She identifies divergent thinking and creativity as the main cultural agile competencies affecting the process of taking decisions in an intercultural context. She states that creative people who can think out of the box are highly demanded, especially in international environments, where the decisions to take and the problems to face are both new and challenging.

Organizational and team cultural intelligence and creativity

Leadership

Sternberg (2012) points out that, like any habit, creativity can be encouraged or discouraged. Supporting an environment for creating new ideas not only refers to a physical spot, but also to creating the appropriate conditions for it in an organization, taken from a proper type of leadership. Amabile (1998) identifies six different managerial practices affecting creativity: challenge, to match people with the right assignments; freedom, to provide people with enough autonomy; resources, in the form of time and money; work-group design, for guaranteeing diversity; supervisory encouragement, to serve as role models; and organizational support, through a company's values, recognition and communication. This kind of leaderships recalls transformational leadership in which leaders inspire employees to go beyond their abilities and assigned tasks, both through task and relations support (Amabile, Schatzel, Moneta, and Kramer, 2004).

Transformational leadership

Transformational leaders are defined as those who inspire their subordinates to release their full potential for completing their tasks in order to meet their organization's goals (Bass, 1985). Keung and Rockinson-Szapkiw (2013) find that there is a significant positive relationship between cultural intelligence and transformational leadership in international school leaders. This find suggests that individuals with high cultural intelligence are able to manage more effectively in multicultural environments. Cheung and Wong (2011) demonstrate that transformational leadership is positively related to an employee's creativity.

A leader's task and relations support moderates this relationship. They also state that transformational leadership promotes an employee's self-efficacy. Employees are then motivated to solve work problems, generate new ideas, and also, as the cultural intelligence construct states, focus energy on their intercultural relationships.

Living abroad and the experiential learning theory

Globalization requires managers to be able to deal effectively with different cultures in multicultural environments. This ability has been defined as cultural competence, global mindset or global competence. As a result, developing competent global managers is a source of competitive advantage for companies. There are three identified main methodologies for training and developing global leaders: didactic learning programs, experiential opportunities, and intensive experiences (Caligiuri, 2006). Caligiuri (2006) states that developmental international assignments should be carried out within the context of broad managerial development programmes in order to avoid underutilization of newly developed knowledge and skills when expats return home. Ng *et al.* (2009) propose a theoretical model based on Kolb's experiential learning theory (ELT) in order to expose how CQ capabilities affect global leaders' ability to learn from their experiences (Kolb, 1984). They show that individual CQ capabilities enhance learning through international experiences.

With regard to creativity, Leung *et al.* (2008) find that multicultural experiences increase creative performance, that the connection between multicultural experience and creativity is higher in intensive immersing experiences and that awareness boosts the creative benefits of the multicultural experience.

Boundary spanners

Shaping creative projects in organizations and aligning them in existing structures requires special abilities involving knowledge, negotiation, motivation, awareness and choosing adequate tools for communicating ideas. Boundary spanning activity enables creative projects to be integrated and developed across organizations. Andersen and Kragh (2015) extend the boundary spanning from a practice to a management process. This approach requires managing different actors, mostly creative teams, but not always, separated from each other by internal and/or external boundaries of time, geography, occupation, culture and ownership. Andersen *et al.* (2013) identify three groups of boundary spanning activities: selecting and mobilizing team members from external organizations, promoting a shared activity and common perspective and combining and integrating ideas across different fields.

Multicultural teams and creativity

Amabile (1998) describes three components of creativity: expertise, creative-thinking skills and motivation. These three components interact better in teams if different points of view, ideas and expertise are combined. It means implementing diversity as a starting point for a team's composition. This diversity can be easily reached by composing multicultural teams. Motivation varies across cultures, and some cultural values such as power distance, collectivism and uncertainty avoidance affect how individuals create new ideas and how they find them useful or not (Erez and Nouri, 2010). Original ideas are created after individuals use different perspectives for approaching challenges. This need is constrained by an individual's culture since it establishes values and norms that cause automatic responses to some behaviours, preventing the search for new and different solutions (Chiu and Kwan, 2010). Simonton and Ting (2010) state that experiences with cultural diversity lead to the development of creativity. Multicultural teams incorporate a variety of cultural approaches naturally since different cultural clusters mean a variety of interpretations for the same challenge. Multicultural teams offer an environment for the multiplicity of different points of view, ideas and expertise that Amabile (1998) identified as accelerators for creativity. Multicultural teams also act as a source of motivation for boosting creativity. The degree of cultural diversity on multicultural teams also influences team performance over time. Here, performance improves only if team members exhibit high levels of cultural intelligence (Moon, 2013). Moon (2013) finds that the greater the cultural diversity among team members, the more essential the team members' CQ in relation to team performance. Divergent thinking is the process of generating many, different ideas, and is characterized by the successful solving of heuristic problems (Williams, 2004). Divergent thinking in multicultural teams as the result of expertise, different approaches to the same problem, and the convergence of new ideas into a solution requires some important issues to be dealt with in a team, such as the creation of trust and how team decision processes are established. People are attracted to others who are similar to them, in terms of similar background and views. In the same way, culture may constrain creativity since we tend to create categories according to our knowledge, values, beliefs and past behaviours; a category's structure plays a central role in many processes; and our imagination is structured by a set of properties characteristic of that category. For instance, when people generate exemplars in a novel conceptual domain (e.g., animals on the planet Mars), even the most creative examples resemble highly accessible exemplars (e.g., animals on Earth with eyes and legs or known science fiction exemplars) (Ward, 1994). Cultural intelligence is relevant here from two different perspectives. From an outsider's point of view, that is, trying to understand how a team works, a high-CQ person is capable of observing, categorizing and analysing team members' actions. From an insider's point of view, i.e. a team member, a high-CQ person is able to understand a team's dynamics (metacognitive CQ) and go beyond the difficulties of forming a multicultural team (Earley, Ang, and Tan, 2006). We expect to find higher levels of creativity in those multicultural teams that show higher levels of cultural intelligence. On the other hand, the relationship between cultural diversity and creativity will be weaker in teams that show lower levels of cultural intelligence.

Conclusion

The present chapter helps us to understand the relationship between cultural intelligence and the management of creativity by developing a conceptual framework based on a list of identified common elements. Identifying these common elements helps to establish a relationship between cultural intelligence and creativity.

Cultural intelligence is not static. It can be developed, so our proposed framework is also a tool for managing creativity based on cultural intelligence. Our framework includes items regarding three different levels: an individual level; a team level; and an organizational level, as well as a group of propositions to be validated in further research.

With regard to the individual level, we state that all four CQ dimensions are directly related to creativity, but multilingualism acts as a moderator in the relationship between cognitive and behavioural CQ and creativity. At the same time, cognitive, metacognitive and behavioural CQ act as moderators in the relationship between extraversion and creativity, and all four CQ dimensions act as a moderator in the relationship between openness to experience and creativity. We also state that designing international experiences based on ELT and CQ produce higher levels of creativity as one of the outcomes.

On the team and organizational levels, we state that teams exhibit a higher level of creativity since they have higher levels of cultural diversity, higher levels of motivational CQ and high cultural intelligent managers. At the same time, if these managers implement a transformational management style, it acts as a moderator for their teams on the positive relationship between cultural intelligence and creativity. Finally, those employees working on boundary spanning positions show higher levels of cultural intelligence and creativity.

There is a lack of research linking cultural intelligence and creativity. There is also a lack of research into the management of creativity, especially with regard to what companies really need to boost creativity, and, therefore, create a pool of ideas in order to innovate. We propose some suggested research in this field:

- Developing the different propositions suggested in this chapter.
- Identifying common competencies related both to creativity and cultural intelligence and building methodologies for developing them.
- Identifying the needs that companies have for managing creativity and trying to provide solutions through new models.

Our proposed framework helps managers to plan how to boost creativity in their organizations. This process can be summarized as consisting of three different stages: selection of candidates, training and development, and change management. Our framework allows creativity to be managed by applying cultural intelligence as a tool for it. It means that assessing cultural intelligence can be used to recruit creative talent or identify areas of personal development. CQ assessment can also be useful in building multicultural teams. Finally, our framework allows a plan for change management to be formulated including the management of creativity in the company's value chain.

This chapter approaches the management of creativity from an original point of view since it provides a framework for further research and a holistic view of the use of cultural intelligence for boosting creativity in organizations. Developing cultural intelligence boosts creativity at all the different levels in which creativity takes place: individual, in teams and at an organizational level. Our framework is a starting point for originating methodologies that allow creativity to be systematically developed because, as Sternberg (2012: 3) states: '*Creativity is a habit*'.

References

Alon, I. and Higgins, J. M. (2005) "Global leadership success through emotional and cultural intelligences," *Business Horizons, 48*(6): 501–512.

Amabile, T. M. (1982) "Social psychology of creativity: A consensual assessment technique," *Journal of Personality and Social Psychology, 43*(5): 997–1013.

Amabile, T. M. (1998). "How to kill creativity," *Harvard Business Review, 76*(5): 76–87.

Amabile, T. M., Schatzel, E. A., Moneta, G. B. and Kramer, S. J. (2004) "Leader behaviors and the work environment for creativity: Perceived leader support," *Leadership Quarterly, 15*(1): 5–32.

Andersen, P. H. and Kragh, H. (2015) "Exploring boundary-spanning practices among creativity managers," *Management Decision, 53*(4): 786–808.

Andersen, P. H., Kragh, H. and Lettl, C. (2013) "Spanning organizational boundaries to manage creative processes: The case of the LEGO Group," *Industrial Marketing Management, 42*(1): 125–134.

Anderson, N., Potocnik, K. and Zhou, J. (2014) "Innovation and creativity in organizations: A state-of-the-science review, prospective commentary, and guiding framework," *Journal of Management, 40*(5): 1297–1333.

Ang, S. and Inkpen, A. C. (2008) "Cultural intelligence and offshore outsourcing success: A framework of firm-level intercultural capability," *Decision Sciences, 39*(3): 337–358.

Ang, S., Van Dyne, L. and Koh, C. (2006), "Personality correlates of the four-factor model of cultural intelligence," *Group & Organization Management, 31*(1): 100–123.

Bandura, A. (1977) "Self-efficacy: Toward a unifying theory of behavioral change," *Psychological Review, 84*(2): 191–215.

Bass, B. M. (1985) "Leadership and performance beyond expectations," New York: Free Press, Collier Macmillan.

Caligiuri, P. (2006) "Developing global leaders," *Human Resource Management Review, 16*(2): 219–228.

Caligiuri, P. (2013) *Cultural Agility: Building a Pipeline of Successful Global Professionals*, San Francisco, CA: John Wiley & Sons.

Caligiuri, P. and Tarique, I. (2012) "Dynamic cross-cultural competencies and global leadership effectiveness," *Journal of World Business, 47*(4): 612–622.

Cheung, M. F. Y. and Wong, C.-S. (2011) "Transformational leadership, leader support, and employee creativity," *Leadership & Organization Development Journal, 32*(7): 656–672.

Chiu, C. and Kwan, L. Y.-Y. (2010) "Culture and creativity: A process model," *Management and Organization Review, 6*(3): 447–461.

Costa, P. T. and McCrae, R. R. (1992) "Four ways five factors are basic," *Personality and individual differences, 13*(6): 653–665.

Csikszentmihalyi, M. (1988) "Society, culture and person: A system view of creativity," in R. J. Sternberg (Ed.) *The Nature of Creativity*, Cambridge: Cambridge University Press, pp. 325–339.

Csikszentmihalyi, M. (1996) *Flow and the Psychology of Discovery and Invention*, New York: Harper Collins.

Csikszentmihalyi, M. (1999) "Implications of a systems perspective for the study of creativity," in R. J. Sternberg (Ed.) *Handbook of Creativity*, Cambridge: Cambridge University Press, pp. 313–338.

Earley, P. and Ang, S. (2003) "Cultural intelligence: Individual interactions across cultures," Stanford, CA: Stanford University Press.

Earley, P., Ang, S. and Tan, J. (2006) "CQ: Developing cultural intelligence at work," Stanford, CA: Stanford University Press.

Erez, M. and Nouri, R. (2010) "Creativity: The influence of cultural, social, and work contexts," *Management and Organization Review*, 6(3): 351–370.

Hofstede, G., Hofstede, G. J. and Minkov, M. (1991) *Cultures and Organizations: Software of the Mind* (Vol. 2), London: McGraw-Hill.

Hommel, B., Colzato, L. S., Fischer, R. and Christoffels, I. K. (2011) "Bilingualism and creativity: Benefits in convergent thinking come with losses in divergent thinking," *Frontiers in Psychology*, 2(November): 1–5.

Keung, E. K. and Rockinson-Szapkiw, A. J. (2013) "The relationship between transformational leadership and cultural intelligence: A study of international school leaders," *Journal of Educational Administration*, 51(6): 836–854.

Kolb, D. A. (1984) *Experiential Learning*, Englewood Cliffs, NJ: Prentice-Hall.

Leung, A. K. Y., Maddux, W. W., Galinsky, A. D. and Chiu, C. Y. (2008) "Multicultural experience enhances creativity: The when and how," *American Psychologist*, 63(3): 169.

Livermore, D. A. (2013) *Expand Your Borders: Discover 10 Cultural Clusters*, Cultural Intelligence Center, Panda Bear Circle, Michigan.

Lovvorn, A. S. and Chen, J.-S. (2011) "Developing a global mindset: The relationship between an international assignment and cultural intelligence," *International Journal of Business and Social Sciences*, 2(9): 275–283.

Lubart, T. I. and Sternberg, R. J. (1998) "Creativity across time and place: Life span and cross-cultural perspectives," *High Ability Studies*, 9(1): 59–74.

Martins, E. C. and Terblanche, F. (2003) "Building organisational culture that stimulates creativity and innovation," *European Journal of Innovation Management*, 6(1), 64–74.

Meyer, E. (2014) *The Culture Map: Breaking Through the Invisible Boundaries of Global Business*, New York: PublicAffairs.

Moon, T. (2013) "The effects of cultural intelligence on performance in multicultural teams," *Journal of Applied Social Psychology*, 43(12): 2414–2425.

Ng, K. Y., Van Dyne, L. and Ang, S. (2009) "From experience to experiential learning: Cultural intelligence as a learning capability for global leader development," *Academy of Management Learning and Education*, 8(4): 511–526.

Prabhu, V., Sutton, C. and Sauser, W. (2008) "Creativity and certain personality traits: Understanding the mediating effect of intrinsic motivation," *Creativity Research Journal*, 20(1): 53–66.

Rudowicz, E. (2003) "Creativity and culture: A two way interaction," *Scandinavian Journal of Educational Research*, 47(3): 273–290.

Runco, M. A. (2005) "Motivation, competence, and creativity," in A. J. Elliot and C. S. Dweck (Eds), *Handbook of competence and motivation*, New York: Guilford, pp. 609–623.

Schein E. H. (2004) *Organizational Culture and Leadership*, 3rd edition, San Francisco, CA: Jossey-Bass.

Shannon, L. M. and Beglet T. M., (2008) "Antecedents of the four-factor model of cultural intelligence", in S. Ang and L. Van Dyne (Eds) *Handbook of Cultural Intelligence: Theory, Measurement and Applications*, New York: Routledge, pp. 41–55.

Simonton, D. K. (2000) "Creativity: Cognitive, personal, developmental, and social aspects," *American psychologist, 55*(1): 151.

Simonton, D. K. and Ting, S. S. (2010) "Creativity in Eastern and Western civilizations: The lessons of historiometry," *Management and Organization Review, 6*(3): 329–350.

Srinivas, K. M. (1995) "Globalization of business and the Third World: Challenge of expanding the mindsets," *Journal of Management Development, 14*(3): 26–49.

Sternberg, R. J. (2006) "Creating a vision of creativity: The first 25 years," *Psychology of Aesthetics, Creativity, and the Arts, 1*(2): 2–12.

Sternberg, R. J. (2012) "The assessment of creativity: An investment-based approach," *Creativity Research Journal, 24*(1): 3–12.

Sternberg, R. J. and Detterman, D. K. (Eds) (1986) *What is Intelligence?: Contemporary Viewpoints on its Nature and Definition*, Santa Barbara, CA: Praeger Pub Text.

Sternberg, R. J. and Lubart, T. (1991) "An investment theory of creativity and its development," *Human Development, 34*(1): 1–31.

Sternberg, R. J. and Lubart, T. I. (1996) "Investing in creativity," *Psychological Inquiry, 4*(3): 229–232.

Sung, S. and Choi, J. (2009) "Do big five personality factors affect individual creativity? The moderating role of extrinsic motivation," *Social Behavior and Personality, an International Journal, 37*(7): 941–956.

Thomas, D. C. and Inkson, K. (2005) "Cultural Intelligence: People skills for a global workplace," *Consulting Management, 16*: 5–9.

Triandis, H. C. (1994) *Culture and Social Behavior*, New York: Mcgraw-Hill Book Company.

Triandis, H. C. (1996) "The psychological measurement of cultural syndromes," *American Psychologist, 51*(4): 407–415.

Triandis, H. C. (2006) "Cultural intelligence in organizations," *Group & Organization Management, 31*(1): 20–26.

Van Dyne, L., Ang, S., Ng, K. Y., Rockstuhl, T., Tan, M. L. and Koh, C. (2012) "Sub-dimensions of the four factor model of cultural intelligence: Expanding the conceptualization and measurement of cultural intelligence," *Social and Personality Psychology Compass, 6*(4): 295–313.

Ward, T. B. (1994) "Structured imagination: The role of category structure in exemplar generation," *Cognitive Psychology 27*(1): 1–40.

Whaley, A. L. and Davis, K. E. (2007) "Cultural competence and evidence-based practice in mental health services: A complementary perspective," *American Psychologist, 62*(6): 563.

Williams, S. D. (2004) "Personality, attitude, and leader influences on divergent thinking and creativity in organizations," *European Journal of Innovation Management, 7*(3): 187–204.

4 Creative capabilities and the regenerative power of creative industries

Local and global ingredients

Chahira Mehouachi, David Grandadam,
Patrick Cohendet and Laurent Simon

Creativity: between the individual and the collective

The current shift from an information-based economy towards a creative economy has fostered an unprecedented infatuation with creativity among politicians, academics and practitioners. There is a large consensus today that creativity is a critical and strategic capability (Leonard-Barton, 1995; Styhre and Sundgren, 2005; Napier and Nilsson, 2006; Teece, 2009) that can ensure competitive advantages for firms and better economic development and promotion of urban regeneration as well as social well-being (Florida, 2002; Scott, 2006; Cooke and Lazzeretti, 2008; Pratt, 2008; Landry, 2012; Csikszentmihalyi, 2014).

Despite this widespread interest in the concept, creativity is still conceived as a genuinely individual and spontaneous activity, inherently difficult to organize and control, and pertaining to the realm of irrationality (Bilton, 2007). Unsurprisingly, creativity has mainly been understood in the literature as an individual attribute of creative geniuses (Amabile *et al.*, 1996; Lubart, 2001; Feinstein, 2006). Creative insights and processes have been primarily investigated at the individual level (Ford, 1996; Oldham and Cummings, 1996; Amabile, 1997; Perry-Smith, 2006), whereas the antecedents of creativity that have been studied are the psychological attributes of creative persons and talents. Consequently, psychological theories have long dominated the literature on creativity (Simonton, 1999; Sternberg, 1999; Kaufman and Sternberg, 2010; Glover *et al.*, 2013).

This supremacy of the individual is being challenged in light of the critical importance of the collective for creativity. There is growing evidence that creative processes can emerge, take form and lead to creative and innovative outputs at the collective level (Woodman *et al.*, 1993; Drazin *et al.*, 1999). In other words, creative insights can occur at the collective as well as at the individual level (Bharadwaj and Menon, 2000; Taggar, 2002; Hargadon and Bechky, 2006).

Concepts such as collective creativity or organizational creativity emphasize the idea of the group and the organization as creative actors with their own creative capabilities (Gilson and Shalley, 2004; Pirola-Merlo and Mann, 2004; Barczak *et al.*, 2010). For most authors, collective creativity is part of the broader construct of organizational innovation which has shed light on many different processes internal to the firm, but does not yet fully grasp the main dynamics of collective creativity, as well as the multiple levels on which these processes occur and from which creative insights emerge and evolve. The study of collective creativity and its antecedents is underexplored in the literature. The antecedents of creativity that have been investigated are mainly situated within the internal context of organizations including, apart from the group interactions, the role of incentive structures and organizational cultures in influencing collective creativity (Amabile *et al.*, 1996; 1998; Woodman *et al.*, 1993; Isaksen and Lauer, 2002). This is due to the embedded nature of collective creative processes as well as the multiple levels on which these processes occur and from which creative insights emerge and evolve (one notable exception is the work by Drazin *et al.*, 1999). The notion of collective in itself is quite varied and incorporates a plethora of actors, each of which stands on different levels of analysis.

In order to deal with the intricacies of this concept and understand the complexity of collective creativity, many authors advocate interactionist approaches. These approaches are depicted in the literature as a useful theoretical tool for integrating different traditions of research focusing on different kinds of creativity, and for disentangling the different capabilities and processes pertaining to collective creativity. The rationale is that managing creativity requires an understanding of how the creative process, the creative product, the creative person and the creative situation interact with one another (Woodman and Schoenfeldt, 1990; Amabile, 1988; Woodman *et al.*, 1993; Isaksen and Lauer, 2002). "The creative output [. . .] for the entire system stems from the complex mosaic of individual, group and organizational characteristics and behaviours occurring within the salient situational influences (both creativity constraining and enhancing) at each level of social organization" (Woodman *et al.*, 1993, p. 298). Thus, far from denying the primary role of individual creativity, these approaches establish complementarities between the existing literature and research focused on collective creativity.

The rising recognition of interactionist approaches has opened up the way to a new stream of research investigating collective creativity. As they stand today, however, these approaches equate collective creativity with organizational creativity. That is to say that the main bulk of studies focuses on the intra-organizational context. Examinations of the origins and processes of creativity at the inter-organizational level are not inexistent. Yet, they limit the scope of analysis to territorialized forms of interactions. Cities, clusters or creative territories are examples of perimeters that delimit inter-organizational interactions when studying collective creativity and its antecedents. This seems, however, at odds with the several examples in the literature detailing creative insights and processes that take place outside the single firm's boundaries and through inter-organizational interactions that cross the borders of territories and link spatially dispersed actors.

Many studies show that global linkages between localized pools of creativity can enhance industrial performance and avoid lock-in effects (Bathelt *et al.*, 2004; Maskell *et al.*, 2006; Maskell, 2014). In this respect, studying the role of inter-organizational interactions in the development of collective creativity cannot be limited to localized regions and territories harbouring creative clusters or firms. It requires the examinations to be extended to inter-organizational interactions occurring at the industrial level regardless of their co-localization.

Going beyond organizational creativity: what is the role of industrial creativity?

In this chapter, we argue that one interesting collective perimeter that allows the integration of inter-organizational interactions in studies of collective creativity is the industrial level. Industries can be conceived as collective actors, quite distinct from their environment and from other collectives composing them or interacting with them. They can be endowed with collective creative capabilities and harbour varied creative processes which are best perceived at the industrial level of analysis. A "creative capability" at the industrial level would convey and serve to capture the capability of the industry as an inter-related set of ecosystems and niches aimed at producing novel and original ideas (both in qualitative and quantitative terms) and devoted to bringing these ideas to the consumers as marketable goods and/or services allowing creative actors to make a living from their creative work (as depicted partially in Van Heur, 2009).

Many authors argue that firms are not only concerned with the organization of their own units; they also need to proceed with the strategic arrangements of the industry that determine the collective future and survival of this industry. Van de Ven and Garud (1989, 1993) point out that individual firms in a given activity need to build a common platform (or "infrastructure"), viewed as a quasi-common good, which allows collective learning and ensures sustainability of the whole industry. As detailed in Table 4.1, such an industrial community

> not only includes private firms developing similar, complementary, or substitute technologies, but also all the other actors in the public and private sectors who play key roles in the development of an infrastructure for innovation. This infrastructure includes (1) institutional arrangements to legitimate, regulate, and standardize a new technology, (2) public resource endowments of basic scientific knowledge, financing mechanism, and a pool of competent labour, as well as (3) proprietary R&D, manufacturing, marketing, and distribution functions that are required to develop and commercialize an innovation.
>
> (Van de Ven, 1993, p. 339)

This innovation infrastructure can have important impacts on the collective learning and innovation processes occurring at the industry level (Van de Ven and Garud, 1993). Since creativity and innovation are theorized in the literature as the results of interactive processes of problem solving engaging different actors (preferably endowed with different types of knowledge and skills) (Bathelt *et al.*, 2004), we can conclude that an innovation infrastructure, by influencing and conditioning the quality of inter-organizational cooperation and the processes of problem solving, can heavily impact overall creativity and innovation within an industry.

Table 4.1 A social system framework for understanding innovation development and industry emergence

---

Components of community infrastructure for innovation

Institutional arrangements

- Legitimation (creation of trust)
- Governance (norms, rules, regulations, laws)
- Technology standards

Resource endowments

- Scientific/technological research
- Financing and insurance arrangements
- Human competence pool (training and accreditation)

Proprietary functions

- Technological development functions: R&D, testing, manufacturing, marketing
- Innovation network/resource channel activities: appropriation of common goods (science, financing, labour) vendor-supplier-distributor channels
- Market creation and consumer demand

Source: Adapted from Van de Ven and Garud (1989).

This infrastructure thus appears as an industrial feature that can condition the capability of an industry, as a whole, to generate collective creativity. Understanding the essence, organization and underlying processes of this innovation infrastructure can enhance our understanding of the creative capability of an industry, and the way it unfolds and evolves.

From the literature, we can surmise many factors that can influence the composition and overall organization of this common industrial innovation infrastructure as well as their underlying processes. Many of these factors are related to the tendency of creative actors to cluster and organize their inter-organizational interactions within territorialized agglomerations. Creative agents have a tendency to agglomerate in so-called creative hubs to manage the non-routine nature of creative work and production processes and their high-requirements in terms of expertise and skilled-labour (Caves, 2000; Yoon and Malecki, 2010; Scott, 2006; Christopher and Storper, 1989). These hubs are typically industrial districts situated in large urban areas where the co-localization between diverse actors promotes directly the development of the production and innovation activities and indirectly through the constitution of social relationships.

Relating the creative capability of an industry to its constitutive creative clusters seems intuitive and logical. Yet the contributions of global pipelines to collective creativity especially at an inter-organizational level are still underexplored (Bathelt and Cohendet, 2014; Lorenzen and Mudambi, 2013). It does not allow us to understand how the various building blocks of the creative capability of an industry fit and work together. Thus, despite a considerable body of research over the past decade into creative clustering, we are still lacking knowledge on how entire industries can develop a collective creative capacity and maintain it over time.

All these elements gathered together suggest that the organization of processes of creativity at an industrial level can be a critical issue for firms as well as regions and nations. It calls for the examination of the capability of an industry as a whole, comprising complex networks of organizations, to produce and manage creativity. Such an examination would extend existing interactionist approaches beyond the intra-organizational level to a particular inter-organizational perimeter: the industry.

This chapter aims to address some of the gaps underlined above by putting forward an investigation of industrial creative capabilities through an examination of one creative industry, namely the video game industry. Through this case study we strive to understand the essence of this concept and highlight a specific organization of the processes of collective creativity at the industrial level that enhances the overall creativity of this collective actor. We also clarify some of the antecedents of the creative capability inherent to the video game industry by high-lighting several interactions occurring at the inter-organizational level and the way they contribute to the overall creativity of this industry through locally embedded and globally distributed circuits and channels. The creative capability in our case study is dependent on the particular organization of inter-organizational interactions and exchanges that support a positive dynamic of knowledge creation and circulation both at the local level, within local innovative ecosystems, and at the global level in de-territorialized and relatively stable networks. We shed light on the Montreal video game cluster as an illustrative example of a local innovative ecosystem. We show how the organization of this ecosystem combined with its insertion in a web of global pipelines contributes to the overall creative capability of the industry. In doing so, our study intends to go beyond the territorialized forms of inter-organizational interactions in order to integrate the role of global linkages and de-territorialized networks in facilitating and enabling collective creativity at the industrial level. In the following sections we first briefly present the video game industry before depicting the organizational and spatial underpinnings of the creative capability of this industry.

The video game industry: a particular creative industry

The video game industry, as a creative industry is an interesting context for our investigation. Creative industries are largely considered the forerunners of knowledge-based economies and epitomize many of the specific features of knowledge-intensive activities including the prototypical features of temporary systems, their project-based organizations and their tendency toward local clustering, while conveying many paradoxes and tensions (Caves, 2000; Eikhof and Haunschild, 2007; DeFillippi *et al.*, 2007; Murphy and Pauleen, 2007). The video game industry is no exception to this rule.

This industry is an example of innovative industries where leading-edge knowledge constantly changes, thus obliging firms to constantly innovate and adapt their processes and organizations as a result (DeFillippi *et al.*, 2007). It is also the scene of many tensions, and, like many other creative industries, has gone through several periods of growth and recession during its evolution.

Yet this industry is also particular as far as several aspects are concerned: its cyclical evolution, the hybrid nature of its products, and so on. A video game is a complex product, mixing computer engineering, graphic arts, character development and story-telling, all integrated in what is coined as "game-play", the design of an enjoyable and challenging experience for the player. The video game industry is also a two-sided market. At the industrial level, the activities related to software (conception and development of the editorial and technological contents of the game) are separated from those associated with the hardware (conception and manufacturing of platforms and devices that are used to run the game software). The development of video games is mainly carried out by studios, whereas editors are generally responsible for the marketing and commercialization of the games (Johns, 2006). The heavy requirements in creative inputs and originality are some of the reasons that have prevented the entire industry from being concentrated on console manufacturers and large editors.

Strategically speaking, and in terms of industrial structure and organization, the development and production activities were traditionally dominated by gatekeepers (9 console manufacturers, publishers and distributors), which led to a situation in which managerial and profit logics were privileged, whereas risk taking and a search for creativity and originality were critically undermined. Until recently, consoles (home and handheld) dominated the market as the main hardware entailing an oligopolistic structure for the hardware market with three main actors: Microsoft, Nintendo and Sony. Console video games require high development costs and the mobilization of highly specialized talents. These requirements weighed heavily on software activities and their actors, especially studios, and, combined with the difficulties in finding investors, have entailed high dependencies on console manufacturers and editors who were generally the only actors willing to invest in these projects. This situation significantly weakened the bargaining powers of studios worldwide, their financial performances, and processes of innovation and creativity. It also favoured the dominance of a managerial logic privileging sequels and exploitative innovations.

These weaknesses are also entailed by the requirements for innovation in this industry. The specificities of the industry and the attributes of the knowledge involved in video game development complicate the development and organization of the prototypical production and innovation process. The hybrid nature of video games offers a wide range of possibilities for product innovations. Studios have the possibility to innovate at editorial level and/or at the technological level. They can choose to introduce exploitative innovations consisting of me-too products similar to existing games that take advantage of new consumption trends and emerging genres or launch explorative games consisting of very original products compared with the existing offer.

In response to these threats and requirements, video game companies have devised many solutions both at the strategic and organizational levels. Strategically speaking, the introduction of online gaming and establishment of new Business Models have helped restore some balance between the managerial and creative logics and enhance the creative capabilities of video game companies. Technological developments have brought about new opportunities, while disrupting the industry in many ways. In combination with the development of casual games, the virtualization of the marketing and retailing has opened up the way to new business models and lessened the bargaining powers of traditional editors and distributors. These changes have also challenged the geography of the industry by fostering the development of new niches and markets.

The video game companies are structured in a way that has allowed their actors to improve their processes of innovation and creativity through a better organization of their processes of knowledge creation and exchange. Through these organizational solutions, video game companies, especially among software actors, have been able to establish a balance between the different logics animating their industry and impacting their collective creativity.

This organization is based, on the one hand, on innovative and different localized ecosystems situated in many regions, which allowed the video game companies to enjoy the benefits of creative clustering. On the other hand, many global flows and bridges were established and helped to link these ecosystems and avoid the sterilization of their creativity and innovativeness for the sake of the collective creativity of the overall industry.

Articulating local ecosystems with global networks in the video game industry

An examination of the current global distribution of the major creative actors and processes in the video game industry shows a strong spatial division of creativity and a worldwide organization including, on the one hand, very innovative local ecosystems which act as creative hubs where the agglomeration of skills is unmatched elsewhere. On the other hand, the creative power of the industry also relies on global pipelines and networks linking these ecosystems to each other and linking these ecosystems to new spaces of video game creation and consumption in developing countries.

Another important feature of this geographical organization is its unequal spatial distribution. The nodal centres of creativity are concentrated in developed countries which have driven the production activities and consumption trends of the industry since its creation. This unbalanced distribution is however challenged. The emergence of new markets and new pools of talents has contributed to an important geographical shift and is changing the dynamics of innovation and overall creativity of this industry.

The first part of this section highlights the creative capability of the local creative ecosystems by focusing more specifically on the local video game cluster in Montreal as an illustrative example. The second part develops the global side of the organization by underlying the creative capability of the video game industry.

The Montreal local ecosystem of video games

The video game ecosystem in Montreal is undoubtedly one of the most important in the world, with over 130 companies dedicated to video games in 2015.

Many of these firms are internal studios to the biggest video games companies in the world: Ubisoft, Warner Games, Electronic Arts or Eidos, to name just a few. Along these local multinational branches, Montreal also counts several small- and medium-sized enterprises supported by local entrepreneurs such as Behaviour Interactive or Frima.

From approximately 500 employees in 1997, this cluster has grown to include approximately 11,000 employees in 2015, thus concentrating 70 per cent of the Canadian video game industry employment in the Quebec province. With almost $1.14 billion in annual expenditures, Montreal stands today as one of the biggest clusters per capita in the world, after those in California and Japan (Pilon and Tremblay, 2013). Over the years, the dynamism of this cluster, combined with the huge successes of many well-known games, such as Prince of Persia or Assassin's Creed, has helped the city develop its legitimacy as a very creative video game cluster that has attracted creative talents from all over the world.

While there are many reasons that explain the exponential growth this cluster has undergone in such a short time, much evidence suggests that the creativity of this cluster and its power of regeneration cannot be understood by looking solely at the creative talent of its employees or by examining the value chains and networks linking them. Indeed, several studies have highlighted the crucial role played by the interactions and dynamics that take place in the local scene of Montreal to ensure the success and generativity of the video game companies embedded in this creative milieu (Cohendet and Simon, 2007; Cohendet *et al.*, 2010; Grandadam *et al.*, 2013). As such, the innovative video game cluster in Montreal and the originality of its products depend primarily on the dynamics of knowledge creation and transformation that are being played locally. As Bathelt and Cohendet (2014) have emphasized, the "local" should essentially be viewed

Table 4.2 Brief presentation of Montreal-based video game companies

	Established in	Number of employees
Behaviour Interactive (A2M)	1992	150–300
Ubisoft	1997	+3000
Gameloft	1999	300–500
Beenox (Activision)	2000 (2005)	300–500
Frima	2003	150–300
Electronic Arts / Bioware	2004	150–300
Hibernum	2005	100–150
Eidos (Square Enix)	2007 (2011)	500–1000
Ludia	2007	150–300
Budge Studios	2010	50–100
THQ (closed since 2012)	2010	–
Warner Bros.	2010	300–500
Red Barrels	2012	10–50
Roofdog Games	2012	10–50
Ankama	2013	10–50
. . .	. . .	. . .

Source: Adapted from Alliance Numérique (2015).

as an ecosystem where the dynamics underlying the formation of new ideas and knowledge rely on the continuous interplay between, on one side, firms viewed as formal organizations, and, on the other side, a myriad of informal local active units such as communities and other collectives.

To create value, the video game companies tend to place some of their key capabilities, in particular, their absorptive capabilities, in the fertile "soil" of the creative city. As the director of the Ubisoft studio often says, "Montreal is our research lab". Video game firms, beyond their competitive actions, are thus continuously building together, with other local actors, a reservoir of resources and nodes that generates ideas, talents and entrepreneurial collectives. This reservoir is perceived as a local common good that is continuously evolving and based on strategic resources that are constituted at the ecosystem level. These resources include available talents and cognitive resources as well as a slack of constantly blended ideas and knowledge (Cohendet and Simon, 2007).

An important part of this collective construction emerges out of a large variety of informal initiatives that are seldom linked to any hierarchical logic and often lie beyond the control of the formal economic system. These initiatives are undertaken by informal entities acting as knowing communities. In the literature, these communities are defined as informal groups of agents, either internal or external to formal organizations, and characterized by a voluntary engagement in the construction, exchange, reflexivity and sharing of a common cognitive resources

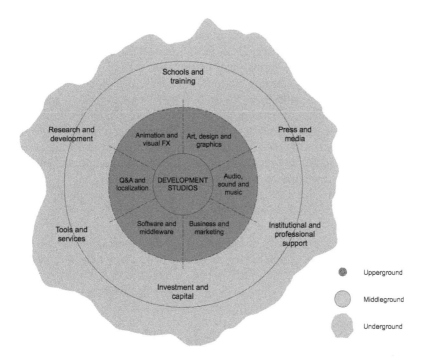

Figure 4.1 The local video game ecosystem.

directory (Brown and Duguid, 1991; Saxenian, 2006; Wenger, 1999; Créplet *et al.*, 2001; Amin and Cohendet, 2004; Cohendet *et al.*, 2006).

In the local ecosystem of Montreal, the observed knowing communities contribute to create different "units of competencies" (Wenger *et al.*, 2002) by doing considerable work in order to re-think, create, maintain and disseminate cognitive resources that allow organizations to revitalize their ideas, knowledge and routines. One of the main generic values of these communities is also their ability to absorb a significant portion of the unavoidable fixed costs associated with building and exchanging knowledge (Amin and Cohendet, 2004). These costs correspond, for instance, to the progressive construction of languages and models of action and interpretation that are required for the implementation of new knowledge and which cannot be covered through the classical efforts of organizations (or markets). This explains why the "informal" (communities), in this particular context, are generally better equipped than formal organizations to produce new ideas, new episteme, new concepts and new knowledge.

Throughout our observations, we have noticed that, despite their inability to directly control the value created though these informal collectives, the video game companies managed to leverage and harness them under certain conditions. These firms – be they early-stage start-ups that look for market opportunities or experienced firms that are integrated into global production networks – tap into the cognitive constructs of different local communities to enhance their innovative capabilities, the generation of new ideas, their access to new trends and uses, the validation of concepts, and even the co-creation of new products (Bathelt and Cohendet, 2014). In turn, the informal is nurtured by the formal through several events, projects and challenges. It is worth noting here that the distinctions and interactions between the formal and the informal are not static and fixed. Part of the "informal" may become "formal" and vice versa. Organizations and other forms of institutions change as the innovative ecosystem evolves and new ideas and talents continuously emerge from informal activities. Ideas sensed in the informal may become projects that will reconfigure several organizations of the formal; talents, attracted and detected in events, festivals and challenges, may become employees in formal organizations; and entrepreneurial informal collectives may be transformed into small business units within studios.

The functioning of such a virtuous interplay is dependent on the quality of the "local common" underlined above, which is partly nurtured by the firm itself, partly supported by other formal organizations (including competitors in the video game domain), and partly orchestrated by public local authorities. To a large extent, this local common can be associated with the notion of "middleground" (Simon, 2009; Cohendet *et al.*, 2010) conceived as a set of intermediary devices and spaces that connect and integrate formal organizations and informal collectives and which can take different forms – places, spaces, events, or projects (Grandadam *et al.*, 2013).

Spontaneous mechanisms occur in places (such as cafés, restaurants, performance halls, art galleries, squares, public areas, old warehouses, specific neighbourhoods, etc.) where heterogeneous group of actors can meet, compare ideas, rethink established theories and practices, and create new models and visions that can become the potential foundation for the development of innovative goods and services (Cohendet, *et al.*, 2010, 2011). Local events allow organizations to detect new talents and individuals in diverse fields (Lampel and Meyer, 2008) and access new ideas and knowledge through global networks (Bathelt and Henn, 2014), thus stimulating the process of institutionalization. Projects provide temporary spaces and places to engage members of diverse communities in common work and enable people with heterogeneous backgrounds and specialities to gather and trade knowledge and practices. These events and projects allow the transformation of part of the informal into the formal by serving as 1) boundary spanner devices to renew and associate heterogeneous knowledge bases, 2) detectors of talents and ideas, 3) platforms that create and enrich social ties, and 4) devices to enrich practices and routines and renew their bases.

Cohendet and Simon (2007) have shown how Ubisoft has willingly decided to decentralize part of its competencies in the fertile soil of Montreal through its communities, thus reinforcing its capacity to absorb new ideas and potential routines that could transform its own ecosystem. The organization has relaxed its hierarchical form and mobilized its internal communities which overlap with informal knowing communities in order to nurture as well as to tap into the local platform of interactions supported by the local middleground. An illustrative example is the case of a musician that was operating in the underground and, though the units of the middleground, was detected by collectives of Ubisoft and then integrated into new projects within the formal organization (Simon, 2009).

As this example suggests, an important component of creativity in the video game industry is based on fertile local ecosystems that are globally distributed.

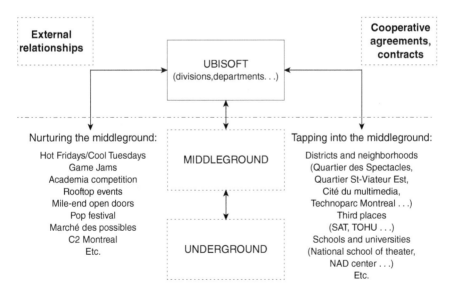

Figure 4.2 Ubisoft and the video game ecosystem of Montreal.

However, beyond these local ecosystems, there are many globalized networks and pipelines linking these ecosystems and supporting the collective creativity of the industry by supporting knowledge creation and circulation.

Resituating the local within the global: the role of global pipelines

In the literature, global pipelines are recognized as critical assets allowing resource flows in and out of clusters (Amin and Thrift, 1992; Bathelt *et al.*, 2004; Coe *et al.*, 2008; Lorenzen and Mudambi, 2013). By linking spatially dispersed local pools of knowledge, global pipelines can facilitate the processes of creativity and innovation and enhance their quality (Bathelt and Cohendet, 2014). They can allow firms to integrate different selection environments endowed with heterogeneous resources and knowledge by ensuring that important information on new markets, trends and technologies is spotted and used in time. These links can also facilitate the functioning of global inter-organizational projects by providing joint-action frames that facilitate interactions between collaborating actors situated in different countries (Bathelt *et al.*, 2004).

Global pipelines are vital to a cluster. First, by opening local creative ecosystems to other environments, these global pipelines can help avoid "lock-in" situations (Martin and Sunley, 2006) and enhance the quality of the local talent pool by attracting specialized skills from other regions. Global pipelines provide weak ties that can mitigate the negative side of strong ties that can easily dominate a local cluster. These links can also enhance local growth by allowing many late-comer clusters within globalized competitive markets to catch up with more advanced clusters for value creation and capture (Lorenzen and Mudambi, 2013).

Our observations of the video game industry confirm the advantages of global linkages, especially in the case of the local cluster of Montreal where actors mobilize many different global linkages to ensure the openness, the continuous regeneration of the local milieu and the creativity of its members. In many aspects, the nature of these linkages in the video games industry and the way they contribute to the overall quality of creative milieus such as the one in Montreal are quite unique and can add to our knowledge of the way these global pipelines act on and interact with local creative hubs.

At the regional level, Montreal is seen by many, its internal actors and outsiders alike, as a geo-cultural bridge. Being at the intersection between the European market and the American Market with its Hollywood-based culture is an important asset for the local ecosystem of video games in Montreal. This dual culture combined with the many resource endowments of the town has attracted several foreign editors who have created local branches in the city and encouraged important inter-regional mobility, especially from Europe. Of course, the Quebec government's subsidies supporting job creation in the sector have played a crucial part in attracting multinational enterprises specialized in video games development, thus contributing to the local dynamics in terms of knowledge co-creation and innovations. The proximity with the American market has encouraged many American acquisitions of local companies specialized in computer graphics and video games and facilitated the development of many important games based on licences of Hollywood movies and other cultural brands.

The global linkages maintained by the local creative ecosystem in Montreal are strongly related to the local branches that several video game multinational enterprises have established in the region. Beginning with Ubisoft in 1997, several international editors have followed and created local studios to benefit from the local subsidies and pools of talents available in Montreal, as well as to benefit from the local buzz in the cluster. In Montreal, these studios have contributed in many different ways to the development of global bridges of knowledge exchanges between the video game cluster and external contexts, markets and cultures. First, they allowed local talents to access the internal resources and knowledge pools available internally in these multinational enterprises. They also helped train the skilled pool of creative talents in the milieu either through internal training programmes or through more direct initiatives.

The corporate spin-offs from these multinational enterprises have also contributed to linking the global flows of knowledge with the existent local milieu and its creativity. After working many years for the big studios, many of the creative talents have chosen to be entrepreneurs and to create their own studios. Behaviour, Frima, Ludia, Budge or Beenox are examples of such initiatives which have contributed to the diffusion of global knowledge and resources within the local milieu and to its mobilization by local actors.

The global connections linking the Montreal ecosystem to others localities also include the portfolios of global partnerships between the studios in the city and editors or studios elsewhere. In this respect, many of the video game companies in Montreal, be they small- or medium-sized enterprises or local branches of multinational enterprises, have expanded their production network to other countries. Several of these partnerships are long-term vertical linkages that are part of global value chains reuniting the video game firms of Montreal and partners established in other countries. Many of these partners are editors and/or studios situated in other creative local ecosystems similar to the Montreal cluster. However, Montreal video games companies have also important portfolios of partnerships with other studios in developed and developing countries for subcontracting purposes. The reasons for subcontracting are quite varied: pursuit of cost advantages, high-skilled talents or proximity to new markets, etc. As noted in the literature, many of these inter-organizational arrangements can enable independent studios (not belonging to a given editor) to save on their development costs while employing qualified talents and skills regardless of their locations (Scott, 2006). They also allow the adaptation of products to the local cultures and facilitate the penetration of local markets.

Multinational enterprises embedded within the local milieu have also contributed to the establishment of important flows of inter-regional mobility that have significantly enhanced the local ecosystem and its internal dynamics. A considerable number of talented expatriates have moved to the city and have helped trigger the establishment of global flows of knowledge exchanges which go beyond internal exchanges within multinational enterprises. Thus, the global pipelines of the Montreal cluster also include the varied networks of relationships of foreign labour that were attracted to the city and their positive creative dynamics both in terms of products and jobs. These workers are affiliated with many localities and help nurture the global pipelines of the cluster through their relationships with the outside, in a professional context, but also in a more community-oriented context.

In addition to these linkages, the video game industry also harbours several independent non-profit networked organizations that help, at the global level, gather different communities of video game professionals in a formalized and almost permanent fashion. An illustrative example is the IGDA (International Association of Game Developers), which is one of the major, most developed formalized global networks of video game professionals in the industry. By linking the different communities of practice through virtual platforms that support global interactions, possibly on a daily basis, these networks have also contributed to the formation of networks of practice that help the circulation of resources (both human, financial and cognitive resources) and their mobilization to enhance the internal dynamics of knowledge management and innovation within the local video game cluster of Montreal.

Another main element that has contributed to the formation of global linkages in the video game industry is temporary face-to-face meetings and gatherings that have helped, in different ways, to structure the industry as a whole. In the literature, these temporary meetings are perceived as "organized anarchies" that operate in sometimes seemingly chaotic and unpredictable ways (Bathelt and Cohendet, 2014; Bathelt and Gibson 2015). Yet, they connect different institutional environments and support the diffusion of ideas and technologies, while at the same time reproducing institutional differences that exist between regions, national

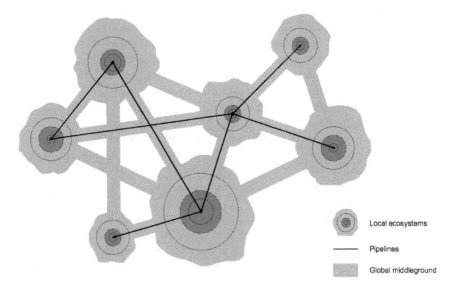

Local ecosystems

Pipelines

Global middleground

Figure 4.3 Local ecosystems, pipelines and the global 'middleground'.

states, technology fields, etc. The video game industry counts many temporary gatherings of economic agents including international trade fairs, conventions, conferences, negotiations, etc. Events such as the Gamescom (in Cologne), the E3 conference (in Los Angeles), or the Game Connection (in Paris) help bring together members of the industry in order to stimulate dynamics of knowledge generation and exchange in the sector. By reuniting these dispersed professionals, temporary gatherings help and connect dispersed formal and informal networks of video game companies including the different communities of practice that animate creative local ecosystems in many regions. These field-configuring events thus serve as "temporary clusters" that connect local production contexts with global value chains, while triggering new opportunities for exchanges (Lampel and Meyer, 2008). They also generate new relations that can be mobilized and transformed into cooperative projects in the future.

From a developmental perspective, these gatherings enhance the overall learning and innovation dynamics in the industry, regardless of the location. On the one hand, they connect advanced producers from developing countries with firms in sophisticated industry clusters at a global level, thus generating opportunities for learning and further upgrading over time. On the other hand, they provide opportunities for firms from leading industry clusters in developing countries to create linkages with each other, thus creating sophisticated knowledge exchange practices and strengthening "creative competitive advantages". These periodical congregations and avenues also contribute to the wide spread of common cognitive and interpretative schemes as well as to the homogenization of industrial practices which can facilitate cooperative work across distance. The video game companies can continue to speak a unified language. This is especially important with regards to all the changes that are impacting the industry and its dominant business models (Baden-Fuller and Mangematin, 2015).

What we wish to emphasize here is that the distant virtual interactions between local creative hubs and ecosystems have been supported by permanent and stable globalized networks, which, overall, have contributed to the formation of several informal knowing communities that cover a global scope and transcend local and national borders. The variety of global pipelines, described above, that link the local creative ecosystem in Montreal to the external environments go beyond simple dyadic relationships between firms. Many of these linkages are part of globalized networked organizations that have clear identities and boundaries and are characterized by a certain stability as opposed to the classical global pipelines described in the literature. The interactions within these global networks are frequent, yet more structured and focused than local relations. The stability of these networks and their formalized nature offer many advantages notably against some of the drawbacks and risks associated with global linkages. Global pipelines require a lot of time and effort to be established and maintained. They are not as spontaneous as local linkages and need regular communication and interactions to continue to exist. Communication processes in global pipelines are contingent by nature and plagued by great uncertainty (Bathelt *et al.*, 2004). Yet, when these global pipelines are stable over a certain period of time and allow for the development of trust and fine-grained information transfer, they can trigger the formation of complex cooperative projects across several local ecosystems.

The observed de-territorialized stable networks helped video game companies overcome the uncertainty related to global pipeline linkages while reducing the time and effort needed for their establishment and maintenance (Bathelt *et al.*, 2004). When combined with temporary gatherings, these networks help the formation of trust even if the conditions of co-localization within the same cluster are absent. They also offer shared spaces of meaning, a common identity and mutual resource endowments that can assist their members in their knowledge search and problem solving.

Global ingredients of industrial creative capability

In this contribution, we argue that the concept of industrial creative capabilities can advance our understanding of collective creativity in various ways. This concept takes the interactionist approach a step further by extending the scope of examination of the interactions intervening in the generation and management of collective creativity to include those occurring at the inter-organizational and industrial level. It also allows the role of dynamics of knowledge creation and exchange occurring at the local and global levels to be taken into account and integrated into the analysis of collective creativity.

Throughout a case study of the video game industry, we have sought to understand how collective creativity unfolds at the level of an entire industry, by highlighting the organization of its underlying processes and some of its antecedents. There are many factors that can influence such a capability. But in this research, we have narrowed the focus to the elements related to the global and spatial organization of the creative processes and activities at the industrial level.

The (global) creative capability of the video game industry appears to emerge as a result of the interactions and articulation between, on the one hand, local creative ecosystems, and on the other, globalized networks and communities linking spatially scattered actors. Each of these networks hosts different, yet complementary, dynamics of knowledge creation and circulation. Thus, the overall knowledge creation and its circulation, at the industrial level, are the result of interwoven processes linking these dynamics and combining them. When adequately combined and articulated, these networks and their dynamics of knowledge help provide global solutions to easing the tensions and paradoxes inherent in the management of creativity.

Theoretically, our line of argument provides a bridge between the theory of clusters and the literature on collective creativity by detailing how the global geography and organization of knowledge distribution in an industry can influence the creativity of its actors. We advocate the applicability of the framework developed by Bathelt *et al.* (2004) to analyse the ingredients of industrial creative capabilities and their functioning. This framework stresses the importance of combining local buzz with global pipelines to ensure the efficiency and performance of clusters especially in terms of knowledge management. We extend this line of reasoning to the level of the industry as a whole. An examination of the creative capability of the video game industry proves that the local and global are, when combined, necessary for the efficiency of knowledge creation and circulation and the management of the paradoxes inherent in creativity. Our observations also suggest that local and global dimensions of knowledge creation are tightly entangled in unique and complex ways. The articulation between both is not straightforward and automatic. The case of the video game industry is illustrative of the important variety in the ways these articulations are established and maintained and the complexity of the issues they raise.

Our results also add significant insights to the main rationales behind the theory of clusters and supplement investigations that have examined how global linkages contribute to the creativity of local clusters. Through our case study, it is clear that the global pipelines are not mere flows of knowledge circulating between territorialized networks. It is thus limiting to consider the global as composed solely of isolated linkages of inflows and outflows of resources and knowledge. The global pipelines we observed are more complex and intricate and include varied forms. Some of them are well described in the literature on creative clustering, such as temporary gatherings, but we have also observed other forms that challenge existent theorizations on how global pipelines interconnect local creative milieus.

Indeed, contrary to the theorizations in the literature which view these channels as dyadic relationships that link a single firm or a limited number of firms to external partners situated elsewhere, our observations highlight the existence of entire stable networks, both formal and informal, with well-defined identities that help connect different local clusters in the industry and support the exchanges of different forms of knowledge. These networks are global in the sense that they are not territorialized and do not have any particular single anchorage in a specific location.

This argument goes beyond a simple global/local dialectic and allows us to conclude that industrial creative capabilities are based on many superposed and overlapping networks and communities, some of which are local ecosystems, whereas others are de-territorialized, global ones.

Our observations show that these trans-local networks and communities act both on local and global levels to provide a soft architecture doubled with a social infrastructure that supports open exchanges of ideas and collective problem solving and enhances the development of a professional culture and common practices throughout the whole industry. This soft architecture facilitates the establishment of different flows between diverse localized communities, ever-evolving networks and diffused collectives, while integrating new devices linking formal institutions to informal units at the global level. By enabling local clusters and their members to access partly localized and partly globalized knowledge bases, this soft architecture enhances the overall creative capability of the industry.

To some extent, what occurs within a given local ecosystem in the video game industry can be extended to a global context. This soft architecture can be considered a global "common", similar in many ways to the local "middleground" and its components described in the literature as a major component of the creative city (Cohendet *et al.*, 2010). Just like a local "middleground", this global soft architecture is enacted through many devices including specific places, spaces, projects and events that support the overall creativity of the industry.

The success and viability of the local creative capability of a given cluster is dependent upon its capability as a collective actor to absorb, process and integrate the new knowledge circulating in the networks of global pipelines. This capability is part of the absorptive capabilities defined in the literature as the ability of a firm to garner external knowledge and use it efficiently in combination with internal knowledge for innovation purposes. In the literature, there is common recognition that the success of global pipelines depends on the absorptive capabilities of local firms and their ability to assimilate the knowledge arriving through extra-local linkages (Bathelt *et al.*, 2004). We extend this rationale to the next level of interactions and argue that a local creative ecosystem needs to develop an absorptive capability that conditions how well local firms articulate localized and global knowledge processes and tap into external knowledge pools situated outside their local ecosystems.

This local capability is not a simple sum of the individual capabilities of a local ecosystem's firms. It is primarily dependent on the quality of the local middleground as well as the nature of the interfaces linking it to the global middleground. These interfaces determine how the global overlaps and interacts with the local milieu and its buzz, and how knowledge emerges and circulates at both levels. It also influences how these bricks of knowledge can be assimilated by firms and may lead to the development of creative and innovative projects. The literature posits that the performance of the production system of a cluster is dependent on finding the right mix between local and extra-local exchanges (Bathelt *et al.*, 2004). We argue that it is not only about finding a right mix, in a deterministic manner, but more about articulating adequately the local and the global through a globally diffused and accessible middleground. Thus, far from being entirely determined, these articulations will depend partly on the strategies of the local and global actors involved in these different networks as well as on the informal ambient global buzz resulting from the dynamics inherent to the global middleground.

To conclude, this collective substratum constituting a global middleground is, from our point of view, one of the major factors that significantly influences the power of attraction, regeneration and resilience of an industry. The following figure summarizes the major antecedents highlighted in this study and their influences in a model, which, we hope, advances our understanding of collective creativity at the industrial level.

However, it is clear that any generalization of these results to other industrial contexts needs to take several limitations and facts into account. First of all, an important limitation of our argument is related to our strong focus on the local creative ecosystem of Montreal. We are aware that the way a local ecosystem develops and/or interacts with global networks is quite dependent on the idiosyncratic features of this ecosystem, including its history and resource endowments. Further studies on other ecosystems that are similar in their performance to the Montreal local cluster, yet different regarding their idiosyncrasies and historical evolution, could be useful in this respect.

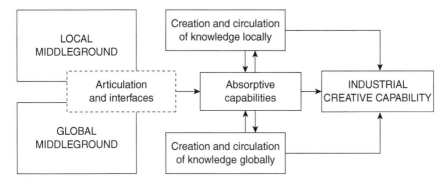

Figure 4.4 Local and global ingredients in industrial creative capability.

In our analysis, we have also intentionally not considered another form of interaction between the formal and the informal: the fact that video game firms may delegate part of their creative effort to specific communities of users, or more generally to the crowd. The reason for this is that this dimension of research is largely covered by the literature (Von Hippel, 2005; Jeppesen and Frederiksen, 2006; Dahlander and Magnusson, 2005; Burger-Helmchen and Cohendet, 2011).

Another limitation of our study lies in our focus on the spatial organization of the processes of knowledge creation and circulation. While this focus helped us provide interesting insights into the role of knowledge dynamics, we are aware that many other factors, such as the collective and deliberate strategies of firms for example, can influence the creative capability of an industry. Investigating the way the antecedents uncovered here can interact with other factors in conditioning industrial creative capabilities is a further line of research.

We also need to underline that the characteristics of the processes of creativity and innovation can vary, of course, from one sector to another, depending on a number of contextual aspects. In the literature, creative industries are clearly presented as a distinct set of economic activities. Yet, a closer look reveals an important internal heterogeneity in this group. They involve, but are not limited to, advertising, arts and crafts, architecture, fashion, film, music, performing arts and video games. This is why the multiplication of industrial contexts and the specification of industrial features and their impacts in the study is an important perquisite for the accumulation of a strong theoretical corpus on the management of creativity and innovation.

In this contribution, we have focused on the video game industry, a digitally native industry. It is clear that the digital nature of the products in this case has facilitated the establishment and functioning of the global networks of pipelines. However, it is important to verify whether the organization and functioning of the observed local and global knowledge dynamics are the same in other creative industries with less digitalized production. This point calls for a further investigation of collective creativity in other creative industries.

References

Amabile, T. M. (1988) A model of creativity and innovation in organizations. *Research in Organizational Behavior*, 10(1), 123–167.

Amabile, T. M. (1997) Motivating creativity in organizations: On doing what you love and loving what you do. *California Management Review*, 40(1), 39–58.

Amabile, T. M., Conti, R., Coon, H., Lazenby, J., and Herron, M. (1996) Assessing the work environment for creativity. *Academy of Management Journal*, 39(5), 1154–1184.

Amin, A. and Cohendet, P. (2004) *Architectures of Knowledge: Firms, Capabilities, and Communities*. New York: Oxford University Press.

Amin, A. and Roberts, J. (Eds). (2008) *Community, Economic Creativity, and Organization*. Oxford: Oxford University Press.

Amin, A. and Thrift, N. (1992) Neo-Marshallian nodes in global networks. *International Journal of Urban and Regional Research*, 16(4), 571–587.

Baden-Fuller C. and Mangematin V. (2015) Business models and modelling business models, *Advances in Strategic Management*, xi–xxii.

Barczak, G., Lassk, F. and Mulki, J. (2010) Antecedents of team creativity: An examination of team emotional intelligence, team trust and collaborative culture. *Creativity and Innovation Management*, 19(4), 332–345.

Bathelt, H. and Cohendet, P. (2014) The creation of knowledge: Local building, global accessing and economic development – toward an agenda. *Journal of Economic Geography*, 14(5), 869–882.

Bathelt, H. and Gibson, R. (2015) Learning in 'organized anarchies': The nature of technological search processes at international trade fairs. *Regional Studies*, 47(6), 985–1002.

Bathelt, H. and Henn, S. (2014) The geographies of knowledge transfers over distance: Toward a typology. *Environment and Planning A*, 46(6), 1403–1424.

Bathelt, H., Malmberg, A. and Maskell, P. (2004) Clusters and knowledge: Local buzz, global pipelines and the process of knowledge creation. *Progress in Human Geography*, 28(1), 31–56.

Bharadwaj, S. and Menon, A. (2000) Making innovation happen in organizations: Individual creativity mechanisms, organizational creativity mechanisms or both? *Journal of Product Innovation Management*, 17(6), 424–434.

Bilton, C. (2007) *Management and Creativity: From Creative Industries to Creative Management*. Victoria, Australia: Blackwell Publishing.

Brown, J. S. and Duguid, P. (1991) Organizational learning and communities-of-practice: Toward a unified view of working, learning, and innovation. *Organization Science*, 2(1), 40–57.

Burger-Helmchen, T. and Cohendet, P. (2011) User communities and social software in the video game industry. *Long Range Planning*, 44(5), 317–343.

Caves, R. E. (2000) *Creative Industries: Contracts between Art and Commerce*. Cambridge, MA: Harvard University Press.

Christopherson, S. and Storper M. (1989) The effects of flexible specialization on industrial politics and the labor market: The motion picture industry. *Industrial and Labor Relations Review*, 42(3), 331–347.

Coe, N. M., Dicken, P. and Hess, M. (2008) Global production networks: Realizing the potential. *Journal of Economic Geography*, 8(3), 271–295.

Cohendet, P. and Amin, A. (2006) Chapter 11. Epistemic communities and communities of practice in the knowledge-based firm. In *New Frontiers in the Economics of Innovation and New Technology: Essays in Honour of Paul A. David.* Cheltenham: Edward Elgar Publishing, pp. 296–322.

Cohendet, P. and Simon, L. (2007) Playing across the playground: Paradoxes of knowledge creation in the videogame firm. *Journal of Organizational Behavior*, 28(5), 587–605.

Cohendet, P., Grandadam, D. and Simon, L. (2010) The anatomy of the creative city. *Industry and Innovation*, 17(1), 91–111.

Cohendet, P., Grandadam, D. and Simon, L. (2011) Rethinking urban creativity: Lessons from Barcelona and Montreal. *City, Culture and Society*, 2(3), 151–158.

Cooke, P. N. and Lazzeretti, L. (Eds) (2008) *Creative Cities, Cultural Clusters and Local Economic Development.* Cheltenham, UK: Edward Elgar Publishing.

Créplet, F., Dupouet, O., Kern, F., Mehmanpazir, B. and Munier, F. (2001) Consultants and experts in management consulting firms. *Research Policy*, 30(9), 1517–1535.

Csikszentmihalyi, M. (2014) *The Systems Model of Creativity: The Collected Works of Mihaly Csikszentmihalyi.* Heidelberg, Germany: Springer.

Dahlander, L. and Magnusson, M. G. (2005) Relationships between open source software companies and communities: Observations from Nordic firms. *Research Policy*, 34(4), 481–493.

DeFillippi, R., Grabher, G. and Jones, C. (2007) Introduction to paradoxes of creativity: Managerial and organizational challenges in the cultural economy. *Journal of Organizational Behavior*, 28(5), 511–521.

Drazin, R., Glynn, M. A. and Kazanjian, R. K. (1999) Multilevel theorizing about creativity in organizations: A sensemaking perspective. *Academy of Management Review*, 24(2), 286–307.

Eikhof, D. R. and Haunschild, A. (2007) For art's sake! Artistic and economic logics in creative production. *Journal of Organizational Behavior*, 28(5), 523–538.

Feinstein, J. (2006) *The Nature of Creative Development.* Stanford , CA: Stanford University Press.

Florida, R. (2002) *The Rise of the Creative Class.* New York: Basic Books.

Ford, C. M. (1996) A theory of individual creative action in multiple social domains. *Academy of Management Review*, 21(4), 1112–1142.

Gilson, L. L. and Shalley, C. E. (2004) A little creativity goes a long way: An examination of teams' engagement in creative processes. *Journal of Management*, 30(4), 453–470.

Glover, J. A., Ronning, R. R. and Reynolds, C. (Eds) (2013) *Handbook of Creativity.* New York: Springer Science & Business Media.

Grandadam, D., Cohendet, P. and Simon, L. (2013) Places, spaces and the dynamics of creativity: The video game industry in Montreal. *Regional Studies*, 47(10), 1701–1714.

Hargadon, A. B. and Bechky, B. A. (2006) When collections of creatives become creative collectives: A field study of problem solving at work. *Organization Science*, 17(4), 484–500.

Isaksen, S. G. and Lauer, K. J. (2002) The climate for creativity and change in teams. *Creativity and Innovation Management*, 11(1), 74–86.

Jeppesen, L. B. and Frederiksen, L. (2006) Why do users contribute to firm-hosted user communities? The case of computer-controlled music instruments. *Organization Science*, 17(1), 45–63.

Johns, J. (2006). Video games production networks: Value capture, power relations and embeddedness. *Journal of Economic Geography*, 6(2), 151–180.

Kaufman, J. C. and Sternberg, R. J. (Eds) (2010) *The Cambridge Handbook of Creativity.* Cambridge: Cambridge University Press.

Lampel, J. and Meyer, A. D. (2008) Guest editors' introduction: Field-configuring events as structuring mechanisms: How conferences, ceremonies, and trade shows constitute new technologies, industries, and markets. *Journal of Management Studies*, 45(6), 1025–1035.

Landry, C. (2012). *The Creative City: A Toolkit for Urban Innovators*. New York: Earthscan.

Leonard-Barton, D. (1995) *Wellsprings of Knowledge: Building and Sustaining the Sources of Innovation*. Boston, MA: Harvard Business School Press.

Lorenzen, M. and Mudambi, R. (2013) Clusters, connectivity and catch-up: Bollywood and Bangalore in the global economy. *Journal of Economic Geography*, 13(3), 501–534.

Lubart, T. I. (2001) Models of the creative process: Past, present and future. *Creativity Research Journal*, 13(3–4), 295–308.

Martin, R. and Sunley, P. (2006) Path dependence and regional economic evolution. *Journal of Economic Geography*, 6(4), 395–437.

Maskell, P. (2014) Accessing remote knowledge – the roles of trade fairs, pipelines, crowdsourcing and listening posts. *Journal of Economic Geography*, 14(5), 883–902.

Maskell, P., Bathelt, H. and Malmberg, A. (2006) Building global knowledge pipelines: The role of temporary clusters. *European Planning Studies*, 14(8), 997–1013.

Murphy, P. and Pauleen, D. (2007) Managing paradox in a world of knowledge. *Management Decision*, 45(6), 1008–1022.

Napier, N. K. and Nilsson, M. (2006) The development of creative capabilities in and out of creative organizations: Three case studies. *Creativity and Innovation Management*, 15(3), 268–278.

Oldham, G. R. and Cummings, A. (1996) Employee creativity: Personal and contextual factors at work. *Academy of Management Journal*, 39(3), 607–634.

Perry-Smith, J. E. (2006) Social yet creative: The role of social relationships in facilitating individual creativity. *Academy of Management Journal*, 49(1), 85–101.

Pilon, S. and Tremblay, D. G. (2013) The geography of clusters: The case of the video games clusters in Montreal and in Los Angeles. *Urban Studies Research*, 2013, 1–9.

Pirola-Merlo, A. and Mann, L. (2004) The relationship between individual creativity and team creativity: Aggregating across people and time. *Journal of Organizational Behavior*, 25(2), 235–257.

Pratt, A. C. (2008) Creative cities: The cultural industries and the creative class. *Geografiskaannaler: Series B, Human Geography*, 90(2), 107–117.

Saxenian, A. (1996) *Regional Advantage*. Cambridge, MA: Harvard University Press.

Scott, A. J. (2006) Creative cities: Conceptual issues and policy questions. *Journal of Urban Affairs*, 28(1), 1–17.

Simon, L. (2009) Underground, upperground et middle-ground: les collectifs créatifs et la capacité créative de la ville. *Management international/Gestiòn Internacional/ International Management*, 13, 37–51.

Simonton, D. K. (1999) *Origins of Genius: Darwinian Perspectives on Creativity*. Oxford: Oxford University Press.

Sternberg, R. J. (1999) *Handbook of Creativity*. Cambridge: Cambridge University Press.

Styhre, A. and Sundgren, M. (2005) *Managing Creativity in Organizations. Critique and Practices*. Basingstoke: Palgrave Macmillan.

Taggar, S. (2002) Individual creativity and group ability to utilize individual creative resources: A multilevel model. *Academy of Management Journal*, 45(2), 315–330.

Teece, D. J. (2009) *Dynamic Capabilities and Strategic Management: Organizing for Innovation and Growth*. Oxford: Oxford University Press.

Van de Ven, A. H. (1993) The emergence of an industrial infrastructure for technological innovation. *Journal of Comparative Economics*, 17(2), 338–365.

Van de Ven, A. H. and Garud, R. (1989) A framework for understanding the emergence of new industries. *Research on Technological Innovation, Management and Policy: A Research Annual*, 4, 195–225.

Van de Ven, A. H. and Garud, R. (1993) Innovation and industry development: The case of cochlear implants. *Research on Technological Innovation, Management and Policy*, 5, 1–46.

Van Heur, B. (2009) The clustering of creative networks: Between myth and reality. *Urban Studies*, 46(8), 1531–1552.

Von Hippel, E. (2005) *Democratizing Innovation*. Cambridge, MA: MIT Press.

Wenger, E. (1999) *Communities of Practice: Learning, Meaning, and Identity*. Cambridge: Cambridge University Press.

Wenger, E., McDermott, R. A. and Snyder, W. (2002) *Cultivating Communities of Practice: A Guide to Managing Knowledge*. Cambridge, MA: Harvard Business Press.

Woodman, R. W. and Schoenfeldt, L. F. (1990) An interactionist model of creative behavior. *The Journal of Creative Behavior*, 24(1), 10–20.

Woodman, R. W., Sawyer, J. E. and Griffin, R. W. (1993) Toward a theory of organizational creativity. *Academy of Management Review*, 18(2), 293–321.

Yoon, H. and Malecki, E. J. (2010) Cartoon planet: Worlds of production and global production networks in the animation industry. *Industrial and Corporate Change*, 19(1), 239–271.

5 Outlining spaces for the emergence and fertilization of creativity

The case of audiovisual festivals in Barcelona

Juan Vidaechea and Montserrat Pareja-Eastaway

Creativity is an ubiquitous concept attributable to territories, organizations and individuals. The productive activities of the cognitive-cultural economy are territorially concentrated, even though their market is global (Scott, 2010; Musterd and Gritsai, 2012; Bontje *et al.* 2011). Producers, on the one hand, tend to cluster to benefit from the performance improvements of the economies of scale and scope that emerge from the joint operation of firms in a specific territory (Scott, 2010: 70). On the other hand, local activities are imbued with the social and cultural character of the environment which, at the same time, offers the appropriate conditions for creativity and cultural development (Hall, 1998). The territory also confers a competitive advantage since competence is not only based on prices, but also on the specific qualitative attributes of the final product, including its specific origin (i.e. Milan and fashion).

The relevance of the territory's conditions in fostering innovation in the creative and knowledge intensive sectors (Bontje *et al.*, 2011) is analysed departing from a literary comparison that will serve as a theoretical introduction to this research in order to outline the theory of the anatomy of the creative city (Cohendet *et al.*, 2010).

The main goal of this research is to apply the 'anatomy of the creative city' framework (Cohendet *et al.* 2010) to the Barcelona Metropolitan Region (BMR) to evaluate and assess festivals in the audiovisual sector as spaces for the emergence and fertilization of creativity. Even though the economic perspective of this approach omits possible tensions between intellectual property exploitation and the intrinsic value of culture, education, social cohesion or identity, this rather utilitarian application of culture, art and creativity may be valuable, with a market-oriented view, for a better understanding of the cooperation and innovation processes among assorted stakeholders rooted in the territory, with a special focus on the cultural sector and the cultural and creative industries of Barcelona.

In addition, this chapter introduces ad-hoc indicators to build up an original model of analysis identified by the acronym 'U+3(i)', which is the main added value of this contribution. Rather than a policy recommendation, this tool for reinterpreting and analysing spaces for the emergence of creativity suggests an original approach relevant to a wide array of actors ranging from cultural managers, creative professionals, students and enthusiasts to policy makers and firms. Audiovisual festivals are understood here to be temporary spaces and events suitable for hosting and facilitating the exchange, generation or stimulation of cognitive processes. Our research suggests a festival classification that takes into account four attributes, according to the activities described in the 'anatomy of the creative city': participation of the three components of the creative city (upperground, underground and middleground), international programming, underground visibility and interaction and interchange of knowledge. As a result, the feasibility and value of this kind of analysis may reinforce the use of this framework as a tool for the design, implementation or evaluation of cultural projects and policies.

Creativity, knowledge and the role of the territory

The different forms of creativity are correlated and intertwined: technological creativity, invention or innovation, economic creativity and entrepreneurship, and artistic and cultural creativity (Florida, 2002: 33). Richard Florida incorporates Simonton's (1999) approach to creativity to claim that an intellect enriched by experience and different perspectives encourages creativity. Thus, the distinct creative forms are mutually reinforced and incentivized by cross-fertilization. This feature would explain the tendency for the concentration of diverse creative practitioners in multifaceted creativity centres throughout history such as Florence in the Renaissance, Vienna in the nineteenth century or many places in the United States today.

According to Florida, 'the creative centers provide the integrated ecosystem or habitat where all forms of creativity – artistic and cultural, technological and economic – can take root and flourish' (Ibid: 218). The reasons for a creative person to move to a specific community are based on the experiences and abundant amenities, openness to diversity, and the opportunity to validate their identities as creative people. However, other perspectives reinforce the attachment to territory of creative and knowledge workers together with job opportunities as key aspects for attractiveness (Musterd and Murie, 2010; Musterd and Kóvacs, 2013).

The innovative activity of a territory can be fostered by the concentration of specialized production structures (Becattini, 1979; Porter, 1998). Urbanization or diversification externalities, meanwhile, refer to the transfer of knowledge that encourages innovation in clusters of companies from different sectors. Jacobs (1969) relies on the complementary nature of knowledge for firms in different sectors or activities to affirm that new ideas developed by an industry can be applied to another. According to Neffke (2009), cited by Bontje *et al.* (2011), such clusters are more beneficial for young firms whereas specialized clusters favour the more mature companies which are the only ones that can benefit from the knowledge externalities. In addition, as Scott (2014) states, there is a precise effort from cities to reinvent themselves using the attributes of the so-called creative and knowledge economy. Thus,

> *even many former manufacturing centers are attempting to upgrade parts of their ageing built stock in efforts to construct some sort of 'creative' future for themselves, above all one that emphatically involves a break with the old economy and that reaches out to more knowledge and culture-intensive forms of production.*
>
> (Scott, 2014: 570)

In addition to a type of production structure or market development, the promotion and location of creative and knowledge intensive economic activities in a regional environment is related to aspects of local history (Bontje *et al.* 2011). Path dependency refers to a series of elements that have been crucial in the historical trajectory of the city or region and largely determine its potential to develop a creative economy. It establishes a causal relationship between the development of networks among actors (individuals and public and private organizations) and their embeddedness in the territory established throughout history, culture and the current regional development in a given territory (see Figure 5.1).

Over the last decade, soft conditions have gained much prominence after Florida's thesis (2002). The importance of soft factors lies in their ability to attract a type of human capital, potential employees or entrepreneurs, called the creative class. The economic success of a city depends on its capacity to attract and retain creative talent

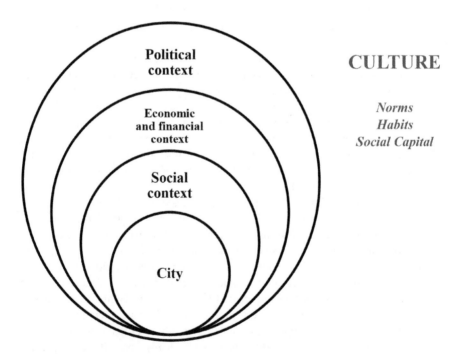

Figure 5.1 The context of the city.
Source: Developed by authors.

in creative and knowledge-intensive industries. To do this, the territory has to offer an appealing environment characterized by the diversity of its people and activities on the one hand, and the tolerance to models of life, cultures and ethnicities on the other. These are the so-called soft factors for attracting talent. In contrast to classical location theories that stress the foremost importance of attracting companies, the author reverses the equation and advocates prioritizing the attraction of the creative class as a strategy for economic development policies.

As explained hereafter, the 'anatomy of the creative city' introduces a perspective for regional development that includes both the business and the personal climate. Competitive advantages in this case are not only pursued through classical theories or soft conditions, but by the achievement of an environment that promotes the conditions for exploration, generation, transfer and exploitation of knowledge, with a symbolic component, by actors in a territory of a different nature.

Epistemic communities and communities of practice: the importance of the *middleground* and the influence of the territory

With the creative city theory sustained by Florida (2002, 2010) as a point of departure, Cohendet *et al.* (2010) develop a complementary normative view on the processes leading to a creative urban environment. The 'anatomy of the creative city' adds the dynamics of emergence and formation of creative processes to the knowledge territory's creative ecology. The formation of creative processes must be understood as the interaction between the actors of the three strata of the territory, resulting in the creation of knowledge. It is a different paradigm from the innovative industrial district or territory whose approach seeks to integrate knowledge.

According to its nature and objectives, the 'anatomy of the creative city' classifies companies and institutions, groups or communities and individuals of the so-called creative class as upperground, middleground and underground, respectively. While companies focus on the exploitation of creativity, individuals are involved in the exploration of new forms of knowledge, understood as new forms of creativity. Meanwhile, and this is the main contribution to characterizing the theory of the anatomy of the creative city, communities are the cornerstone of the creative city, acting as intermediaries between the two layers, navigating between exploitation and exploration processes, facilitating cooperation between creative professionals and developing codes of knowledge and creative externalities for firms. The creative processes in local innovative milieus are therefore distributed along these layers, strata or components or the so-called upperground, middleground and underground which are permeable, complementary and interdependent.

The upperground consists of innovative companies from different sectors, including creative industries and institutions (research centres, universities and art and cultural centres). It is the top level of the creative city, the one analysed by the cluster theory that focuses on the production and use of externalities between organizations. Its contribution to the creative process lies in its ability to finance and unite different expressions, integrate dispersed knowledge from various disciplines and try new forms of creativity in the market (Cohendet *et al.*, 2010: 95). The underground consists of individuals who share identity and lifestyle based on their interest in arts and culture, irrespectively of whether this engagement is for their own pleasure or aimed at developing a specific artistic sector, either during working hours or not (Cohendet *et al.*, 2009: 713). It brings together the creative, cultural and artistic activities outside any organization based on the production, distribution or exploitation that would pervert the underground spirit. The underground culture promotes and defines new trends; it is considered the driving force in the definition of new evolutionary paths of arts and culture (Cohendet *et al.*, 2010: 96).

The middleground is a critical mediator between the underground structure (individuals) and the upperground (firms) where creative externalities are generated. Due to its intermediate position, it fluctuates between organized formal settings and informal mechanisms, promoting the exploration and the exploitation of creativity in cognitive processes that take place in both directions of the vertical axis of the creative city (top-down and bottom-up). This combination of approaches to creativity is found in open spaces as well, and while fab labs and hackerspaces share an explorative approach, the living labs and co-working spaces have an exploitative one (Capdevila, 2015).

The middleground is composed of two types of community that may overlap: epistemic communities and communities of practice. Although they may be related, their roles are different. The first one focuses on the exploration and codification of new knowledge from the underground, and the second on the exploitation of knowledge from the upperground, as described in this section. An epistemic community is a group of individuals with activities outside a company who share a set of commonly recognized topics and obey an agreed procedural authority whose objective is the deliberate creation of knowledge for the benefit of society as a whole, beyond the community itself. Epistemic communities carry out the exploration mechanisms in a creative city's middleground.

Communities of practice are, in the words of Cohendet *et al.*, the applied research section of the middleground. They exploit the ideas of firms and institutions from the upperground. If the processes of the epistemic communities are bottom-up, coding knowledge from the underground to make it understandable to the upperground, the activity of communities of practice is top-down, capturing the ideas of the firms or institutions for interpretation. They are groups or networks of individuals involved in the same activity who continuously communicate their professional practice. The members of a community of practice work together, exchange ideas and opinions, and inform each other of practical, professional or political trends (Lave, 1991). Their role in the anatomy of the creative city is to interpret, enrich and compare ideas from the upperground: the communities of practice exploit creative business and institutions' ideas, improving them gradually and revealing the best practices, and compare them with practices and methods from other fields.

The middleground is thus formed of epistemic communities and communities of practice that are intertwined in knowledge platforms requiring places, spaces, and specific events that open processes of exploration and exploitation, facilitating experimentation and the exchange of concepts and ideas (Cohendet *et al.*, 2011). A fertile middleground provides constant opportunities for the different communities to interact and compare their cognitive processes. It can be understood as a necessary device for channelling the creativity in an environment based on cooperation and competition so that its strength is directly proportional to the ability to generate creative externalities in the territory. By mixing epistemic communities and communities of practice activities, the intermediate layer has a balancing role between local explorations (underground) and potential global exploitation (upperground). In addition, the middleground 'translates, transforms and confronts local ideas with knowledge and practices issued from different parts of the world. It is a node of multiple connections of varying intensity and spatial distance' (Cohendet *et al.*, 2010: 108).

Audiovisual festivals in the BMR: an example of a fruitful middleground?

Film festivals are places for economic, cultural and film exchange that produce economic and cultural value. They ought to meet the demands of a local, national and international audience while being dependent on public funding from various levels of public administration. In addition to their traditional role as an alternative platform for exhibition and distribution, festivals are increasingly involved in film pre-production and production steps (Hing-Yuk Wong, 2011).

As cultural events, festivals have a dual relationship with the territory. On the one side, they are conditioned by the history, characteristics and local population and on the other, they have a diverse impact on the territory where they are held. This impact can be assessed according to their economic, tourist, cultural, physical or social nature (Devesa *et al.*, 2012). In a similar vein, van Aalst and van Melik (2012) summarize the role of a festival for the territory under three types. First, it can be a showcase for the city, contributing to its position as a brand with specific attributes. Secondly, a festival can be a creative destination and a breeding ground for talent. Given its specialization, it can also become a meeting place for audiences, artists and producers. Finally, it can play a role in attracting cultural tourists. Furthermore, festivals can also be entry points for new agents in the industry, such as students or young professionals, resulting in a privileged environment of professional socialization. Being selected at a festival provides public exposure and media coverage for the film, its director, producers and actors, although the impact will depend on the type of event (Rüling *et al.*, 2010).

The empirical evidence that supports the theory of the 'anatomy of the creative city' characterizes events and festivals as essential elements of the creative capacity of the territory (Simon, 2009; Cohendet *et al.* 2010). Consistent with this theory, festivals are studied as determinant events and spaces for the creative capacity of the territory, as one of the loci of innovation in the creative industries where firms, individuals and communities overlap and interact, and as a temporary space of emergence and fertilization of creativity. Therefore, the underlying purpose of this contribution is to explore whether festivals, on the basis of their configuration and programme, can be characterized as a competitive advantage, that is, as a tool for the fertilization and emergence of the territory's creativity in order to promote innovative activity.

The performing arts, music and audiovisual festivals database created by Carreño (2014) and updated by Quima Farré was the point of departure for this research. The sample was slightly modified after a review of the sources and festivals that were not held in 2012 were removed and new festivals added, although the methodology was maintained. The characterization of a festival in this database follows geographical, temporal, programme, conditions of access and event identity criteria: held in Catalonia, with a duration of at least two days, including a minimum of six programming items, open to the public and with a specific festival name (see Carreño, 2014). As explained below, it does not consider quantitative aspects such as budget or attendance, but focuses on its configuration, programme and side events. Thus, the review consists of an analysis of documents, programmes, presentations and other content available on the official web pages of the festivals.

This study is limited to audiovisual and multidisciplinary festivals and focuses on the audiovisual ones held in the Barcelona Metropolitan Region in 2012 and/or 2013. The analysis model U+3(i) is applied to this database. The model incorporates four new qualitative variables that will generate a new approach to festivals.

With regard to the audiovisual typology and geographical scope, there is a high concentration of festivals in Barcelona. A total of 41 out of the 57 festivals identified and analysed in the present sample are held in the Barcelona Metropolitan Region with 32 in the capital, while 16 are hosted by the other provinces in Catalonia. That is, almost three out of four audiovisual festivals in Catalonia are geographically concentrated in Barcelona. Among the audiovisual festivals, there is high diversity in terms of size, theme, activities, and recognition or specialization. For example, both the Sants Marató de Cinema Fantàstici de Terror de Sants and Sitges – Festival Internacional de Cinema Fantàstic de Catalunya address films of the same category, although the former has a local and small footprint, whereas the latter has great media coverage and international recognition in the genre festival network.

The predominance of fantasy and horror genres is to be noted, with three festivals of varied sizes dedicated to it: Fantosfreak, locally oriented, and Festival de Cinema de Terror de Molins de Rei and Sitges – International Fantastic Film Festival, with an international scope. The social aspect of the audiovisual production belongs to the mission of two of them: Dulcinea Curts, with an amateur approach to film production, promotes films covering mental health awareness and the K & O Festival Internacional de Cine Solidario is devoted to the cinema including social, environmental and volunteer topics as a tool for public awareness and the dissemination of these issues.

U+3(i).Variables and indicators for implementation

The aim of this model is to evaluate festival configuration as a space for creativity emergence and fertilization which serves as a breeding ground for talent, a socialization environment and entry points for professionals while promoting cultural and economic exchange. Depending on the characteristics and nature of the activities and programme of each festival, its role in the anatomy of the creative city will be assessed: as a specialized audiovisual supply of international origin that enriches the creative capacity of its public with access to new ideas; as devices that serve to show and reveal underground creative activities; as clusters of individuals, communities and/or companies of the creative city; or as temporary spaces for meeting, exchange and interaction processes.

If the acronym R&D corresponds to Research and Development, or Florida's 3Ts to Technology, Talent and Tolerance, the acronym U+3+I+I+I or U+3(I) can be coined to describe this analysis model as shown in Figure 5.2.

Our model incorporates four qualitative variables operated with 14 qualitative indicators. Before continuing with the description of each of the four variables, it is important to state that the existence of the middleground is assumed in all the festivals included in the database, given the agglomeration of underground members, with similar profiles defined by their interests, tastes, aspirations and, presumably, occupations. Thus, from this perspective, the festival is a middleground device that can be evaluated by attending to four variables (see Figure 5.3).

The preparation of this assessment is based on nominal, comprehensive and exclusive qualitative variables. Data were obtained from the qualitative analysis of each festival programme and events so that the identification of traits is related to the nature, mission and configuration of the festival and not to quantitative data such as budget, attendance, or media coverage, or features of its business model such as funding sources or public or private management of its organization.

After analysing the 41 audiovisual festivals in the of Barcelona Metropolitan Region (see Annex), it is noteworthy that only 10 of them, representing 24 per cent of the sample, offer activities that bring together individuals, groups and companies

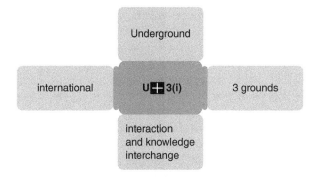

Figure 5.2 Analysis model U+3(i).

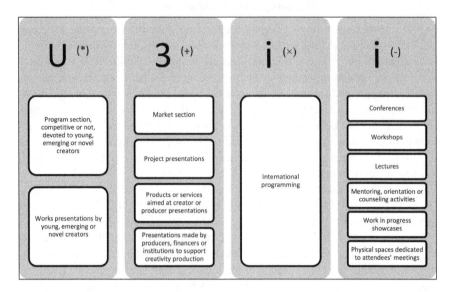

Figure 5.3 Model variables and indicators.

(*) "U" comes from underground, meaning that the festival promotes activities or spaces to bring visibility to the activities emerging from this layer of the creative city.
(+) The "3" identifies the participation of the three components of the creative city according to Cohendet *et al.* (2010): underground, middleground and upperground. The acronym is also used to triple the "i" that follows.
(×) The first "i" refers to the international offer that inspires and encourages the creative collectives in the territory.
(–) The second and third "i" are grouped under the same variable that states the presence of activities or spaces for interaction and knowledge interchange or exchange.

that are the three layers or grounds depicted in the anatomy of the creative city. The remaining three features of the analysis model are mostly present, albeit in different proportions. There are 22 festivals, amounting to 54 per cent, with educational or knowledge oriented transfer activities such as master classes, monographs and presentations. The aim of promoting novel, alternative or unknown artists (underground representatives) through specific programme sections or competitions is part of the mission of 25 of the 42 festivals (61 per cent). The predominant attribute, present in 32 festivals accounting for 78 per cent, is the international programme (see Figure 5.4).

Figure 5.5 presents a hierarchical classification of the festivals under analysis. Applying the model U+3(i) developed for this research, festivals are presented in five groups in ascending order according to their correspondence with model variables. The first group includes one festival that does not meet any criteria. The second consists of nine festivals with one variable. The third set, with two features, is the largest because it encompasses 16 festivals. The third level consists of eight festivals with three traits and, finally, at the top of the hierarchy, there are seven festivals that bring together the four features of the model.

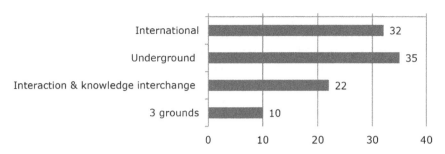

Figure 5.4 Number of festivals displaying each U+3(i) variable.

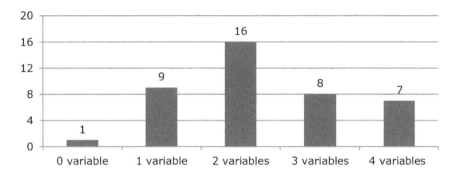

Figure 5.5 Hierarchical classification of festivals according to existing variables.
Source: Compiled by authors.

The seven festivals identified with the four variables of the model U+3(i) are: FILMETS, Festival Internacional de Filmets de Badalona; Sitges Festival Internacional de Cinema Fantàstic de Catalunya; Mecal, Festival Internacional de Cortometrajes de Barcelona; DocsBarcelona; L'Alternativa, Festival de Cinema Independent de Barcelona and Loop Barcelona. Five of the seven are held in Barcelona, while the neighbouring city of Badalona and the town of Sitges host one each. Two of them focus on the documentary genre: DocsBarcelona and IN-EDIT. All have at least one indicator of each of the four variables, even though some exceed this minimum and cover five or more indicators.

Conclusion and discussion

The analysis performed in this study confirms the initial hypothesis: the configuration of the festivals determines their ability to promote the fertilization and emergence of creativity, i.e. their capacity to mediate between exploration and exploitation activities as a middleground device, acting as a nexus in 10 instances between upperground companies and institutions and underground individuals. According to this conclusion, the creative capacity of the territory can be enhanced by the celebration of events that serve both to provide a common space for different kinds of relationships between actors rooted in the city and to offer connections to global trends, creative forms and players. However, the audiovisual festivals in the metropolitan region adjust to the model in different degrees, in all cases adding spaces that promote the flow of creative ideas.

In the light of the analysis model designed for this study, U+3(i), the variety of audiovisual festivals in the Barcelona Metropolitan Region has a shortage of spaces and activities that involve all three layers of the creative city: upperground, underground and middleground. The lack of participation of upperground companies and institutions leads to only 10 of the 41 festivals under analysis presenting the three strata, seven of them showing the four variables of the model. The ability of fertilization with forms of creativity (short films, feature films, video creations) from other countries is at the opposite extreme, given that more than three out of four festivals in the Barcelona Metropolitan Region showcase works of art from international countries.

Audiovisual festivals from the Barcelona Metropolitan Region are configured as a space where creative actors based in the territory can gain visibility and recognition. Sixty-one per cent of festivals include specific sections, competitive or otherwise, for emerging, alternative or unknown creators. Therefore, these events can be characterized as a valuable showcase for individuals and groups in the underground and as a source of talent and inspiration for upperground firms. Moreover, 54 per cent of festivals host interaction and exchange activities, promoting knowledge flows with symbolic components that enrich the artistic creativity of the territory's actors.

The analysis model, U+3(i), and the limited analysis of the Barcelona middleground is this research project's main contribution. From a cultural management point of view, it proposes a new approach to the territory where projects are developed.

- For managers of festivals and events and cultural entrepreneurs, the proposed model U+3(i) introduces a new perspective to the processes that could occur in a festival that complements other strategic management tools. With regard to programme and side events, fund-raising (public or private), the strategy of public and audience relations and the exploration of partnerships and collaboration opportunities with other entities, this model offers multiple points of view depending on the stakeholders: governments, businesses, professional associations, students, enthusiasts, groups and so on.
- For firms in the creative sector, the model offers a perspective that values the importance of integration within the territory, not only in terms of specialization or diversification externalities, both in the economic and knowledge fields, as a result of the concentration of firms, research centres and universities, but also in regard to individuals and groups involved in the exploration and exploitation of creativity. In this respect, festivals stand as a context where companies can benefit from privileged access to forms of creativity that can be globally equipped and exploited.
- For professionals, students and audiovisual enthusiasts, festivals emerge as temporary spaces that promote face-to-face contact and provide learning,

knowledge exchange and inspiration activities and, at the same time, access to global trends, activating interpersonal connections that are useful for vocational and professional purposes. Moreover, they are platforms that provide recognition to authors involved in projects outside the economic logic of exploitation, showing visibility and value to the upperground firms and institutions.

• For cultural policy makers and evaluators, this model offers an additional perspective that focuses on creation, exchange and assessment processes of symbolic knowledge. In light of the analysis in this research, it could be argued that innovation policies aimed at the creative industries should take into account the underground and how it relates to the upperground, how underground creativity comes to the surface, and how it can be commercially exploited and trends set with a global impact so as not to only adapt what is done elsewhere. The upperground can take advantage of this local input/stimulus, the creative ideas arising from the local environment in order to be innovative while, at the same time, the development of local creative communities can benefit from interaction with firms. It is essential to promote, find and encourage liaison mechanisms in the form of common spaces between the strata of the creative city, maximizing their potential while pursuing a balance between exploration activities, with an intrinsic value, and its valorisation with potential global exploitation.

References

Becattini, G. (1979) Dal settore industriale al distretto industriale: Alcune considerazioni sull'unità d' indagine dell'economia industriale, *Rivista di Economia e Politica Industriale*, 1, 35–48.

Bontje, M., Musterd, S. and Pelzer, P. (2011) *Inventive City Regions. Path Dependence and Creative Knowledge Strategies.* Farnham: Ashgate.

Capdevila, I. (2015) Les différentes approches entrepreneuriales dans les espaces ouverts d'innovation. *Innovations*, 3, 87–105.

Carreño, T. (2014) *La gestión de festivales en tiempos de crisis: análisis de las estrategias de gestión financiera y laboral e impacto de la recesión económica.* Tesis doctoral dirigida por Lluís Bonet Agustí. Universitat de Barcelona.

Cohendet, P., Grandadam, D. and Simon, L. (2009) Economics and the ecology of creativity: Evidence from the popular music industry, *International Review of Applied Economics*, 23(6), 709–722.

Cohendet, P., Grandadam, D. and Simon, L. (2010) The anatomy of the creative city, *Industry and Innovation*, 17(1), 91–111.

Cohendet, P., Grandadam, D. and Simon, L. (2011) Rethinking urban creativity: Lessons from Barcelona and Montréal, *City Culture and Society*, 2, 151–158.

Devesa, M., Báez, A., Figueroa, V. and Herrero, L. C. (2012) Repercusiones económicas y sociales de los festivales culturales: el caso del Festival Internacional de Cine de Valdivia, *EURE (Santiago)*, 38(115), 95–115.

Florida, R. L. (2002) *The Rise of the Creative Class: And How It's Transforming Work, Leisure, Community and Everyday Life.* New York: Basic Books.

Florida, R. (2010) *Who's Your City? How the Creative Economy Is Making Where to Live the Most Important Decision of Your Life.* New York: Random House LLC.

Jacobs, J. (1969) *The Economy of Cities*. New York: Random House.
Hall, P. (1998) *Cities in Civilization*. New York: Pantheon Books.
Hing-Yuk Wong, C. (2011) *Film Festivals: Culture, People, and Power on the Global Screen*. London: Rutgers University Press.
Lave, J. (1991) Situating learning in communities of practice, in: J. M. Levine, L. B. Resnick and S. D Teasley (eds) *Perspectives on Socially Shared Cognition*, Washington, DC: American Psychological Association), pp. 63–82.
Musterd, S. and Murie, A. (eds) (2010) *Making Competitive Cities*. Chichester: Wiley-Blackwell.
Musterd, S. and Gritsai, O. (2013) The creative knowledge city in Europe: Structural conditions and urban policy strategies for competitive cities, *European Urban and Regional Studies*, 20(3), 343–359.
Musterd, S. and Kóvacs, Z. (eds) (2013) *Place-Making and Policies for Competitive Cities*. London: Wiley-Blackwell.
Porter, M. E. (1998) *Clusters and the New Economics of Competition*, 6(6), 77–90). Boston, MA: Harvard Business Review.
Rüling, C. C. and Strandgaard Pedersen, J. (2010) Film festival research from an organizational studies perspective, *Scandinavian Journal of Management*, 26(3), 318–323.
Scott, A. J. (2010) Cultural economy and the creative field of the city, *Geografiska Annaler: Series B, Human Geography*, 92(2), 115–130.
Scott A. J. (2014) Beyond the creative city: Cognitive – cultural capitalism and the new urbanism, *Regional Studies*, 48(4), 565–578.
Simon, L. (2009) Underground, upperground et middle-ground: les collectifs créatifs et la capacité créative de la ville, *Management international / Gestiòn Internacional / International Management*, 13, 37–51.
Simonton, D. K. (1999) *Origins of Genius: Darwinian Perspectives on Creativity*. Oxford: Oxford University Press.
Van Aalst, I. and van Melik, R. (2012) City festivals and urban development: Does place matter? *European Urban and Regional Studies*, 19(2), 195–206.

Annex: Barcelona's audiovisual festivals database analysed with the U+3(i) model

Name	Underground	3 grounds	International	Interaction & Interchange
DOCSBARCELONA. International Documentary Film Festival	●	●	●	●
IN-EDIT. Festival Internacional de Cinema Documental Musical de Barcelona	●	●	●	●
FILMETS. Festival Internacional de Filmets de Badalona		●	●	●
L'Alternativa. Festival de Cinema Independent de Barcelona		●	●	●
Loop Barcelona – Screen Festival		●	●	●
Mecal. Festival Internacional de Cortometrajes de Barcelona				●
Sitges. Festival Internacional de Cinema Fantàstic de Catalunya			●	●
Barcelona Visual Sound, Festival Audiovisual de Creació Jove			●	●
Base Film Festival	●		●	●
BccN Barcelona Creative Commons Film Festival	●	●		●
BCN Sports Film			●	●
Festival de Cinema de Terror de Molins de Rei	●	●		
Mostra de Cinema Àrab I Mediterrani	●	●		
Mostra Internacional Films de Dones Barcelona	●		●	
MUSICLIP Festival Internacional de la Música, las Artes Audiovisuales y el Videoclip de Barcelona	●		●	
BANG, Festival de Videoart de Barcelona	●			
D'A, Festival Internacional de Cinéma D'Autor de Barcelona	●		●	●
Dulcinea curts	●			
FESTIMATGE, Festival de la Imatge de Calella	●		●	
Festival Cl'hips	●		●	●
Festival Curtficcions			●	
Festival de Cinema i Drets Humans de Barcelona			●	●

(continued)

(continued)

Name	Underground	3 grounds	International	Interaction & Interchange
FIAB, Festival Internacional del Audiovisual de Barcelona			•	•
FICMA, Festival Internacional de Cinéma de Medi Ambient	•		•	
FLUX, Festival de Vídeo D'Autor	•			•
K&O, Festival Internacional de Cinema Solidari	•		•	
Marató de Cinema Fantàstici de Terror de Sants	•		•	
Mostra Curtmetrages Dr. Mabuse	•		•	•
Non Stop Barcelona Animació	•			
SPC, Sóloparacortos. Festival Internacional de Curtometrages de Temàtica Social de NouBarris	•		•	•
Zinemaldia			•	•
Artfutura, Festival de Culturai Creatividat Digital			•	
Fantosfreak		•		
Festival de Cinema Jueu de Barcelona			•	
Festival Internacional de Cinema Gai i Lèsbic de Barcelona			•	
Festival Internacional de Televisió de Barcelona			•	
FIRE! Mostra Lambda, Mostra Internacional de Cinema Gai i Lesbià			•	
Gandules			•	
Ovni			•	
Sala Monjuïc, Cinema a la fresca				
El Meu Primer Festival				

6 Creativity and entrepreneurship
Culture, subculture and new venture creation

Erik E. Lehmann and Nikolaus Seitz

Introduction

Ever since the seminal work of Schumpeter (1934/2003), creativity and entrepreneurship have been interpreted as the DNA of capitalism and wealth (Scott, 2006): Free competition and its market dynamics selects only the most innovative, thus "efficient" solutions, whereas less well performing ones get abandoned. However, this evolutionary process requires ever-expanding capacities for creative and entrepreneurship activity.

Today, entrepreneurship policy programmes are most highly prioritized issues on almost every economic development agenda across the globe. Nevertheless, what fosters countries' capacities for exploiting new ideas via innovation and entrepreneurship remains fragmented and empirically inconsistent. However, when summarizing the extensive research over the past 40 years, one key insight seems to be evident: instead of being a national phenomenon, creativity and entrepreneurship is a very regional and social event embedded in local communities and their institutions (Audretsch and Lehmann, 2016; Obschonka *et al.*, 2015; Wagner and Sternberg, 2004).

A large body of literature has also emerged that studies the crucial role of culture; it is argued that culture channels creativity and entrepreneurship performance in two interrelated ways. First, from an institutional-based perspective, culture functions as a lubricant enabling people to get creative with each other, share sensible knowledge and take risky chances (Cushing, Florida, and Gates, 2002). Second, being creative and getting entrepreneurial is a state of mind that is shaped by cultural beliefs, perceptions and social ethos (Autio and Acs, 2007; Lee, Florida, and Acs, 2004; Obschonka *et al.*, 2015). The most high performing countries and regions seem to be those that exalt the idea of individuality, self-efficacy, creative-thinking and entrepreneurial behaviour (Acemoglu, Robinson, and Woren, 2012; Hofstede, 1993). For instance, today, San Francisco, Tel Aviv, Berlin, Dublin, London and Stockholm are all start-up hotspots that stylize entrepreneurship as being part of a hip, sophisticated lifestyle. Yet, what "kind of" culture matters is in the midst of current discussions about entrepreneurial ecosystems (Acs, Audretsch, Lehmann, and Licht, 2016; Isenberg, 2011; Mack and Mayer, 2015). Various approaches have been revealed that shed light on various meanings and definitions of culture within different contexts (e.g. Boschma and Fritsch, 2009; Davidsson, 1995; Falck, Fritsch, and Heblich, 2011; Fritsch and Wyrwich, 2012; Lehmann and Seitz, 2016; Obschonka *et al.*, 2015). Results remain inconsistent and often lack both theoretical and empirical rigour.

This article aims to provide a critical review of the current state of the art and presents future implications in the research of culture and its impact on regional entrepreneurship growth. In particular, rather than discussing culture as a whole, we put subcultures at the heart of our analysis of the entrepreneurship ecosystem and its dimensions. The chapter is organized as follows. The following section provides an overview of the vast literature of culture in entrepreneurship and creativity studies, the third section analyses the role of subculture in new venture creation and provides primary statistical evidence from Germany's largest cities, and the fourth section concludes findings and draws implication for future research and policy makers.

Entrepreneurship, creativity and culture

Different perspectives of culture, creativity and entrepreneurship

In the wake of globalization, economies' competitiveness relies on its regions and their ability to create and exploit new knowledge via innovation and entrepreneurship (Audretsch and Belitski, 2013; Audretsch and Feldman, 2004; Audretsch and Lehmann, 2005; Florida, 2013; Paci and Marrocu, 2013). Economic developers across the globe have promoted entrepreneurship – as new venture creation or a start-up activity – as a means of enhancing regional and national growth (Da Rin, Di Giacomo, and Sembenelli, 2011; Ghio, Guerini, Lehmann, and Rossi-Lamastra, 2015; Lehmann and Seitz, 2016). Over past decades, this had led to extensive investments to create an entrepreneurship-ready and sound environment for innovation. In a search for a beneficial environment, academics as well as policy makers have shifted more and more away from physical factors towards human capital and the role of knowledge as a key source of regional entrepreneurship growth. Economists have identified new knowledge creation as a strong predictor for variations in regional entrepreneurial activity and performance (Audretsch and Lehmann, 2005; Clifton and Cooke, 2009; Florida, 2013). As a consequence, countries started expanding their research agendas, raising R&D budgets, offering grants and investing in broad education. For instance, Germany's renowned "Exzelleniniative" or "Leading-Edge Cluster" cluster initiative is one of the most prominent examples along this line (Lehmann and Menter, 2016; Audretsch and Lehmann, 2016). However, even when scholars underline the importance of knowledge and human capital for entrepreneurship, findings also reveal that it is more a necessary condition than a sufficient one (Obschonka *et al.*, 2015). Later, there are signs of a phenomenon that has become known as "the knowledge gap", that is, contrary to expectations, new knowledge production does not automatically lead to higher tiers of entrepreneurship and innovation (Audretsch and Keilbach, 2008; Lee *et al.*, 2004; Obschonka *et al.*, 2015;

Tijssen and Van Wijk, 1999). For instance, most evident in Europe's historically weakness to commercialize new knowledge via entrepreneurship, this paradox sheds light on some underlying forces behind entrepreneurship growth (Obschonka *et al.*, 2015; Torjman and Worren, 2010). In search for a missing link, scholars have recently re-discovered the long neglected role of creativity (e.g. Audretsch and Belitski, 2013; Florida, 1995, 2003; Gabe, 2011; Lee *et al.*, 2004). Creativity features the "ability to transcend ideas, rules, patterns and relationships and transform them into [. . .] meaningful new forms, methods and designs [. . .]" (Florida, 2003, p. 45). Thus, today creativity appears to be crucial because it is the bridging skill that transforms new knowledge into business and innovation. Florida (2003) puts it in a more straightforward way by stating that, contrary to common expectations, it is not knowledge that powers knowledge societies, it is human creativity (Florida, 2003, 2002, 2014).

What sources creativity and entrepreneurship has been extensively studied since the 1980s and approached either from technological and infrastructural patterns (e.g. Porter, 1998, 2000), human capital, or most recently, social capital sided arguments (Audretsch and Feldman, 2004; Coleman, 1988). Recently, scholars shifted their attention towards more culturally driven factors and their impact on local creative and entrepreneurial milieus (Aoyama, 2009; Davidsson, 1995; Florida, 2014; Florida, Mellander, and Stolarick, 2008; Scott, 1999; Torjman and Worren, 2010). It is argued that entrepreneurial orientation, i.e. the willingness of people to create innovative ideas and take risky chances, is highly institutionalized by the cultural context these people are linked to (Audretsch, 2015; Fritsch and Wyrwich, 2012; Hofstede, 1993; Langley, 1993; Obschonka *et al.*, 2015). Culture defines a set of shared beliefs, values and norms of a social group at a given time (Davidsson, 1995; Denzau and North, 1994; Hofstede, 1993). As a part of institutional constraints, culture shapes how people perceive their environment, make their choices and interact with each other (Altinay, 2008; Aoyama, 2009; Davidsson, 1995; Denzau and North, 1994). Regarding creativity and entrepreneurial behaviour, three distinct but intertwined mechanisms behind culture are discussed within the recent literature. Research on the first sheds light on the bridging-and-bounding-effects (e.g. Cushing, Florida and Gates, 2002; Florida, 1995; Maskell and Malmberg, 1999) of culture on creativity and entrepreneurship growth (e.g. Cooke and Wills, 1999; Landry, Amara, and Lamari, 2002; Westlund and Adam, 2010). The second focuses on the entrepreneur's personality and how it is affected by the cultural environment (Krueger Jr, 2003; Obschonka *et al.*, 2015; Rauch and Frese, 2007a, 2007b). The third mechanism, a fast growing body of literature, studies cultural amenities, e.g. artists or museums, and their impact on entrepreneurial and creative milieus (Audretsch and Lehmann, 2016; Boschma and Fritsch, 2009; Breznitz and Noonan, 2014; Falck *et al.*, 2011; Glaeser and Gottlieb, 2006; Glaeser, Kolko, and Saiz, 2001; Glaeser, Rosenthal, and Strange, 2010; Polèse, 2012).

The following sections critically summarize main rationales and findings within these three core streams in research. Further on, we attempt to complement recent discussions by introducing the relevance role of "subcultures" in entrepreneurship and creativity growth.

The human capital perspective

When screening the economic literature, the notion of creativity seems to be caught between two polarities. The first stream, the psychological perspective, sees the individual and its personality as crucial for creativity, whereas the second underlines the role of social networks and institutions (Scott, 1999). Since the first contributions of Cantillon or Say in the early eighteenth century, researchers have eagerly emphasized the special nature of the entrepreneurial personality (Gartner, 1990). Most prominent, Schumpeter (1934) suggests that all entrepreneurs behave in a proactive, opportunity-seeking and risk-taking way by creatively combining new resources. Until now, this archetype of the creative "destructor" is still the most fundamental classification of entrepreneurship and entrepreneurial behaviour in modern economic thought.

The relationship between personality traits and entrepreneurial orientation has become one of the most intensively studied domains in entrepreneurship research (Acs and Szerb, 2007; Gartner, 1990; Rauch and Frese, 2007b). Over past decades, different personality traits have been tested in different settings and levels of analysis and have shown inconsistent results. For instance, Brockhaus and Horwitz (1986) identify three traits that are consistently positively linked to entrepreneurial behaviour: a need for achievement, internal locus of control, and a risk-taking propensity. Mueller and Thomas (2001) find similar characteristics. Sexton and Bowman (1986) reveal that entrepreneurs need autonomy and independence, and are dominant personalities. Furthermore, the ongoing survey of the Global Entrepreneurship Monitor (GEM) team provides evidence that entrepreneurship activity outperforms in countries that are characterized by high secularity while striving values of self-expression and autonomy (Acs, Arenius, Hay, and Minniti, 2004; Bosma, Acs, Autio, Coduras, and Levie, 2008; Reynolds, Hay, Bygrave, Camp, and Autio, 2000; Reynolds, Hay, and Camp, 1999). In addition, recent meta-analyses reveal (Leutner, Ahmetoglu, Akhtar, and Chamorro-Premuzic, 2014; Zhao, Seibert, and Lumpkin, 2010) that entrepreneurial orientation is associated with high conscientiousness, openness and personal extraversion, whereas high levels of neuroticism are negative correlated. Others suggest that optimism, a need for achievement, creativity, self-confidence, self-efficacy and conformity, and discipline, endurance and enthusiasm are defining characters of entrepreneurs (Chell, 2008; Urban, 2006). Against the backdrop of controversial findings, pure personality characteristics appear to be important but not sufficient in explaining different entrepreneurship activity across regions or countries (Denzau and North, 1994; Obschonka *et al.*, 2015). Instead, people decide on parts of their social environment and its constraints (Denzau and North, 1994). What is more, 70 per cent of cross-regional variation in business start-up rates can be explained, at least in the statistical sense, by differences in certain economic and socio-demographic, and the cultural and institutional characteristics of regions (Davidsson and Wiklund, 1997, 2001). For instance, in a context of entrepreneurial orientation, researchers find support for the importance of labour markets, i.e. poor markets foster necessity-driven entrepreneurship (Acs and Szerb, 2007; Saxenian, 1996), the family background, previous organizational experiences, social networks, and the regional and national culture. In particular, over the past decade, a number of authors had underlined the particular role of a society's culture and how it is affecting personal traits and orientations towards entrepreneurship and creativity (Davidsson, 1995; Florida, 2002, 2003; Florida *et al.*, 2008; Lee *et al.*, 2004; Scott, 1999). Culture is relatively persistent over time (Rauch and Frese, 2007a) and can be understood as "the collective programming of the mind that distinguishes members and their values and beliefs from one group to another [. . .]" (Denzau and North, 1994; Hofstede, 1993, p. 19). Research also argues that variations in entrepreneurship and innovation rates across regions are determined by the persisting difference in cultural attitudes and perceptions that can be traced back to both historical roots and other trajectories of regional personality features (Fritsch and Wyrwich, 2012; Obschonka *et al.*, 2015). This becomes even more vivid for the backdrop of a recent study by Fritsch and Wyrwich (2012). While comparing entrepreneurship rates in East Germany from 1925 to 2005, findings reveal that entrepreneurship culture endures even drastic institutional changes, such as the breakdown of socialism or World War II. The qualitative study by Aoyama (2009) also draws a similar picture. By comparing two "entrepreneurial regions" of Japan, it is shown that historical legacy strongly influences business practices and perceptions of entrepreneurship.

However, even when the link between culture and entrepreneurship and creativity growth garnered great reception from academia and policy makers, systemic empirical research, especially related to entrepreneurship and creativity outcomes, is still scarce. Nevertheless, with a broader perspective towards culture and economy, the work of sociologists Weber (1905/2002) and McClelland (1965) can be seen as pioneering. Weber (1930) revealed that a puritan moral code led to the striving for profit and ascetic capital accumulation with no goal other than re-investment, and fuels high work productivity and entrepreneurship growth and therefore, America's ascent. Building on Weber's (1905/2002) approach, McClelland (1965) analyses 22 countries and finds support for the fact that economic growth is strictly related to a culture of individuality and the "need for achievement". These findings match with some ground work by Spence (1985) and Morris, Davis, and Allen (1994) who reveal that the high rates of entrepreneurship in the United States are associated with cultural values such as freedom, independence, achievement and materialism. For instance, Hofstede (1993) suggested other similar culturally based explanations for the economic development in East Asia after the World War II. Shane (1993) investigated the relationship between Hofstede's measures of national culture and innovation growth and shows that societies with low uncertainty acceptance are most closely associated with innovativeness, but that individualism and non-hierarchy structures (power distance) are also related to innovation growth. Wennekers, Thurik, van Stel, and Noorderhaven (2007) even support the relevance of cultural-led attitudes towards risk. In their empirical comparison of 21 OECD countries, it is shown that high levels of uncertainty acceptance reduce the perceived opportunity cost of self-employment and push individuals striving for autonomy and entrepreneurial behaviour. However, Begley and

Tan (2001) show that the social status of entrepreneurship and shame from business failure predict variations in entrepreneurship rates better for East-Asian than Anglo countries. Based on Hofstede's national culture model, Sun (2009) presents a comprehensive meta-analysis showing support that individualism, power distance and uncertainty avoidance in national innovation are correlated with a country's innovation capacity. A similar picture is provided by Rossberger and Krause (2012). Testing the GLOBE culture dimensions, their study demonstrates that uncertainty avoidance, in-group collectivism, and human orientation are crucial for innovative outcomes in 55 of their sampled countries. In a recent study, Lehmann and Seitz (2016) underline the importance of individualism for national innovativeness. Comparing 52 countries plus the 50 US states in their levels of social freedom and innovation capacity, they point to some downside risks that come with rising cultural individualism and heterogeneity. This matches the popular work of Acemoglu *et al.* (2012), whereas economic prosperity, notably a nation's capacity for creative destruction, depends on cultural and political traits that strive people's desire for autonomy and self-efficacy – usually, common in institutional environments that feature high levels of individualism, less autocracy (power distance) and formalism. However, none of the above studies are specifically related to cultural traits on a regional or local level. Recent research has outlined that entrepreneurial culture is primarily rooted in the region, or on a much smaller scale, at local level such as cities, neighbourhoods or districts (Boschma and Fritsch, 2009; Feldman and Audretsch, 1999) rather than societies at large (Davidsson and Wiklund, 2001). Florida (1995/2002/2014) also highlights the role of cultural individualism and tolerance. In a complementary way, Lee *et al.* (2004) relate local creativity and entrepreneurship to the use of a "Bohemian Index", measuring places' open-mindedness and freedom. Davidsson and Wiklund's (1997) findings suggest that autonomy, change orientation, a need for achievement, acceptance of capitalism and valuation of money, and a competitive culture explain variations in regional business venturing rates in Sweden. On a local level, Basu and Altinay (2002) study the readiness to start up a business across London's ethnic minorities. Findings suggest entrepreneurial orientation differs with religious thoughts, collectivism, long-term orientation, and strong family ties.

The social capital perspective

In addition to the human capital thesis of creativity and entrepreneurship, scholars have stressed the role of social capital. Social capital is generally understood as a resource that ties community networks and facilitates their members' interactions (Putnam, 1995). It is embedded in the share of values, beliefs and routines that describe and link people to a certain group or social class (e.g. Adler and Kwon, 2002; Bourdieu, 2011; Coleman, 1994; Fukuyama, 2001; Lin, 2002; Putnam, 1995). Regarding entrepreneurship and creativity, two conflicting lines of argument have been exposed in literature. The first underlines that high levels of social capital accompany high levels of creativity and entrepreneurship, whereas the second line proposes exactly the opposite. It is argued that social capital, i.e. a strong social and cultural fit, ties community members and supports a trustful environment that encourages people to share information and take joint chances on risky ideas (e.g. Adler and Kwon, 2002; Burt, 2000; Fukuyama, 2001; Lin, Cook, and Burt, 2001; Maskell, 2001; Putnam, 1995; Zheng, 2010). In contrast, other researchers warn of the detrimental effects of increasing social capital (e.g. Beugelsdijk and Smulders, 2003; Cushing *et al.*, 2002; Hansen, 1999; Lin, 2002; McFadyen and Cannella, 2004; Morgan, 2007; Nahapiet and Ghoshal, 1998; Portes, 2000; Putnam, 1995). It is also supposed that increasing social capital makes communities reluctant to accept new, outside influences (Adler and Kwon, 2002; Cooke, Clifton, and Oleaga, 2005; Florida, 1995; Granovetter, 1985; Hofstede, 1993; Landry *et al.*, 2002; Lehmann and Seitz, 2016; McFadyen and Cannella, 2004; Portes, 2000; Tura and Harmaakorpi, 2005; Waldinger, 1997). Thus, only low levels of social capital lead to high creative capacities since inspiration, new ideas and knowledge can flow across communities members (e.g. Adler and Kwon, 2002; Ahuja and Katila, 2001; Florida, 1995; Florida, 2002; Fukuyama, 2001; Landry *et al.*, 2002; Lin, 2002).

Although both arguments garnered great response across the academia, empirical evidence is quite conflicting (Westlund and Adam, 2010). Research testing the social capital vs. weak ties hypothesis of creativity and entrepreneurship either concentrates on the regional context (e.g. Barrutia and Echebarria, 2010; Beugelsdijk and Van Schaik, 2005a; Fleming and Marx, 2006; Hauser, Tappeiner, and Walde, 2007; Putnam, 1995; Schneider, Plümper, and Baumann, 2000; Storper and Scott, 2009; Tura and Harmaakorpi, 2005) or micro-units of analysis such as individuals, teams or organizations (e.g. Cooke *et al.*, 2005; Hansen, 1999; Landry *et al.*, 2002; McFadyen and Cannella, 2004; Nahapiet and Ghoshal, 1998). However, only a few studies explore the link on a national level (e.g. Beugelsdijk and Smulders, 2003; Knack and Zak, 2003; Lehmann and Seitz, 2016; Zheng, 2010). Across all levels of analysis, studies show mixed and contradictory results (Westlund and Adam, 2010; Zheng, 2010). At the organizational level, Smith *et al.* (2006) found a non-significant correlation whereas Ahuja (2000) supports a negative one, Cooke *et al.* (2005) a positive one, and Uzzi and Spiro (2005) an inverse U-shaped one between strong social capital and corporate entrepreneurship and innovation performance. At the regional context (Hauser *et al.*, 2007), Akçomak and Ter Weel (2009) or Beugelsdijk and Van Schaik (2005b) found a positive impact whereas Florida *et al.* (2008) or Fleming and Marx (2006) support a negative influence of tie strength and regional entrepreneurship and innovativeness. On the national level, studies are scarce, especially regarding the impact of social capital on national innovation and focus in most cases on general notions of economic development such as GDP or GNI (e.g. Knack and Keefer, 1997; Knack and Zak, 2003; Roth, 2009; Whiteley, 2000). However, Lehmann and Seitz (2015) found a strong linkage between weak social ties, in terms of diversity and personal freedom, and national innovation rates, whereas Dakhli and De Clercq (2004) only partly support a positive influence of social capital on national innovativeness. Against the backdrop of mixed evidence, Westlund and Adam (2010) summarize that it is not clear whether social capital bridges creative spillovers and innovative entrepreneurship or stifles any culture for creativity and entrepreneurship.

The physical capital perspective

Previous chapters have shown that creativity resides in personal capacities and social traits – all products of the cultural and institutional environment individuals are embedded in. In addition to this, a human and social capital perspective of creativity, a third, conceptually "bridging" line of literature, has recently gained great prominence. Pioneering scholars such as Jacobs (1970), Landry (2008) and Florida (2002) have pointed to the supplementary but significant role of local cultural amenities in entrepreneurship and creativity-driven growth. It is argued that cultural industries, such as museums, art galleries, theatres, shopping and entertainment facilities and the presence of a vivid cultural economy (e.g. graphic design, architecture, publishing, music and visual arts, fashion design) unleash local creative and entrepreneurial growth via two distinct but intertwined channels. First, cultural endowments and industries reinforce the local pool and clustering of talents and human capital (Florida, 2014; Lee *et al.*, 2004). Second, both represent stockpiles of local knowledge, ideas and images that inspire artists, designers, scientists and other members of the creative class in their work (Scott, 1999, 2006; Storper and Scott, 2009). Within the first line of argument, the most renowned work is Florida's (2002) cluster theory of the creative class. The creative class describes a social milieu of people that engage in creative problem solving. According to Florida (2002) this even holds for scientists (core creatives) or artists (bohemians) and even professionals (e.g. lawyers, medical doctors, entrepreneurs, business men). In the wake of a global war for talents, these creative and talented people not only become more and more mobile, but sophisticated towards their perceptions of work and leisure time (Florida, 2002). Thus, today not only firms but countries, regions or cities have to mobilize all of their resources to attract those talents and high potentials (Florida, 2014). Florida (2002) reveals that these talents feel attracted to a branded "place of sense" rather than a place with sense. That is, it is no longer about the conventional wisdom "create jobs, and the rest will follow" (Caragliu, Del Bo, and Nijkamp, 2011), but locations have to offer authenticity and a rich supply of cultural (arts and creative industries) and social endowments (diversity, community spirit). As a reinforcing effect, creative class are drawn to its peers, thus, clustering themselves, which spurs local innovation and knowledge capacities and therefore creativity and entrepreneurship.

In addition to this gravitation effect of human capital, the second line argues that cultural endowments span a local system of traditions and sites of ideas, such as museums, galleries, music halls or bars, that create certain kinds of impulses (Breznitz and Noonan, 2014; Glaeser and Gottlieb, 2006; Glaeser *et al.*, 2001; Polèse, 2012): Dramatic architecture, music venues, literature, movie productions and art galleries influence people in their perceptions and may inspire them to get creative on their own (Clark, 2013). Promoting economic growth via cultural attainment has gained popularity in across regional development agendas around the globe. For instance, Sweden set out to attract creative and cultural industries (Andersson and Koster, 2011); the city of Berlin framed its development goals around specialization in cultural and creative industries (Henckel *et al.*, 2008), as did Cologne or Paris. The recent gentrification of Brooklyn's district of Williamsburg (New York) towards an epic centre of a vivid creative scene is associated with local policies to promote cultural production (Curran, 2007, 2010).

Besides these practical examples, from a research point of view, there is ongoing controversy whether the physical presence of cultural endowments and industries really impacts creativity and entrepreneurship, and economic growth (Breznitz and Noonan, 2014; Falck, Fritsch, and Heblich, 2009; Falck *et al.*, 2011; Fritsch and Wyrwich, 2012; Polèse, 2012). Glaeser *et al.* (2008), for instance, insist that, unlike Florida (2002), it is not the cultural setting that drives regional growth; it is the formal knowledge stock, thus, conventional human capital, industry and the presence of research institutions and universities that stimulates innovation and entrepreneurship. Whether cultural attainment has a direct impact on regional entrepreneurship-drive growth is seen as controversial and lacks empirical and conceptual rigour. However, this criticism is always sensitive to the problems of endogeneity and reverse causality. Thus, whether places of the fine arts are more a consequence or sources of creativity and proactive behaviour is difficult to test empirically. For instance, as Glaeser *et al.* (2010) point out, cities with a large fraction of high-skilled and high-earning people tend to have a higher willingness to pay for cultural goods indicating a reverse causality (Morgan and Ren, 2012; Peck, 2005; Rossberger and Krause, 2012). Thus, as a natural experiment, Falck *et al.* (2011) try to overcome the endogeneity problem by going back in history and interpreting the presence of historical cultural amenities. The authors claim that today's regional endowment with human capital is shaped by cultural endowments, using German opera houses from the baroque era as their proxy for cultural richness and local tradition in creativity tradition (Falck *et al.*, 2011). Using a GMM approach, they reveal the importance of creative people for regional growth as Florida (2002) suggests. Nevertheless, they find no evidence that members of the creative class feel attracted by bohemian milieu and cultural attainment.

Against the backdrop of these controversial findings, we suggest that it is not the presence of cultural endowments per se that fuels high rates of entrepreneurship, but the existence of a special cultural atmosphere. In the following section, we define our line of argument and point to, as we believe, the specific role of subcultures and their endowments.

Subculture, creativity and entrepreneurship: an integrative perspective

The emergence of subculture in new venture creation

Studies on subcultures and their impact on societies enlivened research in the twentieth century and appear to have become even more relevant at the beginning of the twenty-first century (Dhoest, Malliet, Haers, and Segaert, 2015). Subcultures define distinctive groups of society that are bound by alternative perceptions, values and beliefs to life as the establishment, thus socio-cultural mainstream (Hebdige, 1995; Schouten and McAlexander, 1995). Ever since, subcultures have become cradles for avant-garde lifestyles (Dhoest *et al.*, 2015; Hebdige, 1995; Schouten and McAlexander, 1995) that later have often been adopted by mainstream culture. For instance, the hillbillies of the 1950s, the hippies of the 1960s, the environment movement of the late 1970s, the punk or club scene and 1990s grunge are all prominent examples of subcultures that have influenced societies' "Zeitgeist".

Even in the context of economics, in particular in the field of entrepreneurship and innovation policy research, subcultures and their impact have attracted more and more attention over the past two decades. It is argued that, as in all other dimensions of social life, even an entrepreneurial spirit and creativity culture is spilled over from a small and pioneering avant-garde of innovative people to the mainstream (Hebdige, 1995; Morgan and Ren, 2012; Schouten and McAlexander, 1995). Thus, fostering innovation and entrepreneurship growth might need the co-location of a vibrant subcultural scene that transcends certain kinds of entrepreneurial spirit. For instance, once it was a small scene of nerdy masterminds that founded Silicon Valley's legacy as a start-up Eldorado. Starting from here, it was the myths about visionary entrepreneurs such as Steve Jobs, Bill Gates or Larry Ellison who made fortunes at a head-snapping speed during the game-changing society that spread a hero-like perception of entrepreneurs across USA and rest of the world. These visionary entrepreneurs act as a role model for an entire generation of founders during the age of the new economy and still influence today's entrepreneurial scene. Even though Silicon Valley is still the hub of the start-up world, we observe vibrant start-up scenes across the globe, in Austin, Nashville, Tel Aviv, Berlin, Moscow, Copenhagen and Leipzig, for example. These cities are not exclusively built on a great share of human capital or industrial production, but are globally recognized for their vibrant subcultural life – in the cases of, for example, Austin, Moscow or Leipzig – more for subculture than traditional cultural attainment. This might indicate that the presence of a vibrant subcultural scene is a better predictor for local entrepreneurship and creativity than the previously tested "conventional" traits of cultural amenities. Thus, entrepreneurs and creative talents are more attracted to music clubs than operas, independent music rather than philharmonics, street-art rather than museums, and so on. In the following, we attempt to provide some descriptive evidence of whether there is a basis for our idea.

Descriptive statistics for Germany

In order to support our argument, we draw on simple scatters, deploying data from 69 German cities with over 100,000 inhabitants. We justify a possible selection-bias by pointing to recent findings that suggest that entrepreneurship, creativity and culture amenities as well as the presence of subcultures are highly sensitive to levels of density and proximity. To capture entrepreneurship performance, we draw on the average number of new business registrations from 2008 till 2012 regardless of industry or type of enterprise. Additionally, we compare these data with start-up outcomes of each region as a proxy of the number of firms associated to the growing information and communication sector (ICT). For our comparison, we trace data on the presence of private and state-owned museums and theatres as a proxy for conventional cultural richness as opposed to previous studies (e.g. Boschma and Fritsch, 2009; Breznitz and Noonan, 2014; Falck *et al.*, 2009, 2011; Polèse, 2012), while trying to capture relevant subcultural elements by drawing on data about self-employed artists, publicists and authors, as well as the number of independent music labels, vegan restaurants and the coverage of alternative practitioners.

Music is a part of self-expression, and has always been a voice of protest and subculture (Nogic and Riley, 2007). Thus, the presence of independent music labels may be an appropriate indicator for vibrant subcultural life. Independent labels compensate market failures since they publish music for small and avant-garde niche markets that are commercially uninteresting for major labels. Usually, when they have proved their potential for the big mainstream audience, music bands switch to larger labels that have the financial power to boost their careers.

Figures 6.1 and 6.2 compare the impact of independent music labels, as a symbol for subculture, vs. the influence of the number of museums, as a proxy for formal cultural amenities, across our data sample of 69 of the largest cities in Germany for both entrepreneurial and creative activity. Both scatter plots

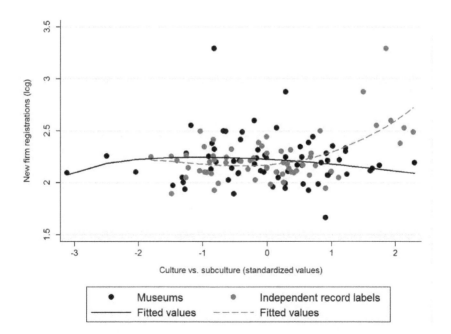

Figure 6.1 New venture creation and independent music record labels.

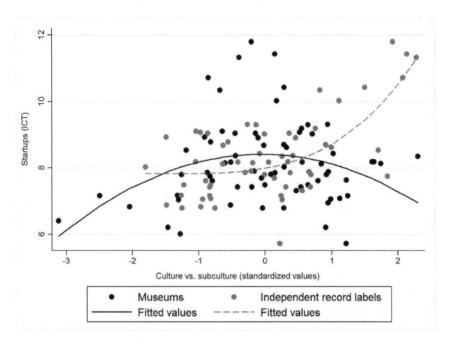

Figure 6.2 Start-up activity and independent music record labels.

indicate that there seems to be a positive effect of rising independent music on both outcomes. However, for the number of museums, the impact does not seem to be very clear – demonstrating an inverse U-shape for creativity outcomes and an almost negligible or slight negative linear relationship between formal culture and entrepreneurship outcomes.

Not surprisingly, Figure 6.3 and Figure 6.4 show similar results. For our comparison, we trace data from federal health insurance (Künstlersozialkasse, KSK) for artists on city level. Artists, including musicians, actors, painters, writers or publicists, have always lived bohemian lifestyles that inspire people and give places a unique cultural spirit (Florida, 2002; Markusen, 2006). However, Figures 6.1 and 6.2 support Florida's (2002, 2014) theory. For entrepreneurship activity which is simply measured by the number of firm registrations, we observe a moderate relationship. In contrast, when treating creative capacity, i.e. number of start-ups associated with ICT, as an outcome we observe a strong positive linkage. In line with previous work, we assume that each type of entrepreneurship activity needs special configurations towards its ecosystem; this includes cultural amenities as well as technical infrastructure. In the case of subculture, we suggest that the presence of a vivid subculture seems to be more important when it comes to start-ups than conventional venturing.

Originally started as a subcultural countermovement, veganism has recently enjoyed popularity across Europe and the US. Unlike vegetarianism, vegan diet

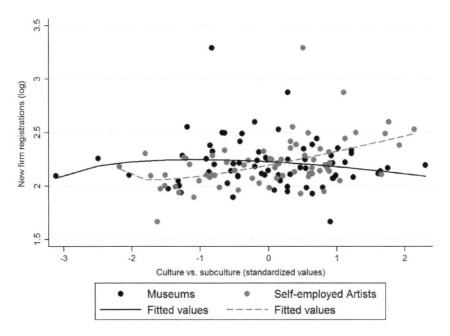

Figure 6.3 New venture creation and self-employed artists.

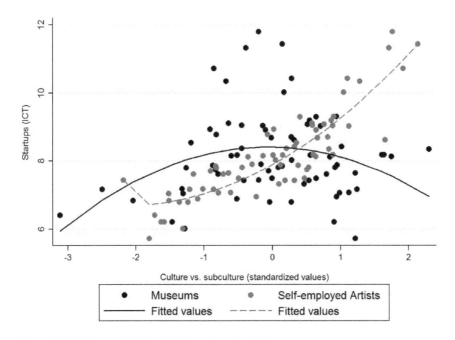

Figure 6.4 Start-up activity and self-employed artists.

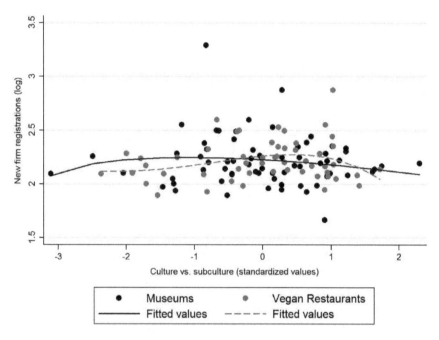

Figure 6.5 New venture creation and vegan restaurants.

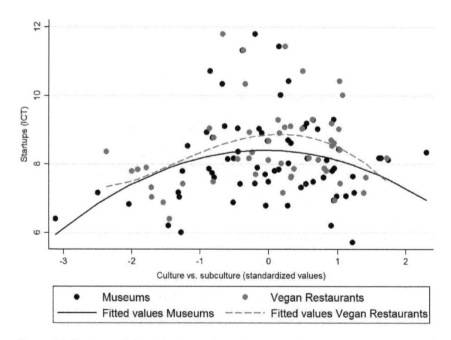

Figure 6.6 Start-up activity and vegan restaurants.

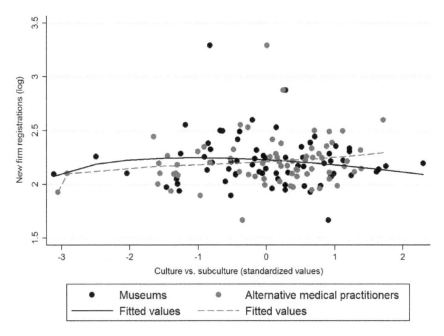

Figure 6.7 New venture creation and alternative medical treatment.

philosophy refuses any kind of animal products for nutrition and often even for clothing. Nowadays, the veggie movement seems to have reached the cultural mainstream. Canteens, cafeterias and even commercial airlines all offer special meals for vegetarians and recently also vegans. The recent survey of YouGov and The Institute for Opinion Polls Allensbach (IfD) (2015) reports that over 10 per cent of Germans are vegetarian while almost 2 per cent are vegan. In order to measure the local importance of subcultural life, we deploy data on the number of vegan restaurants that have been registered with PETA.

However, scatters simply display poor differences between vegans and both conventional new venture creation and start-up growth: Regarding conventional venture activity, the effect of vegan restaurants seems to be negligible. However, for creativity outcomes there seems to be a slight inverse U-shaped link indicating that there might be a kind of threshold effect. However, interpretation is difficult.

Finally, we draw on data regarding practitioners of alternative medicine as a measure of local subculture. Since the 1980s, a healthy and sustainable lifestyle has emerged as a key ingredient for a modern good life and is no longer solely associated with sports enthusiasts, either middle or upper class. Thus, health care, beauty and wellness services garnered a great reception and turned into highly profitable and promising markets. Alternative methods of treatment, such as ancient Chinese medicine, acupuncture or au naturel treatment also enjoy increasing popularity (Barnes, Powell-Griner, McFann, and Nahin, 2004; Eisenberg *et al.*, 1998; Tindle, Davis, Phillips, and Eisenberg, 2005). However, compared

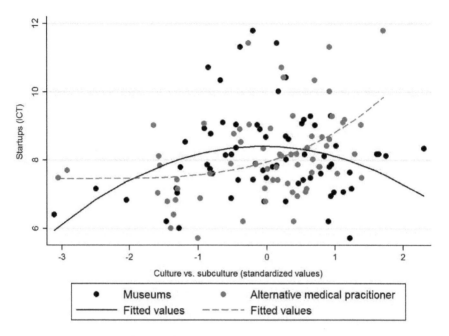

Figure 6.8 Start-up activity and alternative medical treatment.

with conventional school medicine, alternative methods of treatment still remain subcultural (Tindle *et al.*, 2005). Thus, drawing on data on the number of practices offering naturopathy seems to be a reasonable proxy for measuring the presence of subcultural milieus.

Figure 6.8 shows a similar picture compared with previous plots. Two key insights can be revealed. First, as in all other dimensions, the impact of alternative medicine varies with outcomes, thus, showing that it has a clear and strong influence on start-up activity associated with ICT, but only a slight influence on conventional business creation.

Conclusion and discussion

We observe large variations in the supply and allocation of entrepreneurial activity across countries, regions, locations and time. Over the past 40 years, research has found various sources that explain these differences ranging from economic, technological, demographic and institutional factors (Verheul et al., 2002; Wennekers, 2006). Recently, scholars have re-discovered the role of culture in shaping a sound environment for entrepreneurship. Culture is seen as a multi-facet institution that influences social and personal perceptions of life, creativity, market opportunities and risks. It shapes the way we learn from each other and inspires us to be critical and open-minded towards new ideas or our willingness to improve old ones – all essential ingredients for entrepreneurial orientation and behaviour. The purpose of this chapter is to critically review recent literature of culture within the field of entrepreneurship and creativity studies.

We have also attempted to introduce a complementary perspective that, we believe, has only been poorly discussed previously. Therefore, we put the role of subcultures at the centre of our attention and argue that social and economic innovation has always been pushed by a pioneering subgroup of "creative destructors" that share values and beliefs that are different from the culture establishment or mainstream. Thus, rather than studying culture as a whole, it might be more promising to take a closer look at subcultures and their influence on entrepreneurship scenes. We argue that entrepreneurs, and also team members of entrepreneurial firms, are not necessarily the focus group of traditional investments in culture such as opera, theatres, or museums. Thus, we believe that such investments will not necessarily attract and shape new venture creation. Rather, we believe that new venture creation and subcultures are two sides of the same medal – the localized myth of spirit and creativity, but also the individual power and drive just "to be different and do something".

Our descriptive statistics first offer very intuitive evidence and reveal two key insights. First, the impact of "mainstream" cultural attainment against subculture varies with measures of entrepreneurship. That is, both formal as well as subculture has a stronger impact on start-ups (ICT industries) than on conventional entrepreneurial activity, i.e. all firm registrations regardless of industries. Second, there seems to be an inverse U-shaped effect of cultural attainment, whereas subculture is always positively associated with ICT start-up growth.

Thus, considering subculture rather than culture might be a promising frontier in research on entrepreneurship ecosystems and guiding urban and regional planners in establishing a beneficial and sound environment for entrepreneurs and people that get creative.

However, implications for politics may be crude. While investment in mainstream culture is fairly easy, such as subsidizing ticket prizes, investment in new buildings and hiring stars, this could not be done easily in subcultures. It is one main characteristic that subcultures are creating by themselves without hierarchies and political wisdom. Thus, one implication for politics could be to create an area or breeding ground where subcultures could increase and grow up. Like the famous statement of the former mayor of Berlin who once pointed out: "Berlin is poor but sexy" (Audretsch and Lehmann, 2016, p. 44).

References

Acemoglu, D., Robinson, J. A. and Woren, D. (2012). *Why nations fail: The origins of power, prosperity and poverty* (Vol. 4). New York: Crown Business.

Acs, Z. J., Arenius, P., Hay, M. and Minniti, M. (2004). *Global entrepreneurship monitor.* London, UK, and Babson Park, MA: London School and Babson College.

Acs, Z. J. and Szerb, L. (2007). Entrepreneurship, economic growth and public policy. *Small Business Economics*, *28*(2–3), 109–122.

Acs, Z., Audretsch, D. B., Lehmann, E. E. and Licht, G. (2016). National systems of entrepreneurship. *Small Business Economics*, *46*(4), 527–535.

Adler, P. S. and Kwon, S.-W. (2002). Social capital: Prospects for a new concept. *Academy of Management Review*, *27*(1), 17–40.

Ahuja, G. (2000). Collaboration networks, structural holes, and innovation: A longitudinal study. *Administrative Science Quarterly*, *45*(3), 425–455.

Ahuja, G. and Katila, R. (2001). Technological acquisitions and the innovation performance of acquiring firms: A longitudinal study. *Strategic Management Journal*, *22*(3), 197–220.

Akçomak, I. S. and Ter Weel, B. (2009). Social capital, innovation and growth: Evidence from Europe. *European Economic Review*, *53*(5), 544–567.

Altinay, L. (2008). The relationship between an entrepreneur's culture and the entrepreneurial behaviour of the firm. *Journal of Small Business and Enterprise Development*, *15*(1), 111–129.

Andersson, M. and Koster, S. (2011). Sources of persistence in regional start-up rates – Evidence from Sweden. *Journal of Economic Geography*, *11*(1), 179–201.

Aoyama, Y. (2009). Entrepreneurship and regional culture: The case of Hamamatsu and Kyoto, Japan. *Regional Studies*, *43*(3), 495–512.

Audretsch, D. B. (2015). *Everything in its place: Entrepreneurship and the strategic management of cities, regions, and states*. Oxford: Oxford University Press.

Audretsch, D. B. and Belitski, M. (2013). The missing pillar: The creativity theory of knowledge spillover entrepreneurship. *Small Business Economics*, *41*(4), 819–836.

Audretsch, D. B. and Feldman, M. P. (2004). Knowledge spillovers and the geography of innovation. *Handbook of Regional and Urban Economics*, *4*, 2713–2739.

Audretsch, D. B. and Keilbach, M. (2008). Resolving the knowledge paradox: Knowledge-spillover entrepreneurship and economic growth. *Research Policy*, *37*(10), 1697–1705.

Audretsch, D. B. and Lehmann, E. E. (2005). Does the knowledge spillover theory of entrepreneurship hold for regions? *Research Policy*, *34*(8), 1191–1202.

Audretsch, D. B. and Lehmann, E. E. (2016). *The seven secrets of Germany: Economic resilience in an era of global turbulence*. Oxford: Oxford University Press.

Autio, E. and Acs, Z. J. (2007). Individual and country-level determinants of growth aspiration in new ventures. *Frontiers of Entrepreneurship Research*, *27*(19), Article 2.

Barnes, P. M., Powell-Griner, E., McFann, K. and Nahin, R. L. (2004). *Complementary and alternative medicine use among adults: United States, 2002*. Paper presented at the Seminars in Integrative Medicine.

Barrutia, J. M. and Echebarria, C. (2010). Social capital, research and development, and innovation: An empirical analysis of Spanish and Italian regions. *European Urban and Regional Studies*, *17*(4), 371–385.

Basu, A. and Altinay, E. (2002). The interaction between culture and entrepreneurship in London's immigrant businesses. *International Small Business Journal*, *20*(4), 371–393.

Begley, T. M. and Tan, W.-L. (2001). The socio-cultural environment for entrepreneurship: A comparison between East Asian and Anglo-Saxon countries. *Journal of International Business Studies*, *32*(3), 537–553.

Beugelsdijk, S. and Smulders, S. (2003). Bridging and bonding social capital: Which type is good for economic growth, in W. Arts, J. Hagenaars and L. Halman, L. (eds), *The cultural diversity of European unity, findings, explanations and reflections from the European values study*. Leiden: Brill, pp. 147–184.

Beugelsdijk, S. and Van Schaik, T. (2005a). Differences in social capital between 54 Western European regions. *Regional Studies*, *39*(8), 1053–1064.

Beugelsdijk, S. and Van Schaik, T. (2005b). Social capital and growth in European regions: An empirical test. *European Journal of Political Economy*, *21*(2), 301–324.

Boschma, R. A. and Fritsch, M. (2009). Creative class and regional growth: Empirical evidence from seven European countries. *Economic Geography*, *85*(4), 391–423.

Bosma, N., Acs, Z. J., Autio, E., Coduras, A. and Levie, J. (2008). Global Entrepreneurship Monitor. Link: http://www.gemconsortium.org/report/47107. Accessed 24 August 2016.

Bourdieu, P. (2011). The forms of capital. (1986), in I. Szeman and T. Kaposy (eds), *Cultural theory: An anthology*. Oxford: Wiley-Blackwell, pp. 81–93.

Breznitz, S. M. and Noonan, D. S. (2014). Arts districts, universities, and the rise of digital media. *The Journal of Technology Transfer*, *39*(4), 594–615.

Brockhaus, R. H. and Horwitz, P. (1986). The psychology of the entrepreneur. *Entrepreneurship: Critical Perspectives on Business and Management*, *2*, 260–283.

Burt, R. S. (2000). The network structure of social capital. *Research in Organizational Behavior*, *22*, 345–423.

Caragliu, A., Del Bo, C. and Nijkamp, P. (2011). Smart cities in Europe. *Journal of Urban Technology*, *18*(2), 65–82.

Chell, E. (2008). *The entrepreneurial personality: A social construction*, London: Routledge.

Clark, G. M. T. (2013). *Europe's cities in a global economy: Trends, challenges and opportunities*. Paper presented at the Global Cities Initiative, London.

Clifton, N. and Cooke, P. (2009). Creative knowledge workers and location in Europe and North America: A comparative review. *Creative Industries Journal*, *2*(1), 73.

Coleman, J. S. (1988). Social capital in the creation of human capital. *American Journal of Sociology*, *94*, S95–S120.

Coleman, J. S. (1994). *Foundations of social theory*. Cambridge, MA: Harvard University Press.

Cooke, P., Clifton, N. and Oleaga, M. (2005). Social capital, firm embeddedness and regional development. *Regional Studies*, *39*(8), 1065–1077.

Cooke, P. and Wills, D. (1999). Small firms, social capital and the enhancement of business performance through innovation programmes. *Small Business Economics*, *13*(3), 219–234.

Curran, W. (2007). "From the frying pan to the oven": Gentrification and the experience of industrial displacement in Williamsburg, Brooklyn. *Urban Studies*, *44*(8), 1427–1440.

Curran, W. (2010). In defense of old industrial spaces: Manufacturing, creativity and innovation in Williamsburg, Brooklyn. *International Journal of Urban and Regional Research*, *34*(4), 871–885.

Cushing, R., Florida, R. and Gates, G. (2002). When social capital stifles innovation. *Harvard Business Review*, *80*(8), 20.

Da Rin, M., Di Giacomo, M. and Sembenelli, A. (2011). Entrepreneurship, firm entry, and the taxation of corporate income: Evidence from Europe. *Journal of Public Economics*, *95*(9), 1048–1066.

Dakhli, M. and De Clercq, D. (2004). Human capital, social capital, and innovation: A multi-country study. *Entrepreneurship and Regional Development*, *16*(2), 107–128.

Davidsson, P. (1995). Culture, structure and regional levels of entrepreneurship. *Entrepreneurship and Regional Development*, *7*(1), 41–62.

Davidsson, P. and Wiklund, J. (1997). Values, beliefs and regional variations in new firm formation rates. *Journal of Economic Psychology*, *18*(2), 179–199.

Davidsson, P. and Wiklund, J. (2001). Levels of analysis in entrepreneurship research: Current research practice and suggestions for the future. *Entrepreneurship Theory and Practice*, *25*(4), 81–100.

Denzau, A. T. and North, D. C. (1994). Shared mental models: Ideologies and institutions. *Kyklos*, *47*(1), 3–31.

Dhoest, A., Malliet, S., Haers, J. and Segaert, B. (2015). *The borders of subculture: Resistance and the mainstream.* New York: Routledge.

Eisenberg, D. M., Davis, R. B., Ettner, S. L., Appel, S., Wilkey, S., Van Rompay, M. and Kessler, R. C. (1998). Trends in alternative medicine use in the United States, 1990–1997: Results of a follow-up national survey. *Jama, 280*(18), 1569–1575.

Falck, O., Fritsch, M. and Heblich, S. (2009). Bohemians, human capital, and regional economic growth, *International Journal of Urban and Regional Research, 32*, 548–564.

Falck, O., Fritsch, M. and Heblich, S. (2011). The phantom of the opera: Cultural amenities, human capital, and regional economic growth. *Labour Economics, 18*(6), 755–766.

Feldman, M. P. and Audretsch, D. B. (1999). Innovation in cities: Science-based diversity, specialization and localized competition. *European Economic Review, 43*(2), 409–429.

Fleming, L. and Marx, M. (2006). Managing creativity in small worlds. *California Management Review, 48*(4), 6.

Florida, R. (1995). Toward the learning region. *Futures, 27*(5), 527–536.

Florida, R. (2003). Entrepreneurship, creativity, and regional economic growth, in D. Hart (eds), *The emergence of entrepreneurship policy*, Cambridge: Cambridge University Press, pp. 39–58

Florida, R. (2002). *The rise of the creative class and how it's transforming work, leisure, community and everyday life.* New York: Basic Books.

Florida, R. (2013). The learning region, in Acs, A. J. (ed.), *Regional innovation, knowledge and global change*, New York: Routledge, pp. 231–244.

Florida, R. (2014). The creative class and economic development. *Economic Development Quarterly, 28*(3), 196–205.

Florida, R., Mellander, C. and Stolarick, K. (2008). Inside the black box of regional development – human capital, the creative class and tolerance. *Journal of Economic Geography, 8*(5), 615–649.

Fritsch, M. and Wyrwich, M. (2012). The long persistence of regional entrepreneurship culture: Germany 1925–2005 (June 2012). DIW Berlin Discussion Paper No. 1224. Available at SSRN: http://ssrn.com/abstract=2111984. Accessed 24 August 2016.

Fukuyama, F. (2001). Social capital and civil society. *Third World Quarterly, 22*(1), 7–20.

Gabe, T. M. (2011). The value of creativity. *Handbook of Creative Cities.* New York: Edward Elgar Publishing, pp. 128–145.

Gartner, W. B. (1990). What are we talking about when we talk about entrepreneurship? *Journal of Business Venturing, 5*(1), 15–28.

Ghio, N., Guerini, M., Lehmann, E. E. and Rossi-Lamastra, C. (2015). The emergence of the knowledge spillover theory of entrepreneurship. *Small Business Economics, 44*(1), 1–18.

Glaeser, E. L. and Gottlieb, J. D. (2006). Urban resurgence and the consumer city. *Urban Studies, 43*(8), 1275–1299.

Glaeser, E. L., Gyourko, J. and Saiz, A. (2008). Housing supply and housing bubbles. *Journal of Urban Economics, 64*(2), 198–217.

Glaeser, E. L., Kolko, J. and Saiz, A. (2001). Consumer city. *Journal of Economic Geography, 1*(1), 27–50.

Glaeser, E. L., Rosenthal, S. S. and Strange, W. C. (2010). Urban economics and entrepreneurship. *Journal of Urban Economics, 67*(1), 1–14.

Granovetter, M. S. (1985). Economic action and social structure: The problem of embeddedness. *American Journal of Sociology, 91*(3), 481–510.

Hansen, M. T. (1999). The search-transfer problem: The role of weak ties in sharing knowledge across organization subunits. *Administrative Science Quarterly, 44*(1), 82–111.

Hauser, C., Tappeiner, G. and Walde, J. (2007). The learning region: The impact of social capital and weak ties on innovation. *Regional Studies*, *41*(1), 75–88.

Hebdige, D. (1995). Subculture: The meaning of style. *Critical Quarterly*, *37*(2), 120–124.

Henckel, D., Besecke, A., Zahn, A., Godel, B., Herkommer, B. and Eichhorst, C. (2008). *Creative class in Berlin*. Berlin: TU Berlin.

Hofstede, G. (1993). Cultural constraints in management theories. *The Academy of Management Executive*, *7*(1), 81–94.

IfD, 2015, Allensbacher Kurzbericht – Veggie Day: In der Bevölkerung halten sich Zustimmung und Ablehnung in etwa die Waage, www.ifd-allensbach.de.

Isenberg, D. J. (2011). The entrepreneurship ecosystem strategy as a new paradigm for economic policy: Principles for cultivating entrepreneurship. *Presentación ante el Instituto de Asuntos Internacionales u Europeos*.

Jacobs, J. (1970). *The economy of cities*, New York: Random House

Knack, S. and Keefer, P. (1997). Does social capital have an economic payoff? A cross-country investigation. *The Quarterly Journal of Economics*, *112*(4), 1251–1288.

Knack, S. and Zak, P. J. (2003). Building trust: Public policy, interpersonal trust, and economic development. *Supreme Court Economic Review*, *10*, 91.

Krueger Jr, N. F. (2003). The cognitive psychology of entrepreneurship, *Handbook of entrepreneurship research*, New York: Springer, pp. 105–140.

Landry, C. (2008). *The creative city: A toolkit for urban innovators*. Sterling: Dunstan House.

Landry, R., Amara, N. and Lamari, M. (2002). Does social capital determine innovation? To what extent? *Technological Forecasting and Social Change*, *69*(7), 681–701.

Langley, R. (1993). Cultures and organizations: Software of the mind, by Geert Hofstede, *Human Resource Development Quarterly*, *4*(3), 319–325.

Lee, S. Y., Florida, R. and Acs, Z. J. (2004). Creativity and entrepreneurship: A regional analysis of new firm formation. *Regional Studies*, *38*(8), 879–891.

Lehmann, E. E. and Seitz, N. (2016). Freedom and innovation: A cross-country analysis forthcoming in *Journal of Technology Transfer*, doi: 10.1007/s10961-016-9478-3.

Lehmann, E. E. and Menter, M. (2015). University-industry collaboration and regional wealth, *The Journal of Technology Transfer*, doi: 10.1007/s10961-015-9445-4

Leutner, F., Ahmetoglu, G., Akhtar, R. and Chamorro-Premuzic, T. (2014). The relationship between the entrepreneurial personality and the Big Five personality traits. *Personality and Individual Differences*, *63*, 58–63.

Lin, N. (2002). *Social capital: A theory of social structure and action*. Cambridge: Cambridge University Press.

Lin, N., Cook, K. S. and Burt, R. S. (2001). *Social capital: Theory and research*. New York: Transaction Publishers.

Mack, E. and Mayer, H. (2015). The evolutionary dynamics of entrepreneurial ecosystems. *Urban Studies*, 1–16, doi:10.1177/0042098015586547

Markusen, A. (2006). Urban development and the politics of a creative class: Evidence from a study of artists. *Environment and Planning A*, *38*(10), 1921.

Maskell, P. (2001). Towards a knowledge-based theory of the geographical cluster. *Industrial and Corporate Change*, *10*(4), 921–943.

Maskell, P. and Malmberg, A. (1999). Localised learning and industrial competitiveness. *Cambridge Journal of Economics*, *23*(2), 167–185.

McClelland, D. C. (1965). N achievement and entrepreneurship: A longitudinal study. *Journal of Personality and Social Psychology*, *1*(4), 389–392.

McFadyen, M. A. and Cannella, A. A. (2004). Social capital and knowledge creation: Diminishing returns of the number and strength of exchange relationships. *Academy of Management Journal, 47*(5), 735–746.

Morgan, G. and Ren, X. (2012). The creative underclass: Culture, subculture, and urban renewal. *Journal of Urban Affairs, 34*(2), 127–130.

Morgan, K. (2007). The learning region: Institutions, innovation and regional renewal. *Regional Studies, 41*(S1), S147–S159.

Morris, M. H., Davis, D. L. and Allen, J. W. (1994). Fostering corporate entrepreneurship: Cross-cultural comparisons of the importance of individualism versus collectivism. *Journal of International Business Studies,* 65–89.

Mueller, S. L. and Thomas, A. S. (2001). Culture and entrepreneurial potential: A nine country study of locus of control and innovativeness, *Journal of Business Venturing, 16*(1), 51–75.

Nahapiet, J. and Ghoshal, S. (1998). Social capital, intellectual capital, and the organizational advantage. *Academy of Management Review, 23*(2), 242–266.

Nogic, A. and Riley, A. (2007). "So what is the normal amount of bumps allowed in a pit?": Some empirical notes on the (re) construction of a youth music subculture/scene. *Journal of Youth Studies, 10*(3), 317–329.

Obschonka, M., Stuetzer, M., Gosling, S. D., Rentfrow, P. J., Lamb, M. E., Potter, J. and Audretsch, D. B. (2015). Entrepreneurial regions: Do macro-psychological cultural characteristics of regions help solve the "knowledge paradox" of economics? *PloS One, 10*(6), e0129332.

Paci, R. and Marrocu, E. (2013). Knowledge assets and regional performance. *Growth and Change, 44*(2), 228–257.

Peck, J. (2005). Struggling with the creative class. *International Journal of Urban and Regional Research, 29*(4), 740–770.

Polèse, M. (2012). The arts and local economic development: Can a strong arts presence uplift local economies? A study of 135 Canadian cities. *Urban Studies, 49*(8), 1811–1835.

Porter, M. E. (1998). *Clusters and the new economics of competition.* Boston, MA: Harvard Business Review.

Porter, M. E. (2000). Location, competition, and economic development: Local clusters in a global economy. *Economic Development Quarterly, 14*(1), 15–34.

Portes, A. (2000). Social capital: Its origins and applications in modern sociology, in Lesser, E. L. (ed.), *Knowledge and social capital.* Boston, MA: Butterworth-Heinemann, pp. 43–67.

Putnam, R. D. (1995). Bowling alone: America's declining social capital. *Journal of democracy, 6*(1), 65–78.

Rauch, A. and Frese, M. (2007a). Born to be an entrepreneur? Revisiting the personality approach to entrepreneurship, in J. Baum, M., Frese and R. Baron (eds), *The psychology of entrepreneurship.* London: Psychology Press, pp. 41–65.

Rauch, A. and Frese, M. (2007b). Let's put the person back into entrepreneurship research: A meta-analysis on the relationship between business owners' personality traits, business creation, and success. *European Journal of Work and Organizational Psychology, 16*(4), 353–385.

Reynolds, P. D., Hay, M., Bygrave, W. D., Camp, S. M. and Autio, E. (2000). Global entrepreneurship monitor. *Executive Report.*

Reynolds, P. D., Hay, M. and Camp, S. M. (1999). *Global entrepreneurship monitor.* Kansas City, Mo.: Kauffman Center for Entrepreneurial Leadership.

Rossberger, R. J. and Krause, D. E. (2012). *When it comes to innovation, culture matters!: Empirical evidence on the relationship between national culture and innovate outcomes.* Paper presented at the International Conference on Human Resource Management and Professional Development for the Digital Age (HRMandPD). Proceedings.

Roth, F. (2009). Does too much trust hamper economic growth? *Kyklos, 62*(1), 103–128.

Saxenian, A. (1996). Beyond boundaries: Open labor markets and learning in Silicon Valley, in M. B. Arthur and D. Rousseau (eds), *The boundaryless career: A new employment principle for a new organizational era*, Oxford: Oxford University Press, pp. 23–39.

Schneider, G., Plümper, T. and Baumann, S. (2000). Bringing Putnam to the European regions on the relevance of social capital for economic growth. *European Urban and Regional Studies, 7*(4), 307–317.

Schouten, J. W. and McAlexander, J. H. (1995). Subcultures of consumption: An ethnography of the new bikers. *Journal of Consumer Research, 22*(1), 43–61.

Schumpeter, J. (1934/2003). *Theorie der wirtschaftlichen Entwicklung.* Heidelberg: Springer.

Scott, A. J. (1999). The cultural economy: Geography and the creative field. *Media, Culture and Society, 21*(6), 807–817.

Scott, A. J. (2006). Creative cities: Conceptual issues and policy questions. *Journal of Urban Affairs, 28*(1), 1–17.

Sexton, D. L. and Bowman, N. (1986). The entrepreneur: A capable executive and more. *Journal of Business Venturing, 1*(1), 129–140.

Shane, S. (1993). The effect of cultural differences in perceptions of transactions costs on national differences in the preference for international joint ventures. *Asia Pacific Journal of Management, 10*(1), 57–69.

Smith, P. A., Bakker, M., Leenders, R. T. A., Gabbay, S. M., Kratzer, J. and Van Engelen, J. M. (2006). Is trust really social capital? Knowledge sharing in product development projects. *The Learning Organization, 13*(6), 594–605.

Spence, J. T. (1985). Achievement American style: The rewards and costs of individualism. *American Psychologist, 40*(12), 1285.

Storper, M. and Scott, A. J. (2009). Rethinking human capital, creativity and urban growth. *Journal of Economic Geography, 9*(2), 147–167.

Sun, H. (2009). A meta-analysis on the influence of national culture on innovation capability. *International Journal of Entrepreneurship and Innovation Management, 10*(3–4), 353–360.

Tijssen, R. J. and Van Wijk, E. (1999). In search of the European Paradox: An international comparison of Europe's scientific performance and knowledge flows in information and communication technologies research. *Research Policy, 28*(5), 519–543.

Tindle, H. A., Davis, R. B., Phillips, R. S. and Eisenberg, D. M. (2005). Trends in use of complementary and alternative medicine by US adults: 1997–2002. *Alternative Therapies in Health and Medicine, 11*(1), 42.

Torjman, L. and Worren, J. (2010). Building Canada's culture of entrepreneurship: Surebet to startup survival. *Open Source Business Resource*, (February 2010). http://timreview.ca/article/323.

Tura, T. and Harmaakorpi, V. (2005). Social capital in building regional innovative capability. *Regional Studies, 39*(8), 1111–1125.

Urban, B. (2006). Entrepreneurial self-efficacy in a multicultural society: Measures and ethnic differences. *SA Journal of Industrial Psychology, 32*(1), 2–10.

Uzzi, B. and Spiro, J. (2005). Collaboration and creativity: The small world problem. *American Journal of Sociology, 111*(2), 447–504.

Verheul, I., Wennekers, A. R. M., Audretsch, D. B. and Thurik, A. R. (2002). An eclectic theory of entrepreneurship, in D. B. Audretsch, A. R. Thurik, I. Verheul and A. R. M. Wennekers (eds), *Entrepreneurship: Determinants and policy in a European–US comparison*. Boston/Dordrecht: Kluwer Academic Publishers, pp. 11–81.

Wagner, J. and Sternberg, R. (2004). Start-up activities, individual characteristics, and the regional milieu: Lessons for entrepreneurship support policies from German micro data. *The Annals of Regional Science*, *38*(2), 219–240.

Waldinger, R. D. (1997). Social capital or social closure? Immigrant networks in the labor market. *The Ralph and Goldy Lewis Center for Regional Policy Studies*. Working Paper, http://escholarship.org/uc/item/06z6331r.

Weber, M. (1905/2002). *The protestant ethic and the spirit of capitalism: And other writings*. London: Penguin.

Weber, M. (1930). *The protestant ethic and the spirit of capitalism*. Trans. Talcott Parsons, Anthony Giddens. London: Unwin Hyman.

Wennekers, A. R. M. (2006). *Entrepreneurship at country level: Economic and non-economic determinants*. PhD thesis, Erasmus Research Institute of Management (ERIM), Rotterdam.

Wennekers, S., Thurik, R., van Stel, A. and Noorderhaven, N. (2007). Uncertainty avoidance and the rate of business ownership across 21 OECD countries, 1976–2004. *Journal of Evolutionary Economics*, *17*(2), 133–160, doi: 10.1007/s00191-006-0045-1.

Westlund, H. and Adam, F. (2010). Social capital and economic performance: A meta-analysis of 65 studies. *European Planning Studies*, *18*(6), 893–919.

Whiteley, P. F. (2000). Economic growth and social capital. *Political Studies*, *48*(3), 443–466.

Zhao, H., Seibert, S. E. and Lumpkin, G. T. (2010). The relationship of personality to entrepreneurial intentions and performance: A meta-analytic review. *Journal of Management*, *36*(2), 381–404.

Zheng, W. (2010). A social capital perspective of innovation from individuals to nations: Where is empirical literature directing us? *International Journal of Management Reviews*, *12*(2), 151–183.

7 Creativity management

Causation, effectuation and will

Jean-Alain Héraud and
Emmanuel Muller

Introduction

The aim of this chapter is to revisit the *effectuation* theory as a way to introduce creativity in innovation management. We consider this issue in the context of our experience of analysing innovation policies and observing creative behaviours in the field of project management and business consultancy.

The background idea of this chapter is the fact that the theory of innovation is incomplete as long as the idea of creativity is not introduced in the analysis of the cognitive processes involved. In the economic literature, the process of innovation is too often considered as pure knowledge creation (recombination of existing pieces of knowledge, etc.). In management science, as well as in economic geography or in sociology of innovation, it is clear that ingredients other than knowledge are needed: entrepreneurship, serendipity, capability to develop visions, etc.

For a clearer understanding of such issues, it is worthwhile returning first to the seminal works of classical authors such as Marshall, Schumpeter, Hayek . . . in order to see what sort of concept of creativity is present in their understanding of innovation: what are the real characteristics of the "entrepreneur"? Is it an individuality or an element in a complex system? To what extent can we build a representation of radical innovation within a systemic framework, i.e. to "endogenize" creativity in the economy and managerial practices? From the classical and recent literature on inventive and innovative activities, we develop an approach based on three components of creativity: novelty, relevance and "will" factor.

Saras Sarasvathy's contributions will be a key element in our analysis. We want to address the following question in particular: does the effectuation approach to project management introduce the creative dimension that is lacking in the causal approach (of the theories as well as the managerial practices and public policies)? To what extent can business management concepts (and recommendations) be applied to the management of cities or technological clusters? Another field of application we want to explore is the process of creativity and innovation within and between firms in knowledge intensive business services (KIBS). This case specifically illustrates the connection between individual and collective creativity.

Innovation, creativity and the "will" factor

Innovation has largely been theorized in the economic literature as a process of *knowledge production*. In management sciences, other elements are taken into account such as *entrepreneurship*. As a matter of fact, Josef Schumpeter, the great author in economics whose seminal contribution is based on the concept of *entrepreneur*, developed (at least implicitly) a managerial approach to innovation. We will start by reviewing the "mainstream" modelling of innovation as a purely cognitive mechanism and the evolutionist approach, before returning to Schumpeter and looking for an entrepreneurial approach to innovation that is endogenous to the economic system. In this perspective, other traditions of economic thought are also interesting to consider, from Marshall to Hayek. In terms of policy recommendations (innovation policies), it is important to benefit from a realistic view of economic development and the actors who implement creative changes. We therefore conclude this section with a tentative definition of creativity at various levels, from the individual to the territory, and we underline the existence of non-cognitive aspects (linked to personality, local culture, etc.).

Limitations of purely economic approaches to innovation and growth

Arrow's microeconomic *learning by doing* as well as the macroeconomic approach to endogenous growth (initiated by Kenneth Arrow and developed by Paul Romer) were typical contributions to the *economics of knowledge*. Evolutionary economics is also to a large extent focused on the analysis of knowledge mechanisms: see Nathan Rosenberg's *learning by using* or Bengt-Åke Lundvall's *learning by interacting* for an understanding of innovation systems. Such analyses have given fundamental insights, but something is still lacking: the role of the entrepreneur. Mainstream economic models as well as standard evolutionary models do not explain the *intentional* sources of variety that lead to creative endeavours.

As an engine of innovation, the new growth theory considers *knowledge externalities*: spillovers from knowledge producers to knowledge users that play a role of "public good", i.e. a free, inexhaustible factor explaining continuous economic change. Growth is therefore an endogenous phenomenon of the macroeconomic system (real progress in a macroeconomic representation), but the mechanism is spontaneous and automatic. In this description, there is no place for the visionary and risk-taking actors that carry the creative projects at microeconomic level, and how those actors react to the macroeconomic setting, how they can be helped by appropriate structural policies, etc. The only innovation policy to be considered on the basis of such a model is based on public research and public education.

Standard evolutionary approaches also fail to explain the real mechanisms of creative development. The biological metaphor provides an endogenous theory of idea selection in the global system, but no precise description of the ideation process. The knowledge recombination at the basis of idea creation in such models does not express any economic intentionality. It is a model of selection/diffusion of new ideas (in the economy at global level or within firms and other microeconomic organizations through a process of routine selection). Here again, there is no role for entrepreneurs. What are the policy recommendations? Mainly to foster connections between actors in order to produce, at random, more variety in knowledge recombination. This is a possible approach to national systems of innovation or cluster policies, but not very precise and topical.

Managerial approaches complete the analysis by underlining the entrepreneurial dimension of innovation. Qualitative economic change in the long run is driven by actors who are not mainly characterized by their capability to produce and combine knowledge *per se*, but by their visionary attitude and their individual qualities in terms of leadership, resilience, positive risk preference, strategic abilities, etc. The rising economic and managerial literature on *creativity* helps to complement the knowledge-based approach of innovation and to re-focus our understanding of innovation processes (and diffusion mechanisms) on individual and collective *entrepreneurship*.

Towards a systemic theory of entrepreneurship

It is impossible to design a theory of innovation in the framework of economic models only constructed around the principles of equilibrium and optimization, and without taking into account the systemic context of knowledge creation. When Alfred Marshall tried to explain the emergence of the organizational innovation of the first industrial revolution, he built the concept of agglomeration economies and introduced the idea of local culture (*the ideas are in the air*), leading to the very relevant idea that innovation depends on actors that are embedded in concrete territories (the space of innovation systems is not neutral and knowledge is localized). The Marshallian model is also *out of equilibrium*, at least for certain stages of the competition process. This process starts with initial heterogeneity in firms' situations and behaviours; knowledge externalities then enable the firms that are performing less well to imitate the most performing ones and the system can reach an equilibrium. In a way, the Marshallian representation is an evolutionary model of situated innovation.

The Hayekian tradition also brought interesting insight into the economic mechanisms that neoclassical models reduce to a simplistic view of markets working within the overarching principle of equilibrium. As carefully analysed by Kirzner (1997), the Austrian concept of dynamic competitive process implements a tendency to equilibrium – a state that is never met by the system and cannot really be calculated because of constant changes in the environment (products, tastes, technologies, etc.). More precisely, the mechanism called *entrepreneurial discovery* constantly increases mutual awareness among market participants concerning the nature and qualities of goods as well as their price. It is a "discovery process" in the sense that it is "systematically pushing back the boundaries of sheer ignorance" (Kirzner, 1997, p. 62). We are in a situation of Knightian uncertainty and not of computable risk: the entrepreneurs' action consists of finding interesting profit opportunities by a sort of search process that is not the one described in standard search theory (revealing information everybody tries to find in the same race for knowledge) but a process of discovering "unthought-of knowledge" (ibid., p. 73). In the rather realistic view of the economy of modern Austrian theorists, the rivalrous process of competition is not about revealing information people are aware was lacking until now. Participating in the market is always (at least to a certain extent) an entrepreneurial attitude, and this attitude is called "entrepreneurial alertness", which means receptiveness to available (but hitherto overlooked) opportunities.

If the Austrian tradition develops, as described above, a concept of economic creativity that looks fundamentally embedded in the general economic process (entrepreneurial discovery dynamics of markets), what about the Schumpeterian concept of innovation? Building on the legacy of Marshall, Joseph Schumpeter introduced a model of economic evolution by considering that the heterogeneity (variety) of the system is constantly reproduced through the introduction of innovative products, processes, and organizations by creative actors he called "entrepreneurs". But the role of entrepreneurship in his theory of innovation varied and the post-Schumpeterian literature makes a difference between the so-called "Schumpeter.1" and "Schumpeter.2" visions (see, for instance, Burton, 2001). The representation of an innovative economy is not yet fully developed in the first book, the *Theory of economic development* (Schumpeter, 1911), since the source of creativity is exogenous: the emergence of creative actors is not explained within the economic system. In the Schumpeter.2 type of works (*Business cycles* in 1939 or *Capitalism, socialism and democracy* in 1942), the entrepreneur is not "an outsider who enters the economic system guided by animal spirit" (Antonelli, 2015, p. 111), but a creative manager. Product innovation is the result of the strategies of incumbent corporations, no longer the exogenous creation of new entrepreneurs. It seems to be a model of "routinized innovation" that is quite different from the original idea of breakthrough solo-entrepreneurship.

Antonelli (2015) analyses a less known but important text of Schumpeter (*The creative response in economic history*, 1947) which is a sort of late synthesis of Schumpeter.1 and Schumpeter.2 visions. Here the innovator is neither a creative alien nor a perfectly planned manager optimizing R&D programmes, but an economic actor facing unexpected changes in his/her environment (markets of products or factors, technological revolution . . .) and forced to make a *creative response*. Here the entrepreneur (whatever the size of the firm: entrepreneur or *intrapreneur*) is facing a challenge because of an initial situation of disequilibrium: a mismatch between a firm's present situation and the global context. This is the first ingredient for innovation, a systemic tension impacting individual actors. The second ingredient in Schumpeter's view is the support that the system can offer to the potential innovator: knowledge externalities and the competencies of a variety of agents that are able to complement the innovator's endeavour. The innovator appears as an entrepreneur who is embedded in a complex system through at least two mechanisms, an incentive scheme and a supporting context. This last Schumpeterian vision looks more complete and very realistic (and also suggests a rich variety of systemic policy recommendations by taking into account the precise context of potential innovations). Innovation does not appear as a pure alchemy of knowledge. Entrepreneurship is situated at the core of innovation and at the same time, the entrepreneurial mechanism looks endogenous.

We consider Cristiano Antonelli's recent paper on Schumpeter (1947) to be very useful. It not only helps to better understand the late Schumpeter's view, but also to respond at least partially to the remarks made by researchers in management who find "major deficiencies" in the Schumpeterian approach to entrepreneurship and innovation (Burton 2001). The systemic concept of *creative response* in Schumpeter (1947) complements the ideas of "entrepreneurial alertness" and "diffused entrepreneurship" proposed by John Burton. It is also coherent with seminal contributions like those of Amabile and Khaire (2008) who analysed how, in an economic regime characterized by permanent innovation, competitive organizations are forced to manage creatively and out of equilibrium, implementing a sort of collective entrepreneurship. In such a context, the entrepreneur is no longer an isolated individual, his/her creativity is revealed and modulated by interaction within a large system of actors and institutions. We have, for instance, illustrated this observation by studying the role of specific creative individuals (Knowledge Angels) within and between organizations (Muller, Zenker and Héraud,, 2015). Such studies try to implement the Woodman *et al.* (1993) project of designing a *theory of organizational creativity*: understanding creative behaviour in complex social systems.

How creativity, in various forms, contributes to innovation

As discussed above, innovation and entrepreneurship imply knowledge but cannot be reduced to pure knowledge processes. For Sternberg (2008), the most innovative managers are not the most learned, but those who are particularly able to design new representations of the world (possible futures), to think differently (out of existing codes and cognitive routines), and at the same time, be pragmatic enough to transform those new ideas into relevant economic and/or social achievements. We would like to remind using Sternberg's definition that creativity has two dimensions:

- The new idea must be original, unexpected. This is the *novelty* factor.
- It must also be appropriate, i.e. useful, adaptive concerning task constraints. This is the *relevance* factor.

Building on the literature on entrepreneurship, we need to add another fundamental ingredient of innovation: the willingness to change the world. Without such a desire, visions are just dreams. Creative ideas, whatever their level of novelty and relevance, will not change the world without the implication of actors who have the desire to implement them. We do not want to analyse their motivation here: reputation and/or money and/or generosity . . . The important issue is that some individuals or organizations have the desire to act and commit themselves to a specific creative goal.

We will call this the *will* factor.

Now, what is interesting is to look at the precise way the three factors are distributed. Let us take first the example of research as a creative activity. In *scientific* domains, creative achievement is called *discovery*. The latter is sometimes attributed to exceptionally gifted individuals (e.g. Albert Einstein) who were able to "think out of the box" (*novelty* of the model of relativity as compared with current Newtonian physics), for *relevant* knowledge constructions (explaining the trajectory of the planet Mercury or the finite speed of light), and were keen to convince the scientific community (*motivation* for publishing).

Einstein is quite a fascinating model in the history of science, but he is not a paradigm. In the case of Louis Pasteur, the situation looks rather more complex because his discoveries also implied *technological* issues and therefore *invention* (vaccination, fermentation processes, etc.) and even directly *innovation* (for public health, industrial applications, etc.). In fact, Pasteur was not only a scientist, but also an entrepreneur, a manager and a lobbyist . . . In his ventures – and adventures – he was definitely not alone: numerous people and institutions contributed to those applications of nascent microbiology. Many scientific success stories are like Pasteur's: creativity appears multi-faceted, multi-actor, deeply embedded in a complex system of *distributed intelligence*. By "intelligence" we mean not only knowledge but also entrepreneurial strategy – and both are distributed, not individual.

In scientific, technological or commercial (innovation) fields, we generally observe a complex distribution of the three basic factors: the initial *idea* is maybe formulated by some prominent person, but the cognitive revolution was prepared by the "community of knowledge" this person belonged to. The *relevance* of the idea is tested by the same community and often by other communities as well. The *will* factor is mostly carried by the discoverer, inventor or innovator, but the latter needs partners, allies, advisors, business angels and actors that are able and willing to share the vision.

The analysis can be extended to other fields of creativity. Cohendet *et al.* (2014) present the example of communities of artists that prepared the revolutions of the twentieth century such as cubism in Paris. Picasso and Braque had the merit of forging the specific wording and writing a manifesto, but that crucial phase of formalization did in fact finalize a whole maturation process within an artistic community, in a specific location. In a similar way, Cohendet *et al.* (2010) document the contemporary emergence of new paradigmatic forms in creative industries in Montreal.

Referring to Cohendet and his HEC Montreal school of creativity, there are three phases in the ideation process:

1   The *spark*, expressing the breaking of the rules, and leading to the redaction of a manifesto. This phase takes place in an *epistemic community*. The latter is characteristic of artistic and scientific communities whose vocation is to produce original forms of knowledge.

2   The *social construction* (referring to Callon, 1999) where the issue is to share the idea with other circles of people and institutions. This phase takes

place in the concerned epistemic community (codebook writing), but it is in relationship with other communities (of *practice*) because relevance is needed in a larger sense.

3   The *landing*: redesigning the idea in order to make it understandable within current economic and social structures. This means an important effort in terms of relevance and the recruitment of institutional actors such as firms, public organisms, local administrations, etc. Of course, markets are targeted in this phase, either for addressing existing demand or for market creation.

In the preceding analysis we observe the whole range of actors contributing to the creativity in terms of novelty and relevance. We also want to address our third factor: where is the will factor manifested in the production of the breakthrough innovation?

Beyond the process of ideation: the entrepreneurial spirit

During the first phase of the process presented by Cohendet *et al.* (2010), it is evident that the role of individuals is essential: Pasteur, Edison, Picasso, Leary, Zuckerberg, etc. are not only gifted persons, they have a vision and want to change the world (or the representation of the world).

In the second phase, we observe a very complex collective construction, involving chains of translation and adaptation of ideas among and between several communities. But here again, motivation is essential because the transformation of cognitive routines is always painful and costly. Learning a new language is a real investment (exploration) to be made before it can be used (exploitation). Many individuals and organizations must contribute to this process and the final success is not possible without their commitment. This is the reason why certain breakthrough innovations can only start in certain places where cultural parameters in particular play an important role.

As mentioned above, Alfred Marshall explained the emergence of major innovations in specific geographical locations such as Manchester, and he considered the local culture as a fundamental factor of success provided by the system to the entrepreneurs. All the literature on industrial districts, innovative milieus and other sorts of clusters prove the importance of specific entrepreneurial spirit. The specialization of territories can of course be explained by static factors (natural resources, infrastructures, labour cost, etc.) but cognitive assets must also be introduced. A part of the latter territorial characteristics belongs to the field of knowledge economics (educational level and training experience of the population, localized knowledge spillovers from universities, etc.), but a part cannot be explained without taking into consideration the general entrepreneurial spirit (in Max Weber's sense) and the specific "appetite" of the local population for certain forms of ventures. Héraud (2011), for instance, explains how common cultural roots and historical heritage influence the way creative cities can develop in specific territories (even across contemporary national borders and linguistic barriers in the case under consideration).

In the third phase (the *landing*), the role of institutions and organizations is essential. Small and large firms play their natural role in the development, organization of production and access to markets. Smaller ones are sometimes more flexible for exploring breakthrough innovative solutions. Larger ones can help to drive innovation thanks to their position as global players and access to financial means. But in every case, nothing will be possible without the personal enthusiasm of individuals in these organizations. Since creative ventures are not measurable in terms of calculated risk (no previous experience implies that there is no objective probability function to assess the financial returns), it is not a banker's job to invest in such projects as Schumpeter would say . . . For policy makers, the situation is similar: the ordinary bureaucrat or politician will not accept projects in a situation of radical uncertainty, but visionary people in local governments can convince their hierarchy or the electors and taxpayers to support a revolutionary idea that could become the icon of the region.

The complex mechanisms of territorial creativity we have described here, associating the individual personality with institutional and organizational settings, is more realistic than the Florida (2002) model of exogenous development through the attraction of "talented" individuals. We must look at the creative behaviour in complex social systems to achieve better policy and management recommendations.

Analysing creativity with the help of the *effectuation* theory of entrepreneurship

As underlined in the previous section, innovation is an economic creative phenomenon that cannot be seriously considered in a theoretical model based on the principle of equilibrium. Consequently, methodological tools derived from the optimization paradigm are very difficult to apply. The assumption of perfect knowledge is not applicable, even using probabilistic functions, since innovation is more *uncertain* (F. Knight's concept of radical uncertainty) than *risky* (in the sense of computable risks analysed in finance and insurance). Furthermore, the principle of "methodological individualism" does not apply, the actor of innovation being embedded in a complex systemic setting. Innovation – at least radical innovation – is by definition out of equilibrium and looks more like the emerging property of the system than the result of individual behaviour in a purely rational framework.

Starting from such a premise, the approach initiated by Herbert Simon and James March seems to be the only relevant theoretical framework. Innovation is an *exploratory* activity of organizations and the only sort of optimization we can consider is to look for an acceptable compromise between exploration and exploitation, as described in March (1991) when presenting the organizational *ambidexterity*. On the basis of the great forerunners of the theory of organization, Sarasvathy (2001a) proposed an interesting view of entrepreneurial activities (project management) in situations where ordinary linear methods such as optimization of means in view of a given goal cannot apply. The relevant approach, effectuation, is a good model for describing the action of the entrepreneur facing a radical strategic change.

The effectuation theory represents a paradigmatic shift in the way we understand entrepreneurship as well as other forms of radically creative activities within (and between) existing organizations. It is, nevertheless, at a "nascent" or "intermediate" stage of development as showed in Perry, Chandler and Markova (2012) and needs more empirical texts. We hope to contribute a little to this research agenda with our studies of KIBS and Knowledge Angels (see section Analysing creativity with the help of the *effectuation* theory of entrepreneurship).

The basic definitions of causation and effectuation are as follows. In causal approaches to project management, *"the focus is on achieving a desired goal through a specific set of given means. Causation invokes search and selects tactics and underlies most good management theories"*. In the effectuation framework, *"the focus is on using a set of evolving means to achieve new and different goals. Effectuation evokes creative and transformative tactics. Effectual logic is the same name given to heuristics used by expert entrepreneurs in new venture creation"* (Read *et al.*, 2011, p. 7).

As summarized by Perry *et al.* (2012, p. 839), the effectuation *vs* causation approach is about: (1) starting with the means instead of the goals; (2) focusing on affordable loss instead of expected returns; (3) emphasizing strategic alliances and pre-commitments instead of competitive analysis; (4) leveraging environmental contingencies instead of exploiting pre-existing knowledge and; (5) seeking to control an unpredictable future instead of trying to predict a risky future. The first two points are shared with models of research in creative organizations such as Mintzberg's *adhocracies*. The fourth point is related to the notion of *serendipity*. The third and fifth principles are the same as in foresight methods like the French school of *prospective* (perspective futures developed in the 1950s by Gaston Berger, the founder of future studies in France; see also Godet, 1994).

Approaching the global rationale of creative activities

We have to underline some logical link between two pairs of opposites in the following traditions: *exploitation/exploration* (March, 1991); *effectuation/causation* (Sarasvathy, 2001a); *novelty/relevance* (Sternberg, 2008). In exploration activities, the aim is to discover and analyse novelties, and the philosophy of action is effectuation. In exploitation activities, assessing relevance is at the core of the business and the philosophy of action is causation. We sum up some characteristics of both worlds in Table 7.1: the world of optimization rationality and the world of breakthrough creativity.

In the *causation* process, which is the regular way to set up a project, the goal is well known and therefore the effect is given. Means are organized so that the goal can be achieved in the most efficient way. Causal links must be clear; then if the problem is clearly formulated and if we have good knowledge of the lines of causality (technological knowledge), we find an optimal solution. This is the typical "problem-solving" attitude of the engineer. The cognitive process is linear in a sense that the sequentiality between the design of goals and the design of the means is respected. The engineering solution, if it is possible, will be perfect in the sense that it expresses absolute rationality. Of course, its development can be less perfect because other elements interfere during the implementation phase.

In the *effectuation* process, goals and means are not sequentially organized. Very often, goals are learned along the discovery path of the project. The general direction is known, but aims are not fixed at the beginning in full detail. In fact, the project starts more from the existing means (assets, knowledge, competences . . .) and the process explores possible futures on the basis of rare means. Nobody looks for completeness in the set of solutions proposed at the beginning of the project. Ideas will appear throughout the process and rational validation is more a question of experimentation than initial calculation.

It is clear that the *effectuation* approach to project management recalls Mintzberg's observations concerning the unstructured nature of incremental decision-making and the *garbage can* model of Cohen, March and Olsen (1972). It is the typical context of research organizations . . . and certainly less typical of mining industries. Nevertheless, in every organization, exploration phases are needed in certain periods of their life and in these phases, managers start decision-making from the solution side as well as from the problem side.

Sarasvathy's model does not confront two strictly alternative ways of organizing a project. It is mainly a theoretical distinction. In concrete projects, the two philosophies of action can be simultaneously or sequentially used. Nevertheless, it is very important to bear this distinction in mind. Creative management, particularly in deliberate exploration programmes, must be mainly inspired by the effectuation model. With our conception of creativity founded on three factors (novelty, relevance, will) in mind, we must now compare the attributes of both philosophies of action.

Effectuation as a creative attitude

Contrasting causation and effectuation, Sarasvathy (2001a, p. 251) looks first at different aspects of the decision-making selection criteria. Causation processes help to choose between means of achieving a given effect, whereas effectuation processes help to choose between possible effects that can be created with

Table 7.1 Some characteristics of the world of optimization rationality and the world of breakthrough creativity

Optimization rationality: Exploitation, relevance, causation	Breakthrough creativity: Exploration, novelty, effectuation
realization	imagination
implementation	design
efficiency	curiosity
planning	serendipity
selection	variation

given means. Therefore, in the first case, a relative *novelty* is expected in terms of technical or organizational ideas, but in the second case, the stress on *novelty* is more important since it aims at future goals. Another aspect mentioned by the author is the type of outcome: market share in existing markets (through competitive strategies) in the case of causation; new markets (created through alliances and other corporative strategies) in the case of effectuation. The degree of novelty is obviously higher in the second case.

The selection criteria are based on expected return in the causation processes and more on affordable loss or acceptable risk in the effectuation processes. Therefore, the *relevance* factor seems to be stricter in the causation than in the effectuation approach.

With regard to the *will* factor, the effectuation processes, require very strong commitment by the leaders. The underlying logics concerning the future are the following: on the causation side, the organization focuses on the *predictable* aspects of an uncertain future; on the effectuation side, the focus is on the *controllable* aspects of an unpredictable future. Predictability is about knowledge; control expresses more willingness and entrepreneurial spirit. Sarasvathy also underlines the fact that the ideal context of the two project management approaches is natural situations for causation and human action for effectuation.

Implications for management and policies

This section attempts, in a first step, to examine the dimensions constituting the will factor with regard to innovation and creativity. In a second step, we try to characterize the will factor as a creative response through the three dimensions. We illustrate the issue with various examples corresponding to different scales of observation. In their concluding comments, Woodman *et al.* (1993) explain that theorists tend to avoid multilevel research because of their theoretical orientations and because of methodological problems in aggregating data across different levels of analysis. We modestly consider separately individual creativity with Knowledge Angels, group creativity with start-ups and organizational creativity at the territorial policy level. We, nevertheless, bear in mind that these levels are in constant interaction – in the sense of Woodman's interactionist perspective on creativity.

What can be learned about the will factor from a management perspective?

Considering the elements discussed in the two previous sections, we argue that the issue raised by the will factor can be helpful for a better understanding of creativity and innovation management. Here, management can be understood in a broader perspective, i.e. not restricted to companies (as will be shown in the next sub-section).The will factor needs to be analysed under several aspects: the desire to act (whatever positive and negative outcomes may occur), the decision-making process of actors who are not "maximizers" in the sense of mainstream economics and finance, and the types of human competencies that fit this model.

As underlined in the beginning of this chapter, the economics of innovation cannot just be an application of the economics of knowledge, and the creative response of the entrepreneur (in Schumpeter's sense) involves desire and imagination. Therefore, the core dimensions of what we call the "will factor" involve specific cognitive attitudes more or less linked to tacit knowledge (competencies), but also the meta-knowledge of decision-making in very incomplete information and, above all, the desire for action. The creative organization is characterized by structures and rules that support the *imagination*, but also the *willingness to act*. Bureaucracy and vertical organizations are, of course, bad contexts if the aim is to support an entrepreneurial spirit among the members of the organization.

Pushing employees out of their comfort zone is sometimes given as a recipe for boosting creativity; it can work if applied to optimistic and resilient persons, but could lead to negative outcomes such as burnout syndrome if the organization still remains hierarchical at the same time (applying strict controls and asking for short run results). In the framework of Sarasvathy's approach to entrepreneurship, we find a better understanding of the role of constraints. Indeed, "studies show that constraints increase creativity" (Read *et al.*, 2011), but the "entrepreneurial response" is mainly a way to use contingencies as resources (ibid., p. 144). This idea is typical of the *effectuation* attitude where contingencies help to trigger a creative process through the exploration of possible futures on the basis of this new information. To sum up the possible reactions: contingencies could be felt as obstacles or at least unnecessary elements (events, information, people . . .) blocking the actor's way if the latter is particularly passive or stubborn; it induces an adaptive response within existing cognitive framework if the actor is reactive; it can push the actor out of his/ her box (the "heroic response"); or can be used "to leverage the revised box in a new direction" (ibid., p. 144). In Sarasvathy's view, even negative contingencies can be turned into positive forces in a person's entrepreneurial career, and this does not necessarily mean that a strategy must be started completely from scratch, but that the new situation can be considered an additional source of inspiration.

Creative people have a strong preference for freedom and not necessary a strong one for money. As expressed in Sarasvathy (2001b), where she develops her theory of "entrepreneurship as economics with imagination", the entrepreneurial spirit is not about optimizing ROI under stochastic conditions, but about freedom: "it is not that the entrepreneur loves risk, it is just that he loves independence (or some other value) more than security" (op. cit. p. 5). With regard to decision-making, it is important to focus imagination on potential success, and not on the objective of a lower probability of failure. The author explains that the creative entrepreneur accepts to "plunge" into a world of success and failures. Conversations with entrepreneurs show that "the entrepreneurial experience is composed of the temporal stream of the varying degrees of success and failures" (ibid). Therefore, intrapreneurship becomes "the art of learning to outlive failures and cumulate successes over time" (ibid). Creative persons can have some sort of fun in overcoming difficulties, because it is part of the game. The worst for them is life without surprises – obviously not the theoretical vision of the rational economic agent in mainstream economics.

Table 7.2 Managing the will factor, some examples of incentives and hindrances

Core dimensions affecting the will factor:	Incentives	Hindrances
(1) Desire & determination	• Pushing out of the comfort zone	• Hierarchy and bureaucracy
	• Freedom over money	• Money over freedom
	• Diversity of the population (co-workers)	• Corporate clones and cast system
(2) Decision-making	• Right to fail	• Employee of the month
	• *Garbage can* model	• Benchmarking
(3) Competencies & skills	• Experimentation and fun factor	• Need for hyper specialization
	• Curious minds	• Rational minds

In light of the previous analyses, we propose the following description of the management of creative activities. The creative attitude is analysed through three dimensions affecting the "will factor": (i) desire and determination; (ii) decision-making and; (iii) competencies and skills. Table 7.2 displays some keywords linked to these issues, opposing the situations and characteristics that seem supporting (incentives) or unfavourable (hindrances) to the creative attitude. Here we try to illustrate Woodman's interactionist perspective: *"creativity is the complex product of person's behavior in a given situation. The situation is characterized in terms of the contextual and social influences that either facilitates or inhibit creative accomplishments"* (Woodward et al., 1993, p. 294).

In the following, we intend to provide illustrations of what can be observed if one considers the introduction of the will factor as one of the keys of creativity management. In order to show the broad spectrum of possibilities, we deliberately choose heterogeneous examples at different scales, i.e. individuals, companies and territorial levels.

Successes and failures help to explore the potentialities, rather than exploiting known recipes or benchmarking external experiences. James March's (1991) model of *ambidexterity* expresses the idea of finding the relevant balance of exploration and exploitation in the management of organizations. The creative firm needs a minimum of exploration and therefore needs some diversity in the human resources (but only rational minds, but also curious minds and a variety of competencies). Globally, the success/failure trajectory of the entrepreneur described by Sarasvathy looks like a "garbage can" model of activity in the sense of March, not the perfectly planned strategy.

Transposing at various scales the effects of the will factor as a creative response

We aim here to describe the role of entrepreneurial spirit in the three dimensions of the will factor for the innovative response at three levels of the system:

the individual level with the Knowledge Angels; the firm's level with start-ups; and the macro level of innovation policies.

The first example deals with *Knowledge Angels* (cf. Table 7.3). According to Muller *et al.* (2015), Knowledge Angels can be defined as creative individuals fostering innovations in KIBS (Knowledge-Intensive Business Services). As such, Knowledge Angels display several key characteristics that are different from what is commonly observed in "average" employees.

Knowledge Angels are (or may be) specific individuals who:

- typically act as consultants (but not necessarily exclusively);
- may have the talent to "sense" (feel, detect) things before they happen, or make them happen (from the subjective point of view of an external observer);
- make a difference in the way knowledge is created, organized and flows within the firm and between the firm and its partners.

Table 7.3 shows some characteristics of Knowledge Angels (KA) from the perspective of the constitutive dimensions of the will factor as a creative response leading to innovation. The dimension of desire and determination is of course strongly developed in these creative people, but it is particularly oriented towards collective activities: in the interviews, the KAs expressed their willingness to support co-workers. Since the success/failure process is not a 0–1 variable, as described in Sarasvathy (2001b), and because assuming the unavoidable constrained sequence of positive and negative experiences is part of the entrepreneurial game, the "fun factor" appears essential.

Decision-making is generally far from the linear model of causation: intuition and imaginative conceptual leaps are typical cognitive elements of the process. The most required competences are curiosity and multi-expertise since KAs must connect different worlds in order to create almost improbable new crossings of ideas, as in Arthur Koestler's model described by Cohendet (2016). Koestler coined the term *"bisociation"* in order to make a distinction between

Table 7.3 The case of Knowledge Angels as an illustration of individual level

Core dimensions affecting the will factor:	KNOWLEDGE ANGELS
(1) Desire & determination	• Search for freedom and self-expression of own creativity • Willingness to support co-workers • Fun factor
(2) Decision making	• Based on intuition, visions and conceptual leaps • Strong interaction with other people, patchwork of opinions
(3) Competencies & skills	• Curiosity and multi-expertise • Ability to navigate between different worlds (separated epistemic communities) and convince conceptually distant partners

"the routine skills of thinking on a single 'plane', as it were, and the creative act, which (. . .) always operates on more than one plan" (op. cit. p. 621). KAs constantly cross planes.

Let us now consider the firm's level with an analysis of the creative characteristics of the start-ups. According to the abundant literature devoted to start-ups and innovation (see, for instance, Freeman and Engel, 2007), it is possible to put forward some elements corresponding to the three dimensions we use for characterizing the will factor as a vector of creative response (see Table 7.4).

The willingness to create new artefacts and processes of services is of course at the basis of such firms. Survival is a constant issue, and therefore long run planning in a causation approach is not possible. Decision-making is mainly a trial and error process. Start-ups must also make their choice under market pressure and in a situation of scarcity of resources (the typical effectuation process following Sarasvathy's description). Such firms strongly rely on individual values, and their governance cannot be easy adapted to the norms of modern financial capitalism. Financing schemes are therefore very specific as well as the needed competences. Serendipity also plays an important role in terms of financing.

The third example focuses on a relatively recent development in policy making at territorial level (as opposed to national level). It concerns *smart strategies* and *entrepreneurial discovery processes* as strategies for regional development. The core idea of smart specialization urges the entrepreneurial forces of a region to take action and define the role of policy as that of a moderator (Foray, David and Hall, 2011). The wording "entrepreneurial discovery" seems to have been borrowed from Austrian economics and Hayek is quoted in Foray (2015, p. 25), but here, the precise meaning is the following: the entrepreneurial discovery process "is basically economic experimentation with new ideas", the latter coming to a great extent from scientific discoveries or technological inventions, but it is linked to the more general notion of "entrepreneurial knowledge": knowledge about market growth potential, potential competitors, and "the whole set of inputs and services required for launching a new activity" (ibid., p. 25).

Table 7.4 The case of start-ups as an illustration of company level

Core dimensions affecting the will factor:	START-UPS
(1) Desire & determination	• Willingness to create something new • Pushing forward things never made before • Survival
(2) Decision-making	• Trial and error • Choosing under high-market pressure and scarcity of resources
(3) Competencies & skills	• Entrepreneurship, especially ability to identify oneself in the created company • Ability to attract the right people and the right financial resources at the right time

The concept also underlines the idea of specialization: since regions cannot do everything in terms of developing science, technology and innovation, they have to focus on specific (carefully chosen) domains. In other words, regions should not try to imitate each other but develop distinctive areas of specialization and then strategically concentrate their policy efforts on those "smart specialization domains". In this respect, S3 (which now stands for Smart Specialization Strategies in European Commission slang) is examined in Table 7.5.

The will factor plays an important role in this territorial strategy. If properly understood, S3 regional exercises are not bureaucratic top-down analyses defining a priori opportunities and relative strengths, but interactive processes with local entrepreneurs. In this approach, the most interesting factor of potential creative development is the existence of people who have visions for the territory and are ready to invest their time, individual energy and economic means in new projects. These actors of territorial development are not necessarily pure internal actors; the important thing is to have a project *for* the territory. As underlined by Dominique Foray, starting an entrepreneurial discovery process is particularly crucial for regions that are not among the well-developed regional innovation systems and in this case it is often very relevant to link local innovation activities with big partners out of the territory. It helps avoid lock-in situations and helps to reshuffle the cards by allowing new combinations of resources.

The entrepreneurial discovery process means more than the selection of existing well-known technological or sectoral opportunities; it is an evolutionary mechanism with experiences spread across time in the same way as in the effectuation theory. Therefore, decision-making needs the willingness of individual action instead of bureaucratic and causal selection processes.

The administrative skills should be completely transformed because the issue here is to reveal potential entrepreneurs, help regional actors develop new forms of cooperation and create confidence and optimism. Such a catalytic role is the opposite of classical interventionist policy culture.

Table 7.5 S3 as an illustration of the regional level

Core dimensions affecting the will factor:	EU Smart Specialization Strategy
(1) Desire & determination	• Pushing forward new ways of territorial development • Avoiding lock-in situations and/or declining trends at regional level • Reshuffling the cards to allow new combinations of resources
(2) Decision-making	• Entrepreneurial discovery process (as intended by Foray *et al.*) • Evolutionary selection between techno-scientific and sector-related fields
(3) Competencies & skills	• Convincing the (mostly) regional actors to adopt new forms of cooperation • Creating confidence and policy support in the process of emergence of (mostly unexpected) ideas

Conclusion

In this chapter devoted to the analysis of creative management at various levels, we began by reviewing the classical theories concerning economic change and innovation in order to provide an endogenized framework explaining creativity as an emerging characteristic of complex systems. This complexity specifically arises through the interaction between different levels (how individuals are forced by the macrosystem to find an innovative response and how in return their behaviours transform the system) and different organizations (with the role of specific individuals able to carry and translate ideas between heterogeneous cognitive settings).

We have summarized several approaches of creativity from the (interdisciplinary) literature using a three-dimensional model: every act of creativity involves *novelty* and *relevance* of the basic idea, plus the *will* factor of the microeconomic actor who has to implement the project. The latter dimension is closely related to the notion of entrepreneurship. The *effectuation* theory, developed in the framework of entrepreneurship studies, helps us to understand the general philosophy and concrete procedures that are typical of creative ventures: firm's creation as well as innovative management of existing firms, or public policies such as territorial "smart specialization strategies". It is important for the understanding of the endogenous process of innovation to analyse the will factor not only as an individual phenomenon, but as the result of individual characteristics that interplay with environmental factors: organizational features, social routines, public policies . . .

By examining how the will factor is determined by structural, sociological and cultural patterns that either hinder or promote creativity, we hope to have provided some managerial and policy implications from the theoretical framework. Precise policy recommendations were not the aim of this chapter, but some general elements can be discussed, in the same perspective as Muller, Héraud and Zenker (2013) where we considered several instruments for innovation-driven regional policies. In creative public policies, as in creative firm management, a solution-oriented regular philosophy must be at least complemented by the problem-driven approach inspired by the effectuation theory. "Expecting the non-expected" is a more creative attitude than implementing planning procedures. The intrinsic motivation of creative individuals must not be spoiled by excessive financial incentives, controls and division of labour. The will factor is precious and accompanies the fun factor.

References

Amabile, T. M. and Khaire, M. (2008) "Creativity and the role of the leader", *Harvard Business Review*, 86(10): 100–112.

Antonelli, C. (2015) "Innovation as a creative response. A reappraisal of the Schumpeterian legacy", *History of Economic Ideas*, 23(2): 99–116.

Burton, J. (2001) "Innovation, entrepreneurship and the firm: A post-Schumpeterian approach", *International Journal of Entrepreneurship and Innovation Management*, 1(1): 1–21.

Callon, M. (1999) "Le réseau comme forme émergente et comme modalité de coordination", in M. Callon, P. Cohendet, N. Curien, J-M. Dalle, E. Eymard-Duvernay, D. Foray and E. Schenk (eds), *Réseau et coordination*, Paris: Economica, pp. 16–64.

Cohen, M. D., March, J. and Olsen J. P. (1972) "A garbage can model of organizational choice", *Administrative Science Quarterly*, 17: 1–25.

Cohendet, P. (2016) "Arthur Koestler. Aux origines de l'acte créatif: la bisociation", in Thierry Burger-Helmchen, Caroline Hussler and Patrick Cohendet (eds), *Les grands auteurs en management de l'innovation et de la créativité*. Cormelles-le-Royal: Editions EMS, pp. 615–625.

Cohendet, P., Grandadam, D. and Simon, L. (2010) "The anatomy of the creative city", *Industry and Innovation*, 7(1): 91–111.

Cohendet, P., Grandadam, D., Simon, L. and Capdevila, I. (2014) "Epistemic communities, localization and the dynamics of knowledge creation", *Journal of Economic Geography*, 14(5): 929–954.

Florida, R. (2002) *The rise of the creative class: And how it's transforming work, leisure, community and everyday life*. New York: Basic Books.

Foray, D. (2015) *Smart specialization. Opportunities and challenges for regional innovation policy*. London and New York: Routledge.

Foray, D., David, P. A. and Hall, B. H. (2011) "Smart specialization. From academic idea to political instrument, the surprising career of a concept and the difficulties involved in its implementation", Lausanne: *MTEI Working Paper*, École Polytechnique Fédérale de Lausanne, Management of Technology & Entrepreneurship Institute, College of Management of Technology.

Freeman, J. and Engel J. S. (2007) "Models of innovation: Startups and mature corporations", *California Management Review*, 50(1): 94–119.

Godet, M. (1994) *From anticipation to action. A handbook of strategic prospective*. Paris: UNESCO Publishing (col. "Future-oriented studies").

Héraud, J-A. (2011) "Reinventing creativity in old Europe: A development scenario for cities within the Upper Rhine Valley cross-border area", *City, Culture and Society*, 2: 65–73.

Kirzner, I. M. (1997) "Entrepreneurial discovery and the competitive market process: An Austrian approach", *Journal of Economic Literature*, 35: 60–85.

March, J. (1991) "Exploration and exploitation in organizational learning", *Organization Science*, 2(1): 71–87.

Muller, E., Héraud, J-A. and Zenker A. (2013) "Innovation, territories and creativity. Some reflections about usual and less usual instruments for innovation-driven regional policies", in T. Burger-Helmchen (ed.), *The economics of creativity. Ideas, firms and markets*. London and New York: Routledge, pp. 78–88.

Muller, E., ZenkerA. and Héraud, J-A. (2015) "Knowledge Angels: Creative individuals fostering innovation in KIBS – Observations from Canada, China, France, Germany and Spain", *Management International*, 19: 201–2018.

Perry, J. T., Chandler, G. N. and Markova, G. (2012) "Entrepreneurial effectuation: A review and suggestions for future research", *Entrepreneurship Theory and Practice*, 36(4): 837–861.

Read, S., Sarasvathy, S., Dew, N., Wiltbank, R. and Ohlson, A-V. (2011) *Effectual entrepreneurship*. London and New York: Routledge.

Sarasvathy, S. (2001a) "Causation and effectuation: Toward a theoretical shift from economic inevitability to entrepreneurial contingency", *Academy of Management Review*, 26(2): 243–263.

Sarasvathy, S. (2001b) "Entrepreneurship as economics with imagination", *Society for Business Ethics* http://www.effectuation.org/sites/default/files/research_papers/beq01-economics-imagination.pdf.

Schumpeter J. A. (1911, 1934) *The theory of economic development.* Cambridge, MA: Harvard University Press.

Schumpeter J. A. (1939) *Business cycles. A theoretical and statistical analysis of the capitalist process.* New York: McGraw-Hill.

Schumpeter J. A. (1942, 1950) *Capitalism, socialism and democracy.* New York: Harper and Brothers.

Schumpeter J. A. (1947) "The creative response in economic history", *Journal of Economic History*, 7(2): 149–159.

Sternberg, R. J (ed.) (2008) *Handbook of creativity.* Cambridge: Cambridge University Press.

Woodman, R. W., Sawyer, J. E. and Griffin, R. W. (1993) "Toward a theory of organizational creativity", *Academy of Management Review*, 93(18): 293–321.

8 Management of creativity in a large-scale research facility

Arman Avadikyan and Moritz Müller

Introduction

This chapter considers the case of a public science organization that builds on multiple communities, reaching outside the organization, for internal development of its generic technology and related applications. We describe the internal organizational structures and processes that facilitate knowledge differentiation and integration within the organization, and how community involvement varies according to the maturity of the community.

The issue is of general interest to innovation management. In fast-paced environments, the firm's long-term strategy is less about being in the right markets and more about the capability to generate creative and innovative solutions in existing as well as future markets (Grant, 1996). One promising avenue is to invest in a generic technology that allows for a broad spectrum of specific applications in various markets (Kim and Kogut, 1996). The development of generic technology as well as its applications by one firm alone is often neither desirable nor feasible. Instead, firms rely increasingly on external knowledge and efforts for technology development.

Communities are essential for this process. First, communities facilitate and govern collective knowledge processes as they generate its essential ingredients; in particular shared identities, common language and perspectives, and shared practice. Second, communities may be confined to organizational boundaries, but also span across organizations, or exist even without any formal organization. Therefore, communities help us to get a grip on knowledge creation processes beyond the organizational dichotomy (Håkanson, 2010).

The role of communities in external knowledge sourcing is widely acknowledged in the literature. Involvement of the user community has been found to be instrumental in internal innovation efforts (Hienerth *et al.*, 2014; von Hippel, 1976). External communities may even develop the technology on their own. For example, IBM assigned the development of its generic software, Eclipse, to an open source community, maintaining only one proprietary application (Spaeth *et al.*, 2010). While there are various accounts of cases in which external communities contribute to organizational creativity and innovation, most research focuses on the implications for business models (Chesbrough and Appleyard, 2007) and property rights (West, 2003; Henkel, 2006). Only a few studies investigate how organizations manage to leverage the creative potential of external communities and nearly all of them focus on a single community (mostly open source communities) (Franke and Shah, 2003; Lakhani and von Hippel, 2003; Schweisfurtha and Raasch, 2014; Colombo *et al.*, 2014). This chapter provides an account of how multiple external communities work together to drive technological development within the organization.

We investigate this issue for a public science organization that develops and runs a synchrotron; a large-scale generic technology platform with various (future) scientific applications. The skeleton of the case is as follows. The technological system is largely modular, and so is the organization. All organizational units are firmly embedded within external communities which drive continuous development of each module in the system (Avadikyan *et al.*, 2014; Hussler *et al.*, 2016). Since the parts are inter-connected, technological problems found in one part may trigger problem-solving activities in another part of the synchrotron, and internal organizational processes serve to integrate the needs and inputs across communities. We argue that it is the interplay of this triad – a modular technological system, a modular organization, and heavy involvement of multiple communities – which may serve as the basis for internal development of the system in the long term. The remainder of the chapter fleshes this argument out.

Creativity in science and technology

In this chapter we consider creativity as a collective knowledge creation process with a focus on technological development and scientific production (see, for example, the discussion of Fleming *et al.*, 2007). The following provides a short overview of how that perspective relates to the previous literature.

In management studies, creativity is often conceptualized as the creation of novel and useful ideas (Amabile, 1988; Burt, 2004). Creativity is of interest because it fuels the innovation process which is about the implementation of new ideas by organizations and their adoption by markets (Burger-Helmchen, 2013). Both creativity and innovation build on pre-existing elements such as ideas, a theory, a technology, perspectives, processes, methods, or traditions to create new outcomes. Novelty is thus never 'ex nihilo', but results from novel combinations among pre-existing elements. Considering all relevant elements as belonging to a body of knowledge gives rise to the theoretical idea that creativity is essentially a knowledge creation process in which extant pieces are re-combined to create new knowledge.

There is an ongoing debate regarding to what extent it is useful to consider the creative process as residing in the individual or rather in groups, organizations or other collectives. Influenced by psychology, management research first emphasized personal traits of creative individuals and asked which social context or situation could foster individual creativity (Amabile, 1988) – for example, the idea that a creative individual needs to have some freedom in what to aim at and how to arrive at creative outcomes. Another important ingredient for individual creativity, mentioned earlier on, is the interaction with other individuals in order to obtain new facts, knowledge and fresh perspectives which may be recombined in the creative process. Proponents of collective knowledge and creativity argue that the aggregate is more than the sum of its parts because the knowledge of individuals is integrated and extended through collective activity (see Nonaka *et al.*, 2000, for a review and Erden *et al.*, 2008, for more recent development).

Collective learning, however, is potentially subject to a trade-off concerning how much can be learned, on the one hand, and how efficiently it can be learned on the other. Social network research discusses how this trade-off relates to social interaction patterns. Coleman (1988) argues that recurrent interaction within close-knit groups of actors creates social capital – in the form of trust, shared language, and common perspectives – which makes inter-individual knowledge transfer and joint learning more efficient. However, due to the fact that agents in close-knit groups tend to be similar, creative outcomes tend to be less radical. Thus, actors holding a brokerage position, i.e. they reach out to socially distant actors that hold more different knowledge, may be more creative (Burt, 2004). Fleming (2007) suggests a further trade-off related to social structure. Based on an analysis of patents, he finds that inventors occupying brokerage positions produce more radical recombinations, while close-knit groups support their subsequent deployment. Several more recent papers have shifted the level of analysis to the network level supporting the general idea that knowledge recombination and social recombination are two sides of one coin (Börner *et al.*, 2004; Frigotto and Riccaboni, 2011). For example, Frigotto and Riccaboni (2011) compare the dynamics of co-author networks across four scientific sub-disciplines. They argue that social interaction patterns stabilize with the maturity of the sub-discipline. Consequently, organizations will pursue different community involvement strategies depending on the maturity of the targeted community (Hussler *et al.*, 2016).

The role of communities in organizational creativity and innovation became first visible through ethnographic studies of work practice in firms (Lave and Wenger, 1991; Orr, 1996). These studies triggered the insight that communities that engage in a common practice provide the context for collective learning and problem solving (Brown and Duguid, 1991). This way, communities facilitate knowledge creation and integration in the firm which is fundamental for organizational creativity (Grant, 1996; Hargadon and Bechky, 2006; Kogut and Zander, 1996). For example, communities provide their members with shared identities and a common language, which is instrumental for efficient communication and, hence, coordination (Kogut and Zander, 1996). Communities, however, are not necessarily confined by organizational boundaries (O'Mahony and Lakhani, 2011). And there is not a single but multiple communities within any larger organization. Consequently, within an open innovation context, management needs to consider multiple external communities as well. When the boundaries of the firm are blurred, organizational creativity becomes the capability to leverage community efforts and integrate knowledge across communities whose members are mostly outside the organization (Powell *et al.*, 1996).

This arguably abstract idea becomes more concrete in the case of technology platforms. There are plenty of examples of technology platforms, especially in IT. Any operating system, such as Microsoft Windows or Linux, is a technology platform that can be used to run various application programs. Similarly, smart phones constitute a platform for software applications. In the biotech industry, most small biotech companies build on a technology platform, be it a molecule that may serve as a carrier for various medical agents, or a specific method to cut and paste gene sequences. In particular, in high-tech industries, technology platforms and their applications are developed in collaboration. The most visible and extreme cases are probably open source platforms. Our case study is concerned with a synchrotron, i.e. a large-scale technology platform that may be used for multiple (future) scientific and technological applications (Merz and Biniok, 2010; Peerbaye and Mangematin, 2005; Robinson *et al.*, 2007). Such organizations are embedded in multiple external communities, creating an entire ecosystem that fuels its internal innovation dynamics (Avadikyan *et al.*, 2014). Therefore, the following case offers the opportunity to generate insights into the management of internal and external communities for the technological development of a generic technology and its applications.

The case of a synchrotron

Synchrotrons in science

A synchrotron is a generic research instrument with broad application scope (Shinn and Joerges, 2002; Shinn, 2005). At its simplest, a synchrotron is a large complex machine (about the size of a football field) that accelerates electrons to almost the speed of light to produce extremely bright radiation. This radiation feeds into various instruments to explore the physical and chemical properties of various materials and biological systems. Fields of application include, among others, biology and health, earth and environmental sciences, advanced materials, engineering and manufacturing, cultural heritage and archaeology as well as fundamental physics.

The broad spectrum of applications is made possible through a modular design. One central component, the accelerator, is physically connected to multiple application specific components called beamlines. The main function of the accelerator is to produce beam light. Electrons are injected into the accelerator where they reach the speed of light and emit radiation of a broad spectrum – from infrared to hard X-rays. Beamlines use the radiation to run scientific experiments. A beamline constitutes a genuine laboratory where various samples are prepared and analysed during experiments. Each beamline is specialized and designed according to a given wavelength domain and according to one or several experimental techniques. Thus, the generic technology offered by the synchrotron is adapted to the needs of various scientific (sub-)disciplines through differentiation of the beamlines.

Diversification of synchrotrons into new scientific applications was made possible by technological development of generic technology. The emergence of synchrotron radiation use dates back to the 1940s when a small community of scientists (physicians and chemists) discovered its value in exploring the structure of matter. Since then synchrotron radiation facilities have developed through successive generations. The latest are third generation synchrotrons built since the 1990s. They have achieved significant improvements and opened up new experimental possibilities. It was in this period that synchrotrons were developed as large user dedicated research facilities to support a rapidly growing and increasingly diversified user community.

As a research facility and experiment platform where science is made with leading edge instruments, a synchrotron is a place where scientific and technological activities and developments are inseparable (Simoulin, 2012; Hallonsten, 2009). Interactions between science and technology have been key for continuous development of the technology (for science-technology interactions see de Solla Price, 1984; Rosenberg, 1992). The development of the technology itself constitutes a creative process. On the other hand, the synchrotron is a scientific instrument used in the creative process 'science'. Creative processes at the synchrotron thus tend to produce both scientific as well as technological novelties.

Since the main mission of a synchrotron is to provide services to the scientific community, and synchrotron technology itself is developed within a scientific community, communities are naturally influential for its technological development. Collaboration within the larger worldwide synchrotron community has played a major role in the innovation dynamic. As noticed by Haensel (1994, p. 16) referring to the first three hard X-ray machines of the 3rd generation:

> Over the long run the three projects ran parallel and profited enormously from each other [. . .] There are numerous examples of worldwide cross-fertilization. [. . .] where the first steps have been done on one side of the ocean and the systematic development on the other.

Furthermore, external users from different scientific communities play a critical role in the emergence of new synchrotron applications. Users constitute a driving but also active force in the renewal and continuous innovation dynamics of synchrotrons (Simoulin, 2012; Hallonsten, 2009).

Case study data

We investigate the Soleil synchrotron, in operation since 2007. The case study has been conducted within a larger project called EvaRIO (Evaluation of Research Infrastructures in Open innovation and research systems), supported by the Infrastructure subprogram of the European Commission during the 7th Framework Programme. The project was led by Mme S. Wolff and jointly conducted by a team of researchers from the research laboratory BETA (Bureau d'Economie Théorique et Appliquée), University of Strasbourg. It aimed at providing an evaluation framework for large research infrastructures based on relatively broad case studies (EvaRIO, 2013a, 2013b, 2013c).

During the project, data on the synchrotron was gathered from various sources. We collected documents from and about Soleil. Furthermore, 25 semi-structured interviews with an average duration of 2 hours were conducted by at least two BETA researchers. In detail, we interviewed 8 members of the Soleil top management team, 6 beamline leaders and scientists, 2 instrumentation suppliers and 9 beamline users. Each interview was tape recorded and transcribed in full verbatim. We collected about 46 hours of recording time. Conversations over lunch and/or dinner provided us with more highly valuable information. For this chapter, we undertook a content analysis of the transcripts. The quotes cited in the following parts of the chapter are used to illustrate our findings.

Interview findings regarding user community involvement have been corroborated by a quantitative bibliometric analysis for two beamlines. For the analysis, we collected all peer-reviewed publications of external users and beamline scientists that have been published between 2005 (three years before inception of the synchrotron) and 2012 by Thomson Reuters' Web of Science. We extracted all publications individually for each scientist and verified for each publication that it had been correctly attributed. We categorized each paper as being based on research at the focal synchrotron, at another synchrotron, or whether no use was made of a synchrotron. In order to do so, a list of all publications involving the focal synchrotron was obtained from the focal synchrotron itself. Automated search of WoS fields was used to identify publications involving other synchrotrons. Information drawn from the papers includes the journal impact factor (to proxy the extent of creativity), co-authorships (to measure joint knowledge creation), and the scientific field of the journal (to measure the field of specialization of scientists). Concepts and measures are further explicated along with the analysis below.

Organizing technological development at the synchrotron

The technological architecture of the synchrotron is mirrored in its organization. The synchrotron is a loosely coupled modular system, in the sense that technological developments in one module tend to interact relatively little with developments in another module. Loose coupling allows for uneven technological development of individual components and hence for a relatively strong division of decision-making and knowledge (Sanchez and Mahony, 1996; Brusoni *et al.*, 2001). In fact, each component of the synchrotron, the accelerator as well as individual beamlines, is managed by a dedicated organizational unit.

The accelerator unit, in charge of the development of the radiation source for all beamlines, is organized around several functional competence units and involves expert physicians, geometricians and engineers. Efforts at the accelerator system level are strongly focused on system innovations and dynamic integration aspects of the technological platform (Henderson and Clark, 1990; Brusoni and Prencipe, 2001; Brusoni *et al.*, 2001). A good example illustrating this integration-differentiation process is the development of customized accelerator-beamline interfaces (called undulators).

If we install a new beamline or upgrade an existing one, we generally develop a new undulator with unique specificities. This provides us with great flexibility. We have different types of undulators and there are a lot of possible developments. For instance, undulators may have different lengths, use different materials. [. . .] They allow to generate the radiation in new ways. [. . .] We invent new ones continuously [. . .].

(Accelerator system engineer)

Through this late differentiation design strategy (Sanchez, 1995), the accelerator group provides the basis for continued differentiation through the addition of beamlines.

Beamlines are operated by small teams of around six members. The team includes a scientist team manager, other scientists and engineers and often a post-doc or an associate external researcher. Each beamline provides a specific configuration of instruments adapted to the particular needs of the targeted scientific user community. Consequently, new beamlines are developed jointly with members of the relevant communities. In particular, the future beamline manager normally not only has experience in other synchrotrons but is also a member of the community of future beamline users. This scientist develops the technological set-up and the strategy for the future beamline together with the existing synchrotron staff. Once running, the beamline remains under continuous development because of the external development of user needs on the one hand and the internal development of synchrotron technology on the other. The pace of internal and external developments is such that the beamline needs to re-orient its strategy once every five to seven years.

Beamline teams enjoy significant autonomy and deploy a great deal of entrepreneurial spirit in their in-house research projects to confer to their beamlines a distinctive position. Projects concern the development of new experimental methodologies, new instruments and new beamline concepts to open up new experimental opportunities, attract new users and expand synchrotron use to new scientific domains.

We are instigators, awakeners. We have our own research time. We use it to see if a subject is really worth, we make preliminary experiments and when we submit a project to the Program committee we show the preliminary results. This contributes to the acceptance of the risky project, [. . .] 'there are results, it's promising', [. . .] so they fund the project.

(Beamline manager)

All interviewed beamline managers maintained this entrepreneurial attitude towards developing their beamline.

We note that the organization of the main system components, accelerator and beamlines builds on knowledge specialization. Furthermore, most beamlines and also the accelerator teams can be associated with specific scientific or technological communities. Thus, the main organizational structure supports knowledge differentiation. However, managed inter-community interactions within the organization support knowledge integration across components. We argue that such integration efforts are effective because accelerator and beamline teams share a common frame of reference, a broad skill base and have similar background knowledge of 'their' synchrotron technology. Thus, although organizational units belong to different scientific communities, they all share a second identity within the broader organizational community (Dougherty, 2001).

Organizational integration across beamlines is fostered through several transverse laboratories and engineering services. These common laboratories provide critical support in the experimental process and satisfy instrumentation needs across beamlines. Common laboratories strive in their development efforts to have a more integrated and coordinated vision. Although their focus is on developing instruments that fit the specifications and needs of each beamline precisely, they also aim to standardize components across different beamline development projects. Quite often, an innovative instrument is first developed for one beamline and then transferred to several others after technical adjustments.

Integration is further supported by orchestrating research programs involving several beamlines in order to address thematic areas such as ancient materials, cosmetics, or environmental science. This internal networking emphasizes interdisciplinarity and collective problem solving. Platforms create thereby a fluid space where resources are configured and reconfigured according to the scientific problems to be solved.

> Ipanema [the ancient material platform] includes 10 beamlines. [. . .] We are mainly interested in transferring and creating knowledge at the interface between several internal and external disciplines to Soleil. As a platform we have a good knowledge of what can be done by the beamlines, not only the official information. As such we are an interesting entry point. I think that this platform is critical because it allows to forge relations between actors in an unusual way, to develop new tools, to look at things in an atypical way. Particularly methodological aspects within platforms create a critical link between disciplines and between beamlines.
>
> (Platform manager)

Finally, integration between beamline and accelerator communities is facilitated through flexible project based working practices and structures (Hobday *et al.*, 2005; Hoegl *et al.*, 2004). New projects emerge often through frequent communication between beamline and accelerator teams. For these new projects, early coordination helps to internalize critical needs, opportunities and interdependencies at the synchrotron system level in order to orient the creative efforts by beamlines and the accelerator group. Since exploration unfolds in different parts of the organization, local innovations and unforeseen interdependencies may introduce new opportunities, new design problems and require mutual innovative adjustments. Coordination is therefore ensured through regular meetings and information exchange to reallocate and reorient learning efforts across different technological trajectories, reconfigure interfaces, reorganize teamwork and redefine the autonomy zone of beamlines and the accelerator group. Overall, the innovation process is often based on a dynamic balance between autonomous search and team-based integration efforts (Siggelkow and Levinthal, 2003; Westerman *et al.*, 2006; Puranam *et al.*, 2006). The next section shows how external communities keep this wheel turning.

Making use of external knowledge to support creativity and innovation

The synchrotron has been created by the scientific community to serve the scientific community and scientific communities beyond the organization remain important for technological development of the synchrotron. Organizational members are recruited from the relevant community, the community shapes the organization's vision and strategy for technological development, poses technological and scientific challenges to the organization, and helps in resolving them. The relevance of the outside for internal development is reflected by the fact that Soleil is embedded in a rich network of inter-organizational as well as individual collaboration.

This section discusses inter-organizational collaboration between synchrotrons and the interaction of beamline scientists with the user community. In a first part, we provide concrete examples drawn from interviews of how interaction with other synchrotrons shapes internal technological development at the synchrotron. In a second part, we focus on two beamlines. Here we provide evidence from interviews and a quantitative bibliometric analysis on the interaction of beamline scientists with 'their' scientific community.

The synchrotron community

The synchrotron collaborates with various organizations, including among others, private and public research institutions, technology suppliers and state agencies. The relationship with other synchrotrons stands out because it is marked by intense co-opetition, i.e. competition for stakeholders from science and public funding agencies as well as cooperation for technological development.

The evolution of the synchrotron may be described as a technological trajectory (Dosi, 1982). As far as technology is concerned, there is continuous technological improvement along certain, clearly identified dimensions. Participating actors agree on the importance of these lines of development, on what the next steps will be, and what the more distant future will look like. Competition is based on the synchrotrons' capability to shape the technological frontier of the trajectory. Technology advances step-wise as technological problems are solved. The current state of the technology is thus not given by the state of any individual synchrotron, but by the state of the most advanced synchrotron. Other synchrotrons therefore serve as a point of reference for the development of individual synchrotrons.

The influence of other synchrotrons through reference points is in particular visible in the design process of the focal synchrotron from the 1990s onwards.

Its systemic design parameters (e.g. electron energy, total current, emittance) have been fixed by considering external developments in a large set of domains. For example, Soleil planned to start operation with state-of-the-art synchrotron technology yielding a beam intensity of 200 to 300 mA, and subsequently improve through internal development to 500 mA in order to occupy a distinctive position among the synchrotrons.

Collaboration with other synchrotrons through partnerships allows for knowledge transfers across synchrotrons. We observe a multitude of bilateral and multilateral efforts for technological development of the platform (accelerator and cross-beamline technologies) as well as technological development of applications (beamlines).

Several examples showcase the collaborative transfer process either outwards or inwards. Inwards, the use of NEG coating of vacuum chambers to improve beam performance provides a vivid example of collaboration between several synchrotrons (Soleil interviews). The technology was originally developed at the Large Hadron Collider CERN. Other synchrotrons adapted the technology and applied it to specific vacuum chambers. The focal synchrotron was the first synchrotron facility specifically designed to make extensive use of NEG coating technology, extending its use to all straight vacuum chambers. On the other hand, in-house innovations at Soleil were diffused to other synchrotrons. An example is the solid-state amplifiers used in the storage ring to generate the drive power and maintain beam stability. Performance advantages (modularity and reliability) have led several synchrotrons and other facilities (e.g. ESRF, Brazilian synchrotron LNLS, CEA) to adopt the Soleil technology by adapting them to their specific needs. Further collaboration agreements for transfer of the Soleil technology are envisaged (Soleil interviews and Soleil website). Bi- and multilateral consortia, such as TANGO for open source software, develop technology jointly. More broadly, technology diffusion across synchrotrons often resembles technology development within the broader synchrotron community (see for a case in point involving Soleil, Leemann and Dallin, 2013).

This supports the idea that technological development of an individual synchrotron depends on the technological development of the group of synchrotrons. Expectations and objectives regarding future technological development are formed by a group of synchrotrons acting in a common technological trajectory. The common perspective determines the objectives for technological development of individual synchrotrons. In order to reach these objectives, synchrotrons engage in various formal alliances to govern the transfer and joint development of technology. Alliances span the whole technological system since they contribute to the development of the accelerator, technologies across the technological system, as well as beamline technology. Alliances help in defining technological problems and solving them.

Involvement of the user community

While community involvement is essential to all beamlines, its management varies across beamlines. We argue that the management of community involvement depends on the diffusion stage of the technology in the scientific community (see also Hussler *et al.*, 2016). During the early diffusion stages, scientific interaction between synchrotron scientists and (potential) external user scientists is necessary for joint exploration of the technology in novel scientific applications. The theoretical argument is that close social interaction is needed in order to recombine the technological knowledge of the possibilities of the synchrotron and the scientific knowledge of the field where the instruments will be applied (Collins, 1974). Such interdisciplinary knowledge transfer and joint learning may, at the extreme, even lead to the creation of a new scientific community. At the point when the technology was well diffused within a certain scientific community, users learned about the technology. In the management of the user community, joint learning experiences become less of a concern than specialization efforts to make existing processes more efficient and more attractive for the community.

A comparison of two beamlines of our focal synchrotron provides a case in point. One of the two focal beamlines provides X-ray technology, the other infrared technology. The two beamlines are appropriate for a comparative study. They operate largely independently of each other from an organizational, social and scientific perspective. Furthermore, the beamlines are part of the same synchrotron and therefore similar in various aspects: The beamlines are comparable in terms of time of operation (both have operated since late 2007), operating personnel (3 to 5 scientists), number of scientific users (around 350 and 550 for infrared and x-ray), number of users' labs (around 100 for both) and number of projects (around 150 each).

Foremost, the two beamlines differ in their scientific apparatus: The X-ray beamline allows for analysis of crystallized materials through diffraction of hard X-rays. In life sciences, this method is used to investigate the composition and structure of crystallized biological material such as biological molecules. The infrared beamline offers infrared spectroscopy. This method is used in a variety of applications such as the investigation of the nature of (biological) molecules that benefits research in the fields of chemistry, biochemistry and physics and respective applied fields such as instrumentation, materials and diagnostics.

We chose these two beamlines for this case study because they differ in the diffusion stage of their instrumentation in the envisaged user community. X-ray crystallography has been the dominant method used to investigate protein structures in biology for a while. In contrast, most interviewed scientists doing research on infrared have a scientific background in fields where the method offered by the beamline is relatively recent. Infrared is therefore not a substitute for a known instrument, but represents a new instrument that complements the existing scientists' toolbox. Therefore, the beamline has the potential to provide new research avenues in that it allows research questions to be tackled that are different from the ones investigated previously. This is true for research in different scientific fields and even disciplines.

Because targeted communities are at different stages of synchrotron adoption, beamlines need to develop different strategies on how to leverage external scientific communities.

The X-ray beamline focuses on efficiency improvements. Efficiency improvements do not only relate to technological innovations but also organizational innovations. An example could be the introduction of BAG proposals as an alternative to standard proposals for beamline access. Standard proposals take the form of single projects involving often several scientists and concern one or a few blocks of one to five working days on the beamline.

The long time span from application to usage creates some uncertainty at the time of application concerning whether the material to be analysed at the synchrotron will be actually available during the obtained time slot (especially in crystals). Furthermore, during usage of the beamline, unexpected issues may arise, for example regarding the material to be analysed. The uncertainty involved often makes the re-scheduling of experiments necessary.

Against this background, most synchrotron X-ray beamlines adopted the so-called BAG (Block Allocation Group) mechanism. BAGs bundle together more several scientific projects and labs than standard projects. A joint application by several scientific teams for multiple research objectives through a BAG avoids micro-management on behalf of the synchrotron and leaves most re-scheduling decisions to the users.

> There are certain BAGs that are local and certain BAGs that are distant. From the local BAGs (Paris region) they are all going to come. If it's a BAG day, sometimes with up to 2 BAGs, there may be up to 15 or 18 different users that come in 24 hours. We are not going to see all of them, some come in the night, they give themselves a time slot and they call themselves when they are done. If it's a distant BAG, for example from Marseille or Strasbourg, they delegate three users which take the crystals of all the other groups and with some hints they put through the crystals of all others. Hence, they organize among each other. This means that even if we have only three users this might correspond to the work of many other groups.
>
> (Beamline manager)

Further examples would be improve automation at the beamline including the introduction of remotely controlled experiments. What is common to these innovations at X-ray is that they improve the efficiency of beamline usage for external users, and, at the same time, tend to reduce interaction between beamline scientists and external user scientists.

The infrared beamline manager follows a markedly different strategy and tries explicitly to get into close contact with new potential users:

> We had interaction with people that heard about our message to open up towards biology and biomedicine. And so the medical scientists told themselves that now you have the means to investigate our biological essays which go beyond our knowledge which is pragmatic knowledge, using coloration, the observation. [. . .] In any case, I listened to what they said. But when I needed someone, I did not employ someone with a scientific

background in synchrotron physics. I took someone who knew nothing at all about physics but who knew about biospectroscopy and that changed everything. Because he knows how to talk to them, [. . .] He knows better than I do and hence the dialogue works and this is really the element that allows for the transition.

(Beamline manager)

Thus, infrared deliberately hires scientists who have the necessary scientific background to interact closely with potential users and translate their research needs to develop the beamline.

Interview findings are reflected in the (co-)publication behaviour of user and beamline scientists. Table 8.1 provides descriptive statistics on the sample of peer-reviewed publications published by X-ray and infrared users respectively. Consider first the number of papers based on research at the focal synchrotron, another synchrotron, or involving no synchrotron (first three rows of Table 8.1). While the overall number of publications is comparable, X-ray users publish twice as many papers on synchrotron research than infrared users. In both cases, user scientists used the focal or another synchrotron only for a small fraction of their papers; most papers involve no synchrotron. We turn next to the journal impact factors of papers (rows four to six in Table 8.1).

The fact that impact factors for X-ray users tend to be higher than those for infrared users is probably due to discipline effects. We note, however, that papers based on synchrotron research tend to be more successful than those with no synchrotron use. The difference is significant. Based on 10,000 resamples under the null hypothesis that the distribution of impact factors is the same for all papers, we reject the null at a significance level below 0.01 per cent for both beamlines. This suggests that both beamlines contribute positively to scientific output (ignoring the potential bias from selection of beamline proposals). However, the extent to which users rely on close collaboration with

Table 8.1 Beamline user papers published between 2008 and 2012

	X-ray beamline	Infrared beamline
No. papers with research at the		
– focal synchrotron	187 (8%)	64 (3%)
– other synchrotron	291 (12%)	134 (6%)
– no synchrotron	1975 (80%)	2235 (91%)
Impact factor (median) of papers		
– focal synchrotron	5.0	3.8
– other synchrotron	5.2	3.7
– no synchrotron	4.1	3.2
Focal synchrotron papers co-authored		
– with beamline scientists	22 (12%)	53 (83%)
– without beamline scientists	165 (88%)	11 (17%)

X-ray   Infrared

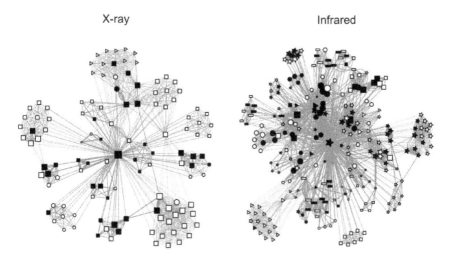

Figure 8.1 Ego-networks of principal beamline scientists at X-ray and Infrared beamline.

beamline scientists is very different depending on the beamline (last two rows of Table 8.1). X-ray users rarely publish with beamline scientists (22 out of 187 papers), whereas infrared users relatively often co-author with beamline scientists (53 out of 64 papers).

Figure 8.1 visualizes the extent to which beamline managers engage within different scientific communities. Each node of the graph represents a scientist and a link connects two scientists when they co-authored a paper. The beamline manager is in the centre connected to all his co-authors (left panel X-ray, right panel infrared). The shape of the node represents the scientific field in which the scientist published most papers (as indicated by the journals' scientific fields): Biochemistry (square), Chemistry (star), Instruments (triangle), Astronomy and Physics (rectangle). Comparing the two ego-networks, we first note that the X-ray beamline manager acts mostly within one discipline (biochemistry of which crystallography is a subfield) while the infrared beamline manager co-authors with scientists from various disciplines. Furthermore, the fraction of co-authors who are also users of the beamline (black) to co-authors who are not beamline users (white) is relatively small at X-ray and high at infrared.

Thus, while both beamlines contribute to the scientific creativity of their users, they do so through markedly different interaction patterns. One explanation can be found in the diffusion stage of synchrotron technology among the different user groups.

In sum, interviews and the bibliometric analysis consistently suggest that the strategy of each beamline responds to the needs of the community to be addressed. Close interaction and joint knowledge creation activity is needed to diffuse an application within the targeted community, or even to create a new community. On the other hand, interaction may be more distant, and perhaps made more efficient if the technology is fully diffused within the community. In either case, a connection between the application and the community is facilitated if beamline scientists are themselves members of the community.

Discussion and conclusion

Our case study observations provide insights into how internal organization and involvement of external communities contribute to continued development of the technological platform 'synchrotron'. The technological architecture appears to be influential to both internal organization and community involvement.

The elements of the technological system are loosely coupled in the sense that development of elements may take place relatively independently of each other. In particular, beamlines, i.e. specific applications of the generic technology, are not directly physically connected, but only indirectly through the more generic accelerator.

The loose coupling of the technology allows for organizational separation. Beamlines develop independently of each other their long-term strategy of which (emerging) communities to target and how to approach them. Involved communities influence the development of components not only through defining (future) needs but also through technology transfers and joint problem-solving activities. On a similar account, we also found that the more generic accelerator infrastructure is continuously developed within a more formally organized 'synchrotron community'. Thus, each of the system's components is developed involving a community that spans beyond the organization.

Both in-depth beamline studies showed that the fact that some organizational members are themselves also active members in the community is essential for effective community involvement. This idea is relatively straightforward. What may be more interesting is that beamlines engaged differently with their communities: one beamline focused on efficiency in service provision for a mature community, while the other beamline engaged in close collaboration activities for knowledge transfer and joint learning within an emerging community.

External community members typically have only one point of contact with the synchrotron. For example a crystallographer's sole point of contact with the synchrotron is typically the X-ray beamline. Individual communities nevertheless influence the overall development of the synchrotron.

Organizational members serve as gatekeepers since they translate and formulate community needs and perspectives for other organizational members. For example, beamline managers often require beam light improvements for their communities, which pose problems to be solved at the accelerator level. Furthermore, technological problems involving several components or interfaces are tackled by project teams that involve scientists from different components. Coordination among all synchrotron members is further facilitated through regular meetings and information exchange to reorient teamwork and learning efforts across the system. In short, various organizational mechanisms are used to integrate and coordinate the input and needs from external communities for internal technological development.

We note that our case involves a public science organization. We believe nevertheless that some of the lessons learned also hold for profit oriented firms that similarly rely on various external communities for the development of a loosely coupled technological system. For these firms, this study provides some useful insights into the management of community *coordination*, which is about how external knowledge can be leveraged for internal creativity. Yet, coordination alone is not sufficient. Community members outside the organization must also be willing to *cooperate*. In our case, incentives for cooperation are clearly given because the objectives of external users and the organization coincide in their need to produce high quality scientific output. Furthermore, all actors are inherently scientists and hence agree on basic principles. In private sectors, community interests may deviate from organizational interests. Since organizations cannot direct the activity of external individuals, an alignment of objectives becomes essential to achieve cooperation. This may be done through appropriate business models (Teece, 1986). Future research may therefore investigate in private organizations how firms are able to manage cooperation as well as the coordination of communities external to the firm.

References

Amabile, T. M. (1988) "A model of creativity and innovation in organizations", *Research in Organizational Behavior*, 10: 123–167.

Avadikyan, A., Bach, L., Lambert, G., Lerch, C. and Wolff, S. (2014) "Dynamique des modèles d'affaires et écosystème: le cas des synchrotrons", *Revue d'Economie Industrielle*, 146(2): 153–186.

Börner, K., Maru, J. T. and Goldstone, R. L. (2004) "The simultaneous evolution of author and paper networks", *Proceedings of the National Academy of Sciences of the United States of America*, 101: 5266–5273.

Brown, J. S. and Duguid, P. (1991) "Organizational learning and communities-of-practice: Toward a unified view of working, learning, and innovation", *Organization Science*, 2(1): 40–57.

Brusoni, S. and Prencipe, A. (2001) "Unpacking the black box of modularity: Technologies, products and organizations", *Industrial and Corporate Change*, 10(1): 179–205.

Brusoni, S., Prencipe, A. and Pavitt, K. (2001) "Knowledge specialization, organizational coupling, and the boundaries of the firm: Why do firms know more than they make?", *Administrative Science Quarterly*, 46(4): 597–621.

Burger-Helmchen, T. (2013) *The Economics of Creativity: Ideas, Firms and Markets*, New York: Routledge.

Burt, R. S. (2004) "Structural holes and good ideas", *American Journal of Sociology*, 110(2): 349–399.

Chesbrough, H. W. and Appleyard, M. M. (2007) "Open innovation and strategy", *California Management Review*, 50(1): 57–76.

Coleman, J. S. (1988) "Social capital in the creation of human capital", *American Journal of Sociology*, 94(S): 95–120.

Collins, H. M. (1974) "The TEA Set: Tacit knowledge and scientific networks", *Science Studies*, 4(2): 165–185.

Colombo, M. G., Piva, E. and Rossi-Lamastra, C. (2014) "Open innovation and within-industry diversification in small and medium enterprises: The case of open source software firms", *Research Policy*, 43(5): 891–902.

de Solla Price, D. (1984) "The science/technology relationship, the craft of experimental science, and policy for the improvement of high technology innovation", *Research Policy*, 13(1): 3–20.

Dosi, G. (1982) "Technological paradigms and technological trajectories: A suggested interpretation of the determinants of technological change", *Research Policy*, 11(3): 147–162.

Dougherty, D. (2001) "Reimagining the differentiation and integration of work for sustained product innovation", *Organization Science*, 12(5): 612–631.

Erden, Z., von Krogh, G. and Nonaka, I. (2008) "The quality of group tacit knowledge", *Journal of Strategic Information Systems*, 17(1): 4–18.

EvaRIO (2013a) *EvaRIO synthesis of results* (Supervisor: Wolff, S.; Contributors: Avadikyan, A., Bach, L., Guittard, C., Héraud, J-A., Hussler, C., Kahn, R., Lambert, G., Lerch, C., Müller, E., Pénin, J. and Wolff, S.), Part I, Final Report, Deliverable D5.2, December 2013, Contract n°262281, FP7, online: http://evario.u-strasbg.fr/final-report (last accessed 11 March 2016).

EvaRIO (2013b) *EvaRIO core study: Adapting the BETA method to the case of the evaluation of the impact of research infrastructures,* (Supervisor: Bach, L.; Technical Support: Flasaquier, M.), Part II, Final Report, Deliverable D5.2, December 2013, Contract n°262281, FP7, online: http://evario.u-strasbg.fr/final-report (last accessed 11 March 2016).

EvaRIO (2013c) *EvaRIO policy recommendations*, (Supervisor: Bach, L., Héraud, J-A. and Wolff, S.; Technical Support: Flasaquier, M.); Part III, Final Report, Deliverable D5.2, December 2013, Contract n°262281, FP7, online: http://evario.u-strasbg.fr/final-report (last accessed 11 March 2016).

Fleming, L., Mingo, S. and Chen, D. (2007) "Collaborative brokerage, generative creativity, and creative success", *Administrative Science Quarterly*, 52(3): 443–475.

Franke, N. and Shah, S. (2003) "How communities support innovative activities: An exploration of assistance and sharing among end-users", *Research Policy*, 32(1): 157–178.

Frigotto, M. L. and Riccaboni, M. (2011) "A few special cases: Scientific creativity and network dynamics in the field of rare diseases", *Scientometrics,* 89(1): 397–420.

Grant, R. M. (1996) "Prospering in dynamically-competitive environments: Organizational capability as knowledge integration", *Organization Science*, 7(4): 375–387.

Haensel, R. (1994) "Synchrotron radiation: 30 years of a fruitful collaboration between the United States and Europe", *Nuclear Instruments and Methods in Physics Research A*, 347(1): 14–16.

Håkanson, L. (2010) "The firm as an epistemic community: The knowledge-based view revisited", *Industrial and Corporate Change*, 19(6): 1801–1828.

Hallonsten, O. (2009) "Small science on big machines: Politics and practices of synchrotron radiation laboratories", PhD Dissertation, Lund Studies in Research Policy, Research Policy Institute, Lund.

Hargadon, A. B. and Bechky, B. A. (2006) "When collections of creatives become creative collectives: A field study of problem solving at work", *Organization Science*, 17(4): 484–500.

Henderson, R. M. and Clark, K. B. (1990) "Architectural innovation: The reconfiguration of existing product technologies and the failure of established firms", *Administrative Science Quarterly*, 35(1): 9–30.

Henkel, J. (2006) "Selective revealing in open innovation processes: The case of embedded Linux", *Research Policy*, 35(7): 953–969.

Hienerth, C., von Hippel, E. and Jensen, M. B. (2014) "User community vs. producer innovation development efficiency: A first empirical study", *Research Policy*, 43(1): 190–201.

Hobday, M., Davies, A. and Prencipe, A. (2005) "Systems integration: A core capability of the modern corporation", *Industrial and Corporate Change*, 14(6): 1109–1143.

Hoegl, M., Weinkauf, K. and Gemuenden, H. G. (2004) "Interteam coordination, project commitment, and teamwork in multiteam R&D projects: A longitudinal study", *Organization Science*, 15(1): 38–55.

Hussler, C., Müller, M. and Wolff, S. (2016) "The effect of large research infrastructures on scientific collaboration networks: Two cases on a synchrotron", *Mimeo*.

Kim, D. and Kogut, B. (1996) "Technological platforms and diversification", *Organization Science*, 7(3): 283–301.

Kogut, B. and Zander, U. (1996) "What firms do? Coordination, identity, and learning", *Organization Science*, 7(5): 502–518.

Lakhani, K. R. and von Hippel, E. (2003) "How open source software works: 'Free' user-to-user assistance", *Research Policy*, 32(6): 923–943.

Lave, J. and Wenger, E. (1991) *Situated Learning: Legitimate Peripheral Participation*, Cambridge: Cambridge University Press.

Leemann, S. C. and Dallin, L. O. (2013) "Progress on pulsed multipole injection for the Max IV storage rings", *PAC 2013 Proceedings*, Pasadena, CA, USA.

Merz, M. and Biniok, P. (2010) "How technological platforms reconfigure science-industry relations: The case of micro- and nanotechnology", *Minerva*, 48(2): 105–124.

Nonaka, I., von Krogh, G. and Voelpel, S. (2000) "Organizational knowledge creation theory: Evolutionary paths and future advances", *Organization Studies*, 27(8): 1179–1208.

O'Mahony, S. and Lakhani, K. R. (2011) "Organizations in the shadow of communities", in Marquis, C., Lounsbury, M. and Greenwood, R. (ed.), *Communities and Organizations: Research in the Sociology of Organizations*, 33, Emerald Group Publishing Limited, pp. 3–36.

Orr, J. E. (1996) *Talking about Machines: An Ethnography of a Modern Job*, Ithaca, NY: Cornell University Press.

Peerbaye, A. and Mangematin, V. (2005) "Sharing research facilities: Towards a new mode of technology transfer?", *Innovation: Management, Policy and Practice*, 7(1): 23–38.

Powell, W. W., Koput, K. W. and Smith-Doerr, L. (1996) "Interorganizational collaboration and the locus of innovation: Networks of learning in biotechnology", *Administrative Science Quarterly*, 41(1): 116–145.

Puranam, P., Singh, H. and Zollo, M. (2006) "Organizing for innovation: Managing the coordination-autonomy dilemma in technology acquisitions", *The Academy of Management Journal*, 49(2): 263–280.

Robinson, D. K. R., Rip, A. and Mangematin, V. (2007) "Technological agglomeration and the emergence of clusters and networks in nanotechnology", *Research Policy*, 36(6): 871–879.

Rosenberg, N. (1992) "Scientific instrumentation and university research", *Research Policy*, 21(4): 381–390.

Sanchez, R. (1995) "Strategic flexibility in product competition", *Strategic Management Journal*, 16(S1): 135–159.

Sanchez, R. and Mahoney, J. T. (1996) "Modularity, flexibility, and knowledge management in product and organizational design", *Strategic Management Journal*, 17: 63–76.

Schweisfurtha, T. G. and Raasch, C. (2014) "Embedded lead users – The benefits of employing users for corporate innovation", *Research Policy*, 44(1): 168–180.

Shinn, T. (2005) "New sources of radical innovation: Research-technologies, transversality and distributed learning in a post-industrial order", *Social Science Information*, 44(4): 731–764.

Shinn, T. and Joerges, B. (2002) "The transverse science and technology culture, dynamics and roles of research-technology", *Social Science Information*, 41(2): 207–251.

Siggelkow, N. and Levinthal, D. (2003) "Temporarily divide to conquer: Centralized, decentralized, and reintegrated organizational approaches to exploration and adaptation", *Organization Science*, 14(6): 650–669.

Simoulin, V. (2012) *Sociologie d'un grand équipement scientifique. Le premier synchrotron de troisième génération*, Lyon: ENS Éditions.

Spaeth, S., Stuermer, M. and von Krogh, G. (2010) "Enabling knowledge creation through outsiders: Towards a push model of open innovation", *International Journal of Technology Management*, 52(3/4): 411–431.

Teece, D. J. (1986) "Profiting from technological innovation: Implications for integration, collaboration, licensing and public policy", *Research Policy*, 15(6): 285–305.

von Hippel, E. (1976) "The dominant role of users in the scientific instrument innovation process", *Research Policy*, 5(3): 212–239.

West, J. (2003) "How open is open enough? Melding proprietary and open source platform strategies", *Research Policy*, 32(7): 1259–1285.

Westerman G., McFarlan, F. W. and Iansiti, M. (2006) "Organization design and effectiveness over the innovation life cycle", *Organization Science*, 17(2): 230–238.

9 Ambidexterity as a means of managing creativity globally

An analysis of the biotechnology industry

Marcus Wagner and Wilfried Zidorn

Introduction

March's seminal study (1991) distinguishes between exploration and exploitation of knowledge within a firm. He defines exploration of knowledge as experimentation with new alternatives and the creation of new capabilities by pursuing fundamental research, experimentation and search. Furthermore, he refers (in the context of exploitation) to the use of existing resources mainly to extend a firm's knowledge portfolio by standardization, scaling and refinement. His research has led several scholars from diverse research fields to apply these concepts. Studies have grown out of this with a special focus on strategic management (e.g. He and Wong, 2004; Uotila *et al.*, 2009); alliances (e.g. Im and Rai, 2008; Lin *et al.*, 2007); technology sourcing and organizational design (e.g. Andriopoulos and Lewis, 2009; Lubatkin *et al.*, 2006; O'Reilly and Tushman, 2004); and innovation management (e.g. Belderbos *et al.*, 2010; Benner and Tushman, 2003; Jansen *et al.*, 2006; Mudambi and Swift, 2014). Although March (1991) describes a trade-off between the two concepts, more recent studies have found that firms are more successful when they focus on ambidextrous innovation strategies that pursue exploration and exploitation at the same time (e.g. Gibson and Birkinshaw, 2004; Grover *et al.*, 2007; O'Reilly and Tushman, 2004). Hence, firms, especially those in high-technology industries, need to balance their exploration and exploitation strategies (e.g. Kim *et al.*, 2012; Lavie *et al.*, 2011; Molina-Castillo *et al.*, 2011). However, there is less agreement amongst scholars on the question of how to balance exploration and exploitation. Some argue that firms should focus on one strategy and dedicate a minimum of their resources to the other (e.g. Gibson and Birkinshaw, 2004; Levinthal and March, 1993). Others claim that a relative imbalance between the two innovation strategies negatively affects firm performance and firms should dedicate equal resources to exploration and exploitation (e.g. Grover *et al.*, 2007; He and Wong, 2004). Furthermore, longitudinal empirical studies on a balancing strategy in literature are scarce (Raisch *et al.*, 2009). Belderbos *et al.* (2010) find an inverted U-shaped relationship between firms' increasing attention to exploration and financial performance but failure to analyse innovation success factors. Based on these considerations, the notion emerges that ambidexterity enables a global management of creativity in the sense that firms are able to switch between and balance exploration and exploitation. This leads us to the research question: what is the optimal balance between exploration and exploitation?

To answer the research question, the first section of the paper briefly reviews previous studies on exploration and exploitation and the attempts made to find an optimal balance between them. Furthermore, the section serves to develop a theoretical background for deriving testable hypotheses. The subsequent section introduces the data and variables that are used for analysis. After presenting and discussing the results, conclusions are drawn and potential areas for future research proposed.

Literature review

This section reviews the existing literature on exploration and exploitation. Traditional, modern, case-specific and empirical studies on the two innovation strategies are presented. The literature from several disciplines is reviewed by analysing the various attempts made to balance exploration and exploitation. These concepts and insights into previous studies are required to derive testable hypotheses.

March (1991) theoretically suggests a trade-off between exploration and exploitation. Even though the two strategies are crucial for a firm to be productive in the short run and innovative in the long run, he finds exploration and exploitation to be essentially incompatible. First, firms have finite resources and pursuing exploration and exploitation simultaneously reveals inefficiencies in resource allocation, that is, firms that dedicate many resources to exploration have fewer resources for exploitation and vice versa. Second, exploration, on the one hand, is experimental and outcomes are *"uncertain, distant and often negative"* (March, 1991: 85). Thus, explorative projects have the tendency to fail. Failure, however, causes firms to strive for newer ideas and concepts, and thus promotes more exploration that leads to a *"failure trap"* (Levinthal and March, 1993: 105). Exploitation, on the other hand, is *"positive, proximate and predictable"* (March, 1991: 85) since it builds on pre-existing knowledge and hence exploitative projects tend to have successful outcomes. Success, however, encourages firms to extend exploitative projects, which leads to more exploitation resulting in a *"success trap"* (Levinthal and March, 1993: 105). Third, organizational processes are different for firms that pursue exploration and firms that engage in exploitation. March concludes that the competition for scarce resources, attention and organizational structures makes exploration and exploitation incompatible (March, 1991; March, 1996; March, 2006). Accordingly, Levinthal and March (1993) suggest two possible balancing strategies. Either, firms should follow a minimum of exploitation and dedicate their remaining resources to exploration or firms should invest a few resources in exploration and use the rest for exploitative projects.

However, scholars have begun to shift their focus away from this trade-off (either/or) view towards a paradoxical (and/both) view on how to effectively balance the two strategies (Gibson and Birkinshaw, 2004). Tushman and

O'Reilly (1996) argue the case with an *ambidexterity* premise which indicates that firms must follow a paradoxical process of balancing explorative and exploitative innovation strategies. However, the paradoxical view creates tensions in balancing the two actions since managers have to decide whether to invest in current or future projects, focus on differentiation or low-cost production, or decide between global business extension or local responsiveness. These resulting tensions may be resolved under certain conditions. Lavie *et al.* (2010) discuss several ambidextrous approaches to effectively implement both strategies. (1) Contextual ambidexterity resolves tensions between exploration and exploitation by actioning both strategies simultaneously at any given organizational level. (2) Organizational separation also makes use of exploration and exploitation simultaneously, but in different organizational units. (3) Temporal separation permits the coexistence of exploration and exploitation within the same organization unit, but at different points in time. And finally, (4) domain separation enables the simultaneous use of both strategies in the same organizational units by pursuing exploration in one domain and exploitation in another.

Firms that make use of these ambidextrous strategies seem to be more successful than firms that see exploration and exploitation as two ends of a continuum in dynamic and fast growing environments (Gibson and Birkinshaw, 2004). Grover *et al.* (2007) analysed the telecommunications industry and found that organizations within this industry use a balanced approach to innovativeness by simultaneously applying dual and paradoxical modes of innovation. O'Reilly and Tushman (2004) found that, after implementing ambidextrous management strategies at USAToday and Ciba Vision, both firms experienced superior firm performance. They found that to outperform competitors, prosper and even survive, firms must excel at both and be aligned with current management techniques and open to innovative new ideas.

He and Wong (2004) were the first to empirically test the ambidexterity hypothesis of Tushman and O'Reilly (1996). They found that balancing the two strategies had a positive effect on firm performance, whereas a relative imbalance between exploration and exploitation negatively influenced firm performance. Auh and Menguc (2005) focused on the food, mining, automotive, construction material and chemical industries and found that survey data confirmed that exploration had a stronger positive effect on firm performance than exploitation. That is to say, more research in experimental fields that are new to the firm yields higher returns than those produced by the development of existing technologies. Furthermore, they found that the balance level of exploration and exploitation has to be adjusted when a firm's strategy or its environmental conditions change.

Summarizing the arguments above, two competing theories emerge on how to effectively balance exploration and exploitation. Levinthal and March (1993) argue that a firm should mainly focus on one strategy by dedicating a minimum of resources to the other. More recent literature, however, has analysed the benefits of ambidextrous innovation strategies by simultaneously and equally focusing on exploration and exploitation (e.g. Grover *et al.*, 2007; He and Wong, 2004; Tushman and O'Reilly, 1996). While there is a consensus among scientists that firms have to be ambidextrous to be successful, there has still been no attempt in literature to analyse the optimal balance between exploration and exploitation.

Development of hypotheses

Levinthal and March (1993: 105) argue that if exploration drives out exploitation, then processes become determined by *"experimentation, change, and innovation by a dynamic of failure"*. Exploration, especially in high-technology industries, is a very complex strategy. It often takes considerable experimentation to achieve a desired objective. However, in many instances even increased experimentation does not yield returns, leaving a firm with nothing but high costs (Giovanetti and Morrison, 2000). Accordingly, failure leads to a search for new ideas that may fail again, and the firm therefore moves towards a *"suboptimal equilibrium"* (March, 1991: 72) or a *"failure trap"* (Levinthal and March, 1993: 105). Furthermore, He and Wong (2004) find that a relative imbalance between the two strategies has negative effects on firm performance. Although a balance between the two strategies seems to be beneficial, a firm that dedicates too many resources to exploration suffers a decrease in performance. Kim *et al.* (2012) find that explorative projects of a firm have a negative overall effect on innovation output. Based on these arguments, one might expect a high relative share of exploration within a firm to reduce innovative performance which leads to the following hypothesis:

> *H1: A negative relationship exists between the relative share of explorative activities in a firm's technology portfolio and its innovative performance.*

Ambidextrous balancing levels between exploration and exploitation are tested by a few empirical studies. Atuahene-Gima (2005) finds that Chinese firms have to pursue both strategies to further develop their products and enter new markets with innovative new products. On the one hand, these firms have to remain productive and competitive with their current products through permanent improvements and reactions to customer needs. On the other hand, they have to invest in future projects through the acquisition of new machines and with innovative ideas on how to attract new customers and enter entirely new markets. Similar results are found by Molina-Castillo *et al.* (2011) when analysing Spanish manufacturing firms using survey data. They find that ambidextrous innovation strategies are important to simultaneously increase the quality of existing products and offer entirely new innovative technologies. Kim *et al.* (2012) show that exploitation and exploration should be combined to patent innovation on the one hand, and to ensure high quality innovation on the other. They find empirical evidence that an ambidextrous strategy is important to be successful in the pharmaceutical industry from an innovation perspective. Following this logic and in line with the findings of He and Wong (2004), we can expect that firms that have the highest innovation output dedicate similar attention to explorative and exploitative technological activities. This leads to the following hypothesis:

> *H2: A firm devoting a similar level of attention to exploration and exploitation positively influences its innovative performance.*

Kim *et al.* (2012) find a negative relationship between exploration and innovation rates. In other words, the greater the engagement in explorative projects, the lower the innovation rate of a firm. However, the results also show that more explorative projects have a positive influence on the innovation impact. That is to say, even if innovation *quantity* decreases with more exploration, the *quality* of innovation rises. Opposite effects are found for exploitation. The higher the dedication to exploitative projects, the higher the innovative performance of a firm, but with decreasing marginal returns. Therefore, these arguments are an indication of a curvilinear relationship of the two strategies and a firm's overall innovative performance. Furthermore, the curvilinear influence of exploration on a firm's innovative performance is assumed to be initially positive. A technology needs to be explored before it can be exploited. Therefore, a minimum of exploration is required for exploitation (Levinthal and March, 1993). To further narrow down the optimal balance level between exploration and exploitation, two types of studies have to be combined. The first type consists of studies that argue that exploration has a negative overall effect on innovative performance, whereas exploitation has a positive effect on innovative performance (e.g. Kim et al., 2012). The second type of studies includes those that define ambidexterity as a firm's relatively equal emphasis on exploration and exploitation (e.g. He and Wong, 2004) and those that argue that ambidextrous strategies lead to higher innovative performance (e.g. Atuahene-Gima, 2005; Kim *et al.*, 2012; Molina-Castillo *et al.*, 2011). First, assuming a curvilinear relationship between the two innovation strategies and innovative performance and including the results of the first type of literature implies that firms that dedicate more resources to exploitation than to exploration perform best from an innovative perspective. Second, reviewing the literature on ambidexterity, firms show the highest innovative performance at the point where the two strategies are roughly equally weighted. When combining the two approaches from literature, an optimal balance of exploration and exploitation is expected to have a slightly higher share of explorative rather than exploitative technological activities. This leads to the following hypothesis:

> *H3: A curvilinear (inverted U-shaped) relationship exists between the relative share of explorative activities in a firm's technology portfolio and its innovative performance.*

Empirical setting

To test for the hypotheses, the study analyses explorative and exploitative patent applications in the biotechnology industry. Significant numbers of biotechnology firms have been established since the mid 1970s. A major breakthrough in the field occurred when *"scientists discovered how to manipulate the genetic structure of cells to induce them to produce specific proteins"* (Pisano, 1997: 12). The last three decades have witnessed a proliferation of biotechnology firms, which has led to fierce competition. This is partly caused by the high economic value of biotechnology solutions and application integration, which has attracted attention from several industries (Cantwell and Santangelo, 2000; Nesta and Saviotti, 2006). The environmental industry, the chemical industry (which works with bio-based materials and bioprocess engineering), the agriculture industry, the food and medical engineering industries and, most importantly for this dissertation, the pharmaceutical industry, have all developed an interest in this emerging technology (Powell *et al.*, 1996). The increasing demands of these customer industries has led to a strong need for rapid product development that has further increased interest (Deeds and Hill, 1996) as well as sparking patent races among the biotechnology firms (Gilbert and Newbery, 1982). In the 1990s, applications for biotechnology patents increased from 1,358 to 3,014 and private investments from USD 10 billion in 1990 to USD 24 billion in 1999 (Audretsch, 2001). This rapid development also led to complex structures within the whole industry, which created a division of labour between biotechnology firms, pharmaceutical firms and universities (Hohberger, 2007). In high-technology industries in particular, innovation is indispensable since it ensures the long-term survival of a firm (Baum *et al.*, 2000; Shan *et al.*, 1994). Therefore, explorative and exploitative innovation is a central issue in high-technology contexts such as the biotechnology industry. Additionally, a focus on one industry helps to control for industry effects, such as scale economies or new technologies, which have been shown to influence results in a complex manner that is difficult to control in multi-industry samples (Pangarkar, 2003). Furthermore, measuring patenting activity among firms within the same industry is clearly more informative than data on patenting spanning industries or countries (Basberg, 1984). These multiple benefits permit an advanced analysis and the biotechnology industry thus provides an excellent setting from which to test the hypotheses. Therefore, a representative sample of the 20 most successful biotechnology firms (MedAdNews, 2004) was created. A filter was applied to ensure that full information on all variables in the dataset was available. This was done for several reasons. First, observations that do not contain any information on patent activity were eliminated, which reduced the sample to 381 observations. Furthermore, the analysis required financial information on the focal firms for the estimation. Several firms in the sample had not been public throughout their economic lifetime, which limited access to their financial data. Therefore, those observations that did not provide such information were excluded from the dataset, which reduced the sample to 251 observations. To test the derived hypotheses, several variables were constructed and these are explained in Table 9.1.

Dependent variable

Patent data for 20 biotechnology firms were used to build the dependent variable (granted patent applications of subsidiaries are added to the patent portfolio of the

Table 9.1 Variable definitions

Variable name	Variable description	Data sources
Dependent Variable		
Patents	Number of patents a firm successfully filed in year t	USPTO
Independent Variables		
Ambidexterity	Balance between the shares of explorative and exploitative patents in year t	USPTO
Exploration share	Share of explorative patents in year t. A patent is defined as explorative if a firm has not filed one within the same patent class in the prior 5 years. This status is kept for the three following years.	USPTO
Control Variables		
Size	Logarithm of total sales of a firm in year t	COMPUSTAT COMPUSTAT Global CRSP
Alliances	Logarithm of alliance events of a firm in year t	CATI CGCP RECAP
R&D intensity	Ratio of R&D expenditures to total assets of a firm in year t	COMPUSTAT COMPUSTAT Global CRSP
Experience	Number of years since the IPO of the firm	Firm profiles
Europe	Dummy variable set to one if the headquarter of the firm is in Europe (base category: US firm)	Firm profiles
Asia	Dummy variable set to one if the headquarter of the firm is in Asia (base category: US firm)	Firm profiles
Acquisitions	Logarithm of the number of acquisitions of a firm in year t	THOMPSON RECAP
Technological change	Change of a firm's patent portfolio	USPTO

parent firm). The yearly count of granted patents sorted by the firm and the year, respectively, was used to create the dependent variable *Patents*. The year when the firm filed the patent was chosen, and not the year when the patent was granted, providing a more accurate measure for a firm's technological activity since the innovation has already taken place when the firm files a patent (Gilsing *et al.*, 2008; Nooteboom *et al.*, 2007).

Independent variables

To create the independent variables, the patent data of the 20 biotechnology firms were subdivided into explorative and exploitative patents. The patents were first sorted according to the corresponding firm, the year and the IPC class. If a patent had been filed in a class where the firm successfully filed a patent during the last five years, it was considered to be an exploitative patent. A patent was defined as explorative whenever a firm was seen to patent a technology for a first time, or for the first time in five years, in an IPC class. This explorative status was then assumed to be current for three consecutive years. The same approach is used by several scholars. (Belderbos *et al.*, 2010; Gilsing *et al.*, 2008; Nooteboom *et al.*, 2007). These studies, however, use the two-digit IPC or USPTO classes to distinguish between explorative and explorative patents. However, this separation method has produced a bias towards exploitative patents. For instance, both Belderbos *et al.* (2010) and Nooteboom *et al.* (2007) label approximately 90 per cent of cases as exploitative patents. Therefore, this study used the full information of the IPC class (e.g. A61K 9/08) to separate the two innovation strategies. This enabled a more detailed separation and more accurately represented the actual technological activity of a firm's technology portfolio, with 50 per cent of all explorative patents in the sample. This separation permitted the creation of the dependent variable, *Exploration share*, which represents the relative share of explorative patents over all patents. To test for curvilinear relationships, this variable was squared and the independent variable, *Exploration share*^{2} created (Haans *et al.*, 2016). To create the independent variable, *Ambidexterity*, two steps were necessary. First, the exploitation share was determined in the same way as the independent variable, *Exploration share*. Second, the inverted Herfindahl Index was used to compare the shares of the two innovation strategies.

$$1 - HDI_{i,t} = 1 - \sum_{i=1}^{N} s_{i,t}^2$$

Within this inverted Herfindahl index, *s* represents the two innovation strategies of firm *i* during time *t*. Depending on the balance level of exploration and exploitation, values between 0 and 0.5 are feasible. If the shares of exploration and exploitation are equal then the independent variable, *Ambidexterity*, takes the value 0.5. If one strategy outdrives the other (e.g. 0 per cent exploration and 100 per cent exploitation), it is captured by the value 0.

Control variables

The relationships that are assumed in the hypotheses are controlled by several control variables. To control for size and technology related effects, the variables *Size (log sales)*, which is the logarithm of the firm's sales in a given year, and *R&D/assets* were created. Large and R&D intensive firms are more likely to benefit from economies of scale by more effectively processing R&D resources, which in turn increases a firm's technological activity (e.g. Griliches, 1990; Leten *et al.*, 2007). Furthermore, we controlled for collaboration-related effects by including the variables *Alliances* and *Acquisitions*. Firms that have many alliances are more likely to have higher levels of technological activity, whereas acquisitions generally have neutral or negative effects on innovation (De Man and Duysters, 2005). A further variable, *Technological change*, was developed to control for changes in a firm's patent portfolio since firms with high exploration shares tend to focus on experimentation and fundamental research and thus tend to patent new technologies (March, 1991). To develop this variable, an approach introduced by Jaffe (1986) to measure the annual changes in patent behaviour within one firm was applied. Hence, technology portfolios of each firm containing the distribution of granted patents among IPC classes were generated. A firm's technology portfolio in each period was captured by a vector F_{it}, with F'_{it} being the transposed vector of F_{it}, the period and the observed firm are indicated by t and i, respectively. The whole equation was inverted and thus, a firm's TC from year t to the subsequent year $t+1$ was measured as follows:

$$TC_{it} = 1 - \left(\frac{F_{it}F'_{it+1}}{\sqrt{([F_{it}F'_{it}])(F_{it+1}F'_{it+1}]}} \right)$$

The values can range from 0 to 1 where 0 indicates no change of the technology portfolio from one period to another and 1 stands for patents that are assigned to entirely different technology classes in the subsequent period. In other words, if the patenting behaviour of firm i in period t equates to the patenting behaviour of the same firm i in the period $t+1$ then the level of TC reaches a value of 0, and if is completely different (in terms of IPC classes), a value of 1. A further variable, *Experience*, is incorporated into the models and is based on the years since the IPO of the focal firms. Furthermore, two types of dummy variables are included. The first type indicates where the firm is headquartered geographically. According to the triad concept of the world economy, the firm may be headquartered in the USA, Asia-Pacific region, or Europe (Ohmae, 1985). Firms that are headquartered in different countries may have different patenting patterns. The second type consists of time dummies and was included to control for a firm's changing behaviour in patenting over time.

Descriptive analysis

A sample overview is provided in Table 9.2. The 20 biotechnology firms are sorted according to their average sales during the time of observation. In the sample, Amgen has the highest average annual sales (USD 4.1 billion) and MGI Pharma the lowest (USD 43 million). On average, firms have about the same number of explorative patents as exploitative patents. However, firms with relative high numbers of filed patents at the USPTO (above 1,000 patents in total) have more exploitative patents. Firms in the sample with only a small number of filed patents tend to have more explorative patents.

Table 9.3 presents the descriptive statistics and correlation matrix. The average firm files 38.32 patents per year, which are equally distributed between the explorative or exploitative categories; it also forms 2.92 alliances, engages in 0.23 acquisitions, has an average annual technological change of 10 per cent, and is primarily located in the USA. There is no strong correlation between the

Table 9.2 Sample overview of the 20 most successful biotechnology firms in the year 2004

Firm	Period	Average Sales	Patents			
		(in Million US$)	Explorative		Exploitative	Total
Amgen	1982–2007	4,104.96	483	34%	919	66%	1402
Genentech	1980–2007	2,223.57	660	23%	2200	77%	2847
Merch Serono	1980–2006	1,870.95	67	77%	23	26%	87
Genzyme	1984–2007	1,806.72	455	54%	389	46%	840
CSL	1989–2007	1,520.48	46	68%	22	32%	68
Gilead Science	1988–2007	1,000.15	236	64%	133	36%	369
Actelion	2000–2007	650.17	24	96%	1	4%	25
Biogen	1980–2007	638.17	250	35%	462	65%	712
Chiron	1982–2007	600.23	644	35%	1193	65%	1837
Cephalon	1989–2007	529.46	200	67%	100	33%	300
Life Technologies	1991–2007	499.24	252	61%	162	39%	414
Medimmune	1990–2007	469.85	144	50%	145	50%	289
Genencor Intern.	1984–2007	356.48	429	42%	588	58%	1017
Millenium Pharma	1995–2007	307.43	91	76%	28	24%	119
Celgene	1997–2001	277.57	2	67%	1	33%	3
Imclone Systems	1988–2007	131.70	50	49%	53	51%	103
Nabi Biopharma	1994–2007	109.83	31	76%	10	24%	41
QLT	1995–2007	66.65	57	75%	19	25%	76
Regeneron Pharma	1990–2007	56.29	111	40%	167	60%	278
MGI Pharma	1988–2007	43.21	9	64%	5	36%	14

independent variables, except the obvious one between exploration share and its square variable. The dependent variable positively correlates with the variables *Ambidexterity*, *Size*, *Alliances*, *Acquisitions*, *Experience* and with the dummy variable for firms that are geographically headquartered in the USA. A negative correlation is found for *Exploration share*, its square variable, *R&D intensity*, *Technological change* and for the dummies of the firms that are geographically located in the other two triad regions of the world economy.

The descriptive statistics reveal that the firms in the sample balance exploration and exploitation equally. This is a first indication that there is an optimal balance between the innovation strategies and confirms the study by He and Wong (2004). However, an empirical regression is required to generalize any findings to the whole biotechnology industry.

Model specification and econometric issues

The dependent variable, *Patents*, is a count variable, strongly skewed to the right, that makes the use of a GLS regression inappropriate. A more appropriate approach to analyse effects on a count variable offers a *poisson regression* (Hausman *et al.*, 1984; Henderson and Cockburn, 1996). However, one basic assumption of the poisson regression is that the mean and the variance of the count variable distribution take an equal value. In particular, for panel data, this assumption is often violated with overdispersion. In the case of the dependent variable, *Patents*, the variance is remarkably higher than the mean and the highly

Table 9.3 Descriptive statistics and correlation matrix

	Mean	S.D.	1	2	3	4	5	6	7	8	9	10	11	12	VIF
1 Patents	38.32	52.76													
2 Exploration share	0.50	0.28	-0.35 *												1.21
3 Exploration share²	0.33	0.32	-0.36 *	0.97 *											1.58
4 Ambidexterity	0.34	0.18	0.21 *	-0.33 *	-0.57 *										1.37
5 Size (log sales)	5.06	2.25	0.47 *	-0.15 *	-0.19 *	0.20 *									2.63
6 R&D/assets	0.18	0.13	-0.21 *	0.03	0.06 *	-0.14 *	-0.52 *								1.46
7 Alliances	2.92	0.98	0.49 *	-0.23 *	-0.29 *	0.30 *	0.43 *	-0.14 *							1.58
8 Acquisitions	0.23	0.44	0.19 *	0.01	-0.05	0.19 *	0.34 *	-0.22 *	0.35 *						1.25
9 Technological change	0.10	0.17	-0.24 *	0.25 *	0.31 *	-0.32 *	-0.05	0.00	-0.34 *	-0.08					1.40
10 Experience	15.69	7.38	0.36 *	-0.17 *	-0.18 *	0.12	0.51 *	-0.27 *	0.21 *	0.16 *	-0.24 *				1.85
11 Asia	0.05	0.22	-0.15 *	0.10	0.11	-0.06	0.15 *	-0.23 *	-0.11	-0.04	0.20 *	-0.28			1.35
12 Europe	0.04	0.20	-0.12	0.14 *	0.19 *	-0.27 *	0.16 *	-0.02	-0.06	-0.01	0.31 *	-0.09	-0.05		1.85
13 US	0.91	0.29	0.20 *	-0.17 *	-0.21 *	0.23 *	-0.22 *	0.19 *	0.13 *	0.04	-0.36 *	0.27 *	-0.74 *	-0.64 *	2.44

Notes: * $p<0.05$; $n = 251$.

significant likelihood-ratio test for all models in the poisson regression confirms overdispersion. As an alternative, a negative binomial regression is applied to test the hypotheses derived above, which permits the variance of the count variable to exceed the mean. More precisely, a random effects negative binomial model, which controls for unobserved heterogeneity among firms, is applied. The Hausman test (Hausman et al., 1984) that compares the coefficients of a fixed-effects and random effects model could not reject the equality of the coefficients, making a random effects model the more efficient choice.

Results

The following section describes the estimation results that are used to test the hypotheses above and are illustrated in Table 9.4. The section also presents the determinants of technological activity (number of patents) of successful biotechnology firms. The Log-Likelihood and the Wald-test values indicate a good overall model fit.

Model 0 is a baseline model that includes the control variables. *Size (log sales)* has a significant positive impact on a biotechnology firm's patent output and thus confirms previous studies (Henderson and Cockburn, 1996; Vanhaverbeke *et al.*, 2007). Larger firms tend to have access to a variety of resources, internally and externally, which supports higher innovation output. Furthermore, the control variable *Technological change* has a negative effect on the dependent variable. That is to say, firms that focus on a diverse technology portfolio tend to have fewer patents granted. Biotechnology firms that perform research that is too diverse are often not fast enough to win patent races against competitors since they do not concentrate their available resources on one technology, which leads to less patent output. Model 1 adds the variable *Ambidexterity* and increases the fit of the model. It has a positive influence on the dependent variable technological activity at a 5 per cent significance level. Therefore, firms that balance their innovation strategies equally tend to have a higher output than firms that have unbalanced innovation strategies. This finding supports H2 and confirms the study by He and Wong (2004) that finds that firms have a higher performance if they pursue balanced innovation strategies. Replacing *Ambidexterity* with *Exploration share* also shows a better overall fit and significance compared with Model 0. *Exploration share* does not have a significant impact on the dependent variable, thus the alternative hypothesis of H2 cannot be rejected. Model 3 adds *Exploration share²* and further improves overall fit and significance. The linear effect of the share which is dedicated to innovation within a biotechnology firm has a positive effect on a firm's technological activity and the quadratic term has a negative influence. This supports H3, which assumes a curvilinear (inverted U-shaped) effect of *Exploration share* on the dependent variable. This effect has decreasing marginal returns with a global maximum for exploration share at 58 per cent.

This effect is visually illustrated in Figure 9.1. The graph shows that the relationship between the independent variable *Exploration share* and the dependent variable is positive. Accordingly, the higher the exploration share, the lower the

Table 9.4 Determinants of technological activity of successful biotechnology firms, 1980–2007

	Model 0	Model 1	Model 2	Model 3
Independent Variables				
Ambidexterity		0.57 (0.24) **		
Exploration share			0.19 (0.15)	1.29 –(0.51) **
Exploration share^2				–1.11 –(0.49) **
Control Variables				
Size (log sales)	0.10 (0.04) **	0.10 (0.04) **	0.10 (0.04) **	0.10 –(0.04) **
R&D/assets	–0.30 (0.35)	–0.27 (0.36)	–0.26 (0.35)	–0.23 –(0.35)
Alliances	0.05 (0.06)	0.07 (0.06)	0.04 (0.06)	0.06 –(0.06)
Acquisitions	0.06 (0.08)	0.05 (0.07)	0.06 (0.08)	0.05 –(0.07)
Technological change	–0.79 (0.33) **	–0.77 (0.33) **	–0.78 (0.32) **	–0.77 –(0.33) **
Experience	0.04 (0.03)	0.04 (0.03)	0.05 (0.03)	0.04 –(0.03)
Asia	0.39 (0.84)	0.35 (0.81)	0.50 (0.86)	0.44 –(0.84)
Europe	–0.03 (0.66)	0.02 (0.64)	0.01 (0.68)	0.07 –(0.66)
Constant	0.17 (0.55)	–0.02 (0.54)	0.03 (0.57)	–0.13 –(0.56)
Year dummies	included	included	included	included
Observations (Groups)	251 (20)	251 (20)	251 (20)	251 (20)
Log Likelihood	–939.1728	–936.3712	–938.3328	–935.6791
Wald Chi^2 (df)	287.52 (33) ***	289.31 (34) ***	291.40 (34) ***	292.75 (35) ***

Notes: *** p<0.01; ** p<0.05; *p<0.1 (two sided tests). Results of a random effects negative binomial model.
Standard deviations in parentheses

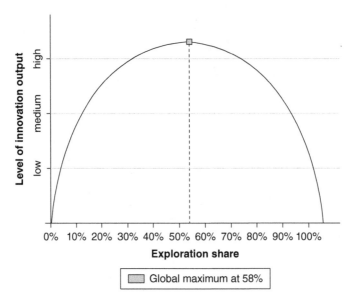

Figure 9.1 Optimal balance between exploration and exploitation.

exploitation share. This positive effect becomes negative when a global maximum is reached and when a successful biotechnology firm engages in 58 per cent explorative innovation and 42 per cent exploitative innovation.

Discussion

Ambidexterity positively influences a firm's innovative performance. That is to say, firms that find methods that allow them to dedicate a similar amount of attention to exploration and exploitation have increased technological activity and perform better from an innovative perspective. There are several studies that find similar results from a theoretical, empirical and practical perspective (Grover *et al.*, 2007; He and Wong, 2004; O'Reilly and Tushman, 2004; Tushman and O'Reilly, 1996). Yet, firms have to find the means to concentrate on both strategies and may adopt two different approaches to do so. A firm may either focus on separation through an extensive alliance portfolio or focus on integration. This suggests firms should combine exploration and exploitation within the same business units (Gibson and Birkinshaw, 2004; Im and Rai, 2008; Lin *et al.*, 2007; Tushman and O'Reilly, 1996). Most importantly however, and what distinguishes this result from others, is that an imbalance between exploration and exploitation leads to inferior innovative performance. This extends the study by He and Wong (2004) who empirically find the same impact on sales growth. An ambidextrous strategy helps firms to stay effective in the short run and to survive, and even to sustain their competitive advantage in the long run (Benner and Tushman, 2003;

Gupta *et al.*, 2006; Lavie *et al.*, 2011). This result offers a valuable clue as to the point at which an optimal balance of the two strategies could be found and so endorses the finding that firms should devote similar amounts of attention to both exploration and exploitation.

A further result gives more precise information on the optimal balance level between exploration and exploitation and thus represents the main result of this study. It shows a curvilinear relationship between the share of explorative innovation strategies and a firm's technological activity, with decreasing marginal returns. That is to say, an inverted U-shaped relationship is found between the share of exploration – the creation of new capabilities by pursuing fundamental research, experimentation and searches – and a firm's innovative performance. The global maximum is therefore determined and shows that successful biotechnology firms engage in 58 per cent explorative innovation and in 42 per cent exploitative innovation. Of course, generalization of this result to other industries may be difficult since industries and firms are influenced by different environmental, organizational and managerial antecedents (Lavie *et al.*, 2010). However, a noteworthy result is that ambidexterity should not be defined as a concept where one innovation strategy dominates another, as in the study of Gibson and Birkinshaw (2004), but as a concept that dedicates similar innovation attention to both strategies, as described by He and Wong (2004).

It is worth diverting briefly to discuss why biotechnology firms profit most from a slight imbalance towards exploration and a rationale may be found in the attributes of the biotechnology industry. Since the 1970s, the biotechnology industry has experienced rapid technology development and a mushrooming of newly established firms, which has led to fierce competition (Pisano, 1997). Rapid product development (Deeds and Hill, 1996) and patent races among competitors (Gilbert and Newbery, 1982) are only a couple of the attributes of this competitive environment. Auh and Menguc (2005) find that firms in competitive environments benefit most from explorative strategies. Furthermore, firms in the biotechnology industry are exposed to a turbulent, dynamic and uncertain environment (Van de Vrande *et al.*, 2009). Jansen *et al.* (2006) find that dynamic environments positively moderate the relationship between explorative innovation and firm performance. In summary, the characteristics of the biotechnology industry enable firms within the industry to benefit slightly more from exploration than firms in less competitive, dynamic environments.

Conclusions

This paper analyses explorative and exploitative innovation strategies in the biotechnology industry. Most of the literature stresses that firms have to engage in both types of innovation to remain effective in the short run and survive in the long run (Benner and Tushman, 2003; Gupta *et al.*, 2006; Lavie *et al.*, 2011). Despite the consensus that the two strategies must be balanced, little is known of what constitutes an optimal balance between the two strategies. Some scholars argue that a firm should dedicate most of its management attention to one innovation strategy and only a minor share to the other (e.g. Gibson and Birkinshaw, 2004). Other scholars argue that this imbalance has a negative impact on firm performance (e.g. He and Wong, 2004). This paper seeks to close this gap in literature by applying a new approach to quantifying explorative and exploitative innovation and by determining the optimal balance of the two strategies with modern analytical methods. A set of hypotheses on the relationship between the exploration share in a firm's innovation strategy and its patent output are derived and then tested. It is shown that firms have the highest innovative performance if they dedicate similar amounts of attention to both explorative and exploitative innovation strategies.

Firms in the biotechnology industry benefit from a reduced imbalance between explorative and exploitative innovation strategies. This extends the study by He and Wong (2004) that found a negative relationship between this imbalance and a firm's financial performance. This result can be analysed in more detail by looking for the optimal exploration share. A curvilinear or inverted U-shaped relationship between a biotechnology firm's explorative innovation strategy and its innovative activity (number of patents) is found. Furthermore, the global maximum that represents the optimal balance between the innovation strategies is found with an exploration share of 58 per cent. Although it confirms previous studies, this result has to be interpreted carefully. Industries and firms are influenced by distinct organizational, environmental and managerial antecedents and it is most plausible that an optimal balance is influenced by these factors (Lavie *et al.*, 2010). However, the finding that can be transferred to other high-technology industries and contexts is that firms should dedicate similar R&D efforts to exploration and exploitation in order to remain effective in the short run and survive in the long run. Thus, this study contributes a new and more accurate approach to distinguishing between explorative and exploitative patents to the literature and adds empirical evidence to Tushman and O'Reilly's (1996) ambidexterity hypothesis.

However, this analysis has some limitations. This study is based almost entirely on one country and thus country-specific characteristics could limit the generalizability of the results. Therefore, the data should be extended by information taken from biotechnology firms around the world. What is more, some firms of interest have not been public throughout their economic lifetime, making financial data unavailable. Therefore, survey research could be used to extend the database.

Further research could also extend this study by applying contingency theory. Lavie *et al.* (2010) argue that several contingency factors have an influence on an optimal balance between exploration and exploitation. Whereas high-technology industries with dynamic environments and fierce competition benefit from a balance bias towards exploration, firms in low-technology arenas may have to pursue other innovation strategies. There may also be differences between service and manufacturing firms (Blindenbach-Driessen and van den Ende, 2014), or firms from the creative industries (Wu and Wu, 2016). Even firms in the same industry are very heterogeneous, for example, as far as size, products, cultures and other contingent factors that may influence an optimal balance between exploration and exploitation are concerned.

References

Andriopoulos, C. and Lewis, M.W. (2009) "Exploitation-exploration tensions and organizational ambidexterity: Managing paradoxes of innovation", *Organization Science* 20(4): 696–717.

Atuahene-Gima, K. (2005) "Resolving the capability: Rigidity paradox in new product innovation", *Journal of Marketing* 69(4): 61–83.

Audretsch, D.B. (2001) "The role of small firms in U.S. biotechnology clusters", *Small Business Economics* 17(1): 3–15.

Auh, S. and Menguc, B. (2005) "Balancing exploration and exploitation: The moderating role of competitive intensity", *Journal of Business Research* 58(12): 1652–61.

Basberg, B.L. (1984) "Patent statistics and the measurement of technological change: An assessment of the Norwegian patent data, 1840–1980", *World Patent Information* 6(4): 158–64.

Baum, J.A.C., Calabrese, T. and Silverman, B.S. (2000) "Don't go it alone: Alliance network composition and startups' performance in Canadian biotechnology", *Strategic Management Journal* 21(3): 267–94.

Belderbos, R., Faems, D., Leten, B. and Looy, B.V. (2010) "Technological activities and their impact on the financial performance of the firm: Exploitation and exploration within and between Firms", *Journal of Product Innovation Management* 27(6): 869–82.

Benner, M. and Tushman, M. (2003) "Exploitation, exploration, and process management: The productivity dilemma revisited", *The Academy of Management Review* 28(2): 238–56.

Blindenbach-Driessen, F. and van den Ende, J. (2014) "The locus of innovation: The effect of a separate innovation unit on exploration, exploitation, and ambidexterity in manufacturing and service firms", *Journal of Product Innovation Management* 31(5): 1089–1105.

Cantwell, J. and Santangelo, G. D. (2000) "Capitalism, profits and innovation in the new technoeconomic paradigm", *Journal of Evolutionary Economics* 10(1): 131–57.

De Man, A.P. and Duysters, G. (2005) "Collaboration and innovation: A review of the effects of mergers, acquisitions and alliances on innovation", *Technovation* 25(12): 1377–87.

Deeds, D.L. and Hill, C.W. (1996) "Strategic alliances and the rate of new product development: An empirical study of entrepreneurial biotechnology firms", *Journal of Business Venturing* 11(1): 41–55.

Gibson, C. and Birkinshaw, J. (2004) "The antecedents, consequences, and mediating role of organizational ambidexterity", *The Academy of Management Journal* 47(2): 209–26.

Gilbert, R.J. and Newbery, D.M.G. (1982) "Preemptive patenting and the persistence of monopoly", *The American Economic Review* 72(3): 514–26.

Gilsing, V.A., Nooteboom, B., Vanhaverbeke, W.P., Duysters, G. and van den Oord, A. (2008) "Network embeddedness and the exploration of novel technologies: Technological distance, betweenness centrality and density", *Research Policy* 37(10): 1717–31.

Giovanetti, G. and Morrison, S. (2000) *Convergence: The Biotechnology Industry Report.* Palo Alto, CA: Ernst & Young.

Griliches, Z. (1990) "Patent statistics as economic indicators: A survey", *Journal of Economic Literature* 28(4): 1661–1707.

Grover, V., Purvis, R.L. and Segars, A.H. (2007) "Exploring ambidextrous innovation tendencies in the adoption of telecommunications technologies", *Engineering Management* 54(2): 268–85.

Gupta, A.K., Smith, K.G. and Shalley, C.E. (2006) "The interplay between exploration and exploitation", *The Academy of Management Journal* 49(4): 693–706.

Haans, R. F. J., Pieters, C. and He, Z.-L. (2016) "Thinking about U: Theorizing and testing U- and inverted U-shaped relationships in strategy research", *Strategic Management Journal*, in press.

Hausman, J., Hall, B.H. and Griliches, Z. (1984) "Econometric models for count data with an application to the patents-R&D relationship", *Econometrica* 52(4): 909–38.

He, Z.-L. and Wong, P.-K. (2004) "Exploration vs. exploitation: An empirical test of the ambidexterity hypothesis", *Organization Science* 15(4): 481–94.

Henderson, R. and Cockburn, I. (1996) "Scale, scope, and spillovers: The determinants of research productivity in drug discovery", *The RAND Journal of Economics* 27(1): 32–59.

Hohberger, J. (2007) *Individual-level collaboration and firm-level innovation in the biotechnology industry*, PhD thesis, Universitat Ramon Llull. ESADE-BS UDC 10803/9205.

Im, G. and Rai, A. (2008) "Knowledge sharing ambidexterity in long-term interorganizational relationships", *Management Science* 54(7): 1281–96.

Jaffe, A.B. (1986) "Technological opportunity and spillovers of R&D: Evidence from firms' patents, profits, and market values", *American Economic Review* 76(5): 984–1001.

Jansen, J., Volberda, H.W. and Van Den Bosch, F.A.J. (2006) "Exploratory innovation, exploitative innovation, and performance: Effects of organizational antecedents and environmental moderators", *Management Science* 52(11): 1661–74.

Kim, C., Song, J. and Nerkar, A. (2012) "Learning and innovation: Exploitation and exploration trade-offs", *Journal of Business Research* 65(8): 1189–94.

Lavie, D., Kang, J. and Rosenkopf, L. (2011) "Balance within and across domains: The performance implications of exploration and exploitation in alliances", *Organization Science* 22(6): 1517–38.

Lavie, D., Stettner, U. and Tushman, M.L. (2010) "Exploration and exploitation within and across organizations", *The Academy of Management Annals* 4(1): 109–55.

Leten, B., Belderbos, R. and Van Looy, B. (2007) "Technological diversification, coherence, and performance of firms", *Journal of Product Innovation Management* 24(6): 567–79.

Levinthal, D.A. and March, J.G. (1993) "The myopia of learning", *Strategic Management Journal* 14(S2): 95–112.

Lin, Z., Yang, H. and Demirkan, I. (2007) "The performance consequences of ambidexterity in strategic alliance formations: Empirical investigation and computational theorizing", *Management Science* 53(10): 1645–58.

Lubatkin, M., Simsek, Z., Ling, Y. and Veiga, J. (2006) "Ambidexterity and performance in small-to medium-sized firms: The pivotal role of top management team behavioral integration", *Journal of Management* 32(5): 646–72.

March, J.G. (1991) "Exploration and exploitation in organizational learning", *Organization Science* 2(1): 71–87.

March, J.G. (1996) "Continuity and change in theories of organizational action", *Administrative Science Quarterly* 41(2): 278–87.

March, J.G. (2006) "Rationality, foolishness, and adaptive intelligence", *Strategic Management Journal* 27(3): 201–14.

MedAdNews (2004) *Top 100 Biotechnology Companies*. http://www.pharmalive.com/magazines/archive.cfm?mag=medad&year=2004 (accessed 7 November 2006).

Molina-Castillo, F.-J., Jimenez-Jimenez, D. and Munuera-Aleman, J.-L. (2011) "Product competence exploitation and exploration strategies: The impact on new product performance through quality and innovativeness", *Industrial Marketing Management* 40(7): 1172–82.

Mudambi, R. and Swift, T. (2014) "Knowing when to leap: Transitioning between exploitative and explorative R&D", *Strategic Management Journal* 35: 126–45.

Nesta, L. and Saviotti, P.-P. (2006) "Firm knowledge and market value in biotechnology", *Industrial and Corporate Change* 15(4): 625–52.

Nooteboom, B., Van Haverbeke, W., Duysters, G., Gilsing, V. and van den Oord, A. (2007) "Optimal cognitive distance and absorptive capacity", *Research Policy* 36(7): 1016–34.

O'Reilly, C. and Tushman, M. (2004) "The ambidextrous organization", *Harvard Business Review* 82(4): 74–81.

Ohmae, K. (1985). *Triad Power: The Coming Shape of Global Competition*. New York: Free Press.

Pangarkar, N. (2003) "Determinants of alliance duration in uncertain environments: The case of the biotechnology sector", *Long Range Planning* 36(3): 269–84.

Pisano, G.P. (1997) *R&D Performance, Collaborative Arrangements, and the Market for Know-how: A Test of the 'Lemons' Hypothesis in Biotechnology*. Boston, MA: Harvard Business School.

Powell, W., Koput, K. and Doerr, L. (1996). "Interorganizational collaboration and the locus of innovation: Networks of learning in biotechnology", *Administrative Science Quarterly* 41(1): 116–45.

Raisch, S., Birkinshaw, J., Probst, G. and Tushman, M.L. (2009) "Organizational ambidexterity: Balancing exploitation and exploration for sustained performance", *Organization Science* 20(4): 685–95.

Shan, W., Walker, G. and Kogut, B. (1994) "Interfirm cooperation and startup innovation in the biotechnology industry", *Strategic Management Journal* 15(5): 387–94.

Tushman, M.L. and O'Reilly, C.A. (1996) "Ambidextrous organizations: Managing evolutionary and revolutionary change", *California Management Review* 38(4): 8–30.

Uotila, J., Maula, M., Keil, T. and Zahra, S.A. (2009) "Exploration, exploitation, and financial performance: Analysis of S&P 500 corporations", *Strategic Management Journal* 30(2): 221–31.

Van de Vrande, V., Vanhaverbeke, W. and Duysters, G. (2009) "External technology sourcing: The effect of uncertainty on governance mode choice", *Journal of Business Venturing* 24(1): 62–80.

Vanhaverbeke, W., Gilsing, V. and Duysters, G. (2007) "Exploration and exploitation in technology-based alliance networks", *UNU-MERIT Working Paper Series 2007–018*.

Wu, Y. and Wu, S. (2016) "Managing ambidexterity in creative industries: A survey", *Journal of Business Research* 69(7): 2388–96.

Index

 Taylor & Francis eBooks

---

Helping you to choose the right eBooks for your Library

Add Routledge titles to your library's digital collection today. Taylor and Francis ebooks contains over 50,000 titles in the Humanities, Social Sciences, Behavioural Sciences, Built Environment and Law.

Choose from a range of subject packages or create your own!

Benefits for you

» Free MARC records
» COUNTER-compliant usage statistics
» Flexible purchase and pricing options
» All titles DRM-free.

Benefits for your user

» Off-site, anytime access via Athens or referring URL
» Print or copy pages or chapters
» Full content search
» Bookmark, highlight and annotate text
» Access to thousands of pages of quality research at the click of a button.

 Free Trials Available
We offer free trials to qualifying academic, corporate and government customers.

eCollections – Choose from over 30 subject eCollections, including:

Archaeology	Language Learning
Architecture	Law
Asian Studies	Literature
Business & Management	Media & Communication
Classical Studies	Middle East Studies
Construction	Music
Creative & Media Arts	Philosophy
Criminology & Criminal Justice	Planning
Economics	Politics
Education	Psychology & Mental Health
Energy	Religion
Engineering	Security
English Language & Linguistics	Social Work
Environment & Sustainability	Sociology
Geography	Sport
Health Studies	Theatre & Performance
History	Tourism, Hospitality & Events

For more information, pricing enquiries or to order a free trial, please contact your local sales team: www.tandfebooks.com/page/sales

Routledge
Taylor & Francis Group

The home of
Routledge books

www.tandfebooks.com